The Dynamics of Complexity, Accuracy and Fluency in Second Language Development

Iwona Kowal

The Dynamics of Complexity, Accuracy and Fluency in Second Language Development

Jagiellonian University Press

REVIEWER

prof. dr hab. Zdzisław Wawrzyniak

COVER DESIGN

Pracownia Register

The book has been financed by the Jagiellonian University from the funds of Institute of German Studies

ISBN 978-83-233-4136-9
ISBN 978-83-233-9474-7 (e-book)

JAGIELLONIAN UNIVERSITY PRESS

www.wuj.pl

Jagiellonian University Press
Editorial Offices: Michałowskiego 9/2, 31-126 Krakow
Phone: +48 12 663 23 80, +48 12 663 23 82, Fax: +48 12 663 23 83
Distribution: Phone: +48 12 631 01 97, Fax: +48 12 631 01 98
Cell Phone: + 48 506 006 674, e-mail: sprzedaz@wuj.pl
Bank: PEKAO SA, IBAN PL 80 1240 4722 1111 0000 4856 332

Table of contents

Acknowledgments

This book is an outcome of almost ten years of work, filled with reading, creating experimental sessions, conducting the experiments, making data analysis, rejecting analyzing tools, adapting new analysis, making reflections, participating in discussions, and having fluctuating feelings about the results and my own capacity to deal a generally acceptable research. But without other people it couldn't be possible to come to the present state. Therefore I would express my gratitude first of all to my family: my husband and my daughters who most directly experienced the dynamics of my emotions related to this research. My great gratitude also goes to Gisela Håkansson and Jonas Granfeldt who accompanied me in the most extensive time and discussed parts of this work. I would thank my colleges from the Language Acquisition Research Group at Lund University: Malin, Henrik, Tanja, Maarja and Anna-Lia for their support, social and psychological presence and overall empathy. I also would like to pay tribute to my colleges from the Institute for Swedish Language and Literature at Jagiellonian University for enabling me a quiet sabbatical and substituting me in the educational part of my work. There are, however 32 students of Swedish Philology that participated in this study, without whose collaboration the project could not have been born. So, I will thank all of you, even if your names cannot appear in these acknowledgements because of the principle of anonymity. I also thank Swedish Institute and Institute for Germanic Languages at Jagiellonian University that gave a financial support for this project.

1

Preface

Nowadays research in all disciplines is becoming increasingly interdisciplinary in character. Scholars utilise knowledge from other disciplines not only in order to better understand the phenomena they are investigating but also to obtain a different perspective, which always makes it possible to solve problems and find answers to questions in every sphere of life. This tendency is remarkable not only in the formal and natural sciences but also in the humanities. In the last few years a new approach, called Dynamic Systems Theory, has rapidly increased in popularity in Second Language Studies. This theory has in fact a long history, going back to Newton's Laws of Motion, and hitherto it has been used primarily in, among others, mathematics, biology and economics. As it investigates complex and changing systems DST can easily be adopted in Linguistics, especially in Second Language Development, where the focus is on complex and variable systems such as the second language learner, the (second) language, the learning environment etc.

When these complex systems develop, they are constantly changing and reorganizing so that in fact we cannot predict when a learner will achieve a certain level in the second language. Dynamic system behaviour is also characterised by considerable variability and they continuously interact with one another. Even a small trigger in the initial phases of the learning period can have a substantial impact on future development, which is comparable to the widely known butterfly effect. Additionally, significant differences always exist between second language learners who themselves are constantly changing. There is also variability within every student. All these properties are basic pre-requisites for investigating second language development from the point of view of dynamic systems theory.

In the present book we will look at the development of Swedish as a second language in young adults, beginning from the first months of their second language instruction and ending after three years of intensive language courses. During the course of this study we will focus on three proficiency dimensions: Complexity, Accuracy and Fluency and their interplay not only at group level, but also, and most importantly, in individual students. Chapter 2 provides an introduction to dynamic systems theory and its implementation for developmental and second language studies. Chapter 3 offers an overview of research conducted on the concepts of Complexity, Accuracy and Fluency in Second Language studies. In Chapter 4 we describe the present project, after which the focus shifts to an analysis of the development of several aspects of Complexity (Chapter 5), Accuracy (Chapter 6) and Fluency (Chapter 7). Finally, in Chapter 8, the interplay between all dimensions is investigated, on the basis of which we will also distinguish between four learner profiles and propose a developmental order for the three investigated dimensions.

The goal of this book is to provide a platform for further discussion of the dynamics of second language development and the interconnectedness of systems involved in this development. With this issue in mind we would also appeal for an individual approach to be taken with every learner and for development to be treated as a constant interplay between many factors. Therefore, it is always important to investigate at least two variables in interaction during the learning process.

2

Dynamic systems theory

When addressing the issue of dynamic systems we must not overlook the concept of motion. This notion includes a set space, a time set, an initial time and initial conditions. The set space is the set of all possible states that certain objects can possess. Motion refers to the change in a state over time. This concept goes back to Newton's Laws of Motion, and dynamic systems theory has in fact its roots in the former. Newtonian mechanics is even treated as "the archetype of deterministic dynamical theories" (Manneville, 2004, p. 25). The laws describe the behaviour of bodies under the influence of forces acting upon them. Motion occurs as a consequence of this action. Motion in classical Newtonian mechanics is considered within three main subfields. Although all of these deal with the same phenomenon each one focuses on a different aspect. Statics investigates the action of forces that leads to the equilibrium of a body. Kinematics describes the motion of bodies, but is not interested in the cause of the motion. Dynamics, in turn, considers the motion of bodies under the influence of forces (Encyclopedia of Science & Technology, 1997). Newton introduced a set of equations, called differential equations, which describe the motion of physical bodies and systems, such as, e.g., the Solar System. Newton's laws of motion have been used primarily to investigate the motion of large bodies. However, they have their limitations in the case of bodies that move at high speed or very small bodies. These kinds of objects are considered within the context of special relativity or quantum physics.

According to Newton's First Law, when a force acts on a body the latter can move as long as that force is acting on it, after which it comes to a state of rest due to gravity or friction. The body can even continue to move at constant speed, which can be illustrated as a straight line. This kind of motion is called linear motion and is the basic form of motion. Linearity means proportionality to the input. A body can thus change direction or velocity, but in linear motion this change will always be proportional to the strength of the acting force that caused the change in direction or velocity. In general, linear motion may be described as a linear function whose solution is presented as a straight line. The basic linear equation is:

$$y = ax,$$

where x and y are variables and a is a constant. When, for example, we assume that x stands for time and y for motion in a space state, the change in position of the object will proceed proportionally, according to the constant a. For example, if value $a = 1$, the object covers a distance of one space unit during one time interval, if value $a = 2$, the object covers a distance of two space units during one time interval. In a graphic presentation of such a function, the gradient of the line depends on the value of a (Figure 2.1).

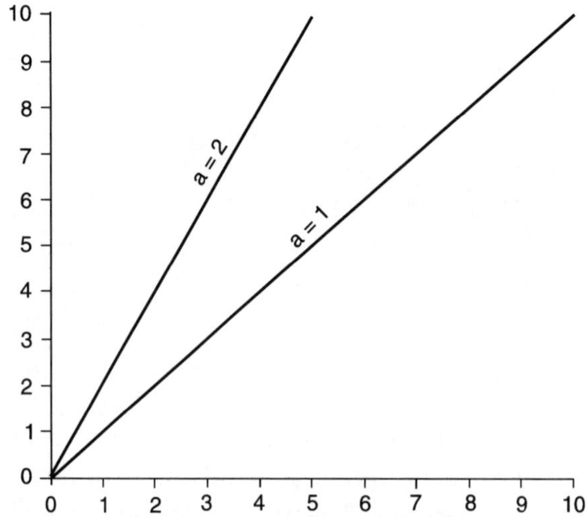

Figure 2.1. An illustration of linear functions where $a = 1$ and $a = 2$, respectively. Unless otherwise specified, all figures in this book are the author's own

The second kind of motion is periodic motion. In this case the object changes its position in regular cycles or intervals that are reproducible and thus predictable. Such a motion occurs, for example, in the Solar System between the Sun and the Earth. It is also visible in the behaviour of the vocal cords when we produce vowels or voiced consonants. Periodic motion can be described by the following function:

$$f(x + P) = f(x),$$

where P is a non zero constant and stands for the period. The function can be interpreted as follows: when we have a point x we will achieve the same point x after the period P (see Figures 2.2a and 2.2b for examples of periodic motion).

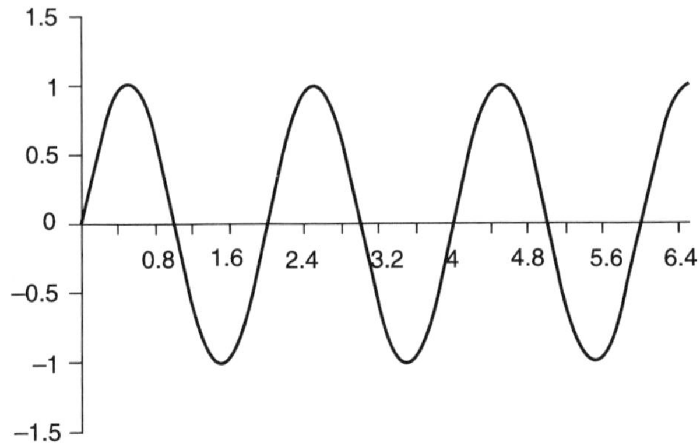

Figure 2.2a. An illustration of periodic function where $P = \sin\pi$

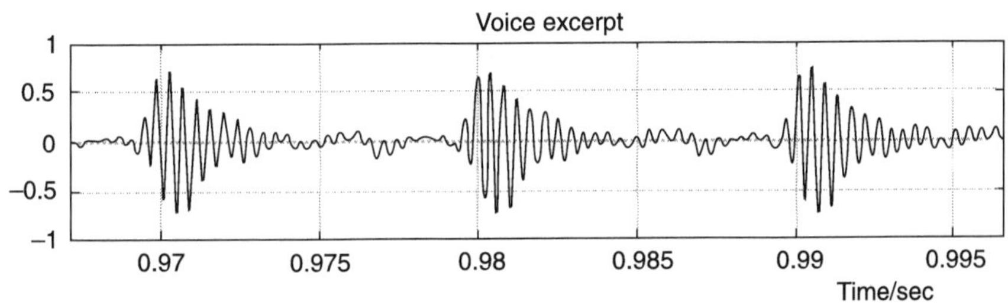

Figure 2.2b. An illustration of the periodic motion of vocal cords during a vowel sound (from Ellis, 2010, p. 762)

The third kind of motion is chaotic motion, which is defined as a form of motion that is "erratic, but not simply quasiperiodic with a large number of periods, and not necessarily due to a large number of interacting particles" (Alligood, Sauer & Yorke, 1996, p. vi). Chaotic motion as a characteristic of dynamic systems was first mentioned in 1975 by Li and Yorke (1975). However, even prior to this researchers had observed the specific behaviour of objects which we now call chaos. Cartwight and Littlewood (1945) reported the random-like behaviour of nonlinear differential equations, while Lorenz (1963) was interested in hydrodynamic systems and used differential equations to describe non-periodic trajectories. In his lecture at the 139th meeting of the American Association for the Advancement of Science Lorenz discussed the question of the unpredictability of the weather that led to what is known as the "butterfly effect," i.e. a sensitive dependence on initial conditions. This principle, together with unpredictability and boundedness, is one of the primary features of chaos (Kaplan & Glass, 1995, p. 27). Sensitive dependence on initial conditions means that two trajectories that are initially arbitrarily close to one another necessarily diverge (Ruelle, 1978; Ruelle & Takens, 1971). Such an abrupt change in behaviour is called bifurcation. Bifurcations occur in dynamic systems when a parameter is changed. There are many different types of bifurcation. The most archetypal equation for chaotic behaviour is the logistic equation devised by the Belgian mathematics Pierre François Verhulst for calculating population growth. The logistic equation takes the following form:

$$x_{n+1} = rx_n(1-x_n),$$

where r is a positive constant that in Verhulst's equation expressed the population growth rate. When r is a small value the system exhibits quite stable behaviour. However, at $r > 3$ the logistic map becomes unstable and bifurcation occurs. Figure 2.3 presents a bifurcation diagram that illustrates the logistic equation presented above.

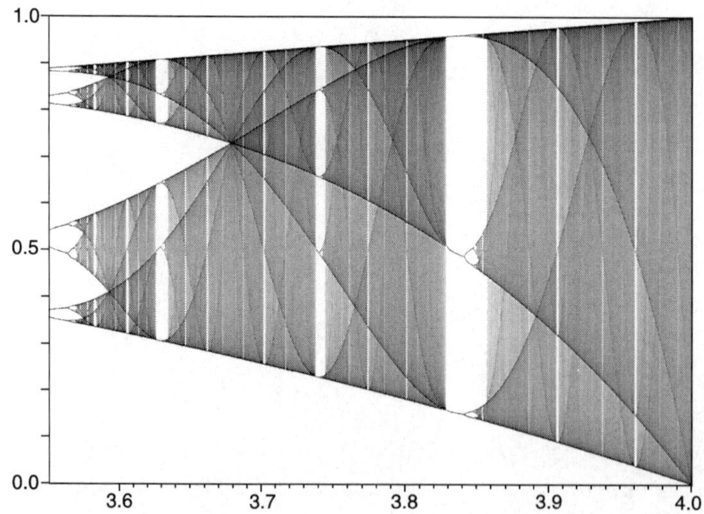

Figure 2.3. A bifurcation diagram (https://commons.wikipedia.org/wiki/File:LogisticmapBifurcationDiagram.png [31.05.2016])

Small changes at the beginning of the process can thus have significant effects at the end of the observed period. To use Lorenz' comparison, the flap of a butterfly's wings in Brazil will set off a tornado in Texas.

The second feature of chaos, i.e. unpredictability, is the logical outcome of non-periodicity and dependence on initial conditions. In conditions of chaos it is also not possible to repeat the sequence of functions that describe the trajectory of a point during a certain period. The third feature – boundedness – means that the points do not leave their own state spaces, even if they move unpredictably. This feature mirrors how the system interacts with its surrounding environment.

Most hitherto research on chaos has made use of the term 'molecular chaos' to describe the complete disorder of the positions and velocities of gas molecules. However, it turns out that molecular motions follow the principles of deterministic behaviour, i.e. behaviour in which a current state is described as a consequence of its preceding states. Such complex fluctuation phenomena are now regarded as 'deterministic chaos' (Bergé, Pomeau & Vidal, 1986) and are studied in many different sciences: mathematics uses a set of differential equations, physicians and chemists employ the term 'chaotic' to describe complex phenomena which occur in systems of closed, deterministic equations (Favre, Guitton, Lichnerowicz & Wolff, 1988). Chaotic motion characterizes phenomena studied by meteorologists, biologists, economists, sociologists, psychologists and even linguists.

Chaos is the main property of dynamic systems. According to the mathematical definition of dynamic systems, they are "a means of describing how one state develops into another state over the course of time" (Weisstein, 2002, p. 844). The term *dynamic* refers to a change in motion. The interconnection between chaotic motion and dynamics can be found in Maxwell's Theory of the Electromagnetic Field. Maxwell called his theory a *Dynamical Theory* due to the fact that the observed phenomena depended on motion (Maxwell, 1865, p. 460). A dynamic system can be any mechanism that evolves deterministically over time. The focus is on evolution and in Dynamic Systems Theory the state of a system is described as a function of time that mirrors the motion of the system (Broer & Takens, 2011). In mathematics and physics dynamic systems can be modelled by means of nonlinear algebraic or differential equations. Dynamic Systems Theory (DST) has been adapted to suit the needs of formal, physical and social sciences. There is, however, a slight difference in the nomenclature applied by various disciplines. While mathematics, physics and chemistry only use the term *dynamical systems*, in biology, economics or psychology both *dynamic systems* and *dynamical systems* occur. In linguistics, on the other hand, the term *dynamic systems* is preferred.

Dynamic changes occur in systems. "A system can be defined as any collection of identifiable elements – abstract or concrete – that are somehow related to one another in a way that is relevant to the dynamics" (van Geert, 2008, p. 180). The elements in a system do not necessarily interact with one other. However, there must be a relationship between them that enables change to occur in the state of the system. Let us take school as an example. This is a system consisting of people (students, teachers, a school director, administrative and technical staff), rules (laws and statutes governing an education system or a national curriculum, rules of behaviour during lessons, in recesses or in the library) as well as physical entities (the school building, the classrooms with their equipment, the cafeteria). Some elements of the system directly interact with one other, for example the teachers and students, while others exist in order to enable this interaction to take place or to keep the system functioning.

Dynamic systems are open systems – in contrast to isolated or closed systems, which only move internally, without exchanging energy or matter. Isolated systems tend to achieve equilibrium and they are resistant to changes triggered from the outside. Open systems, on the other hand, can take resources from the surrounding environment, which leads to change due to a new supply of energy. The most basic open systems are biological systems where the supply of energy causes growth and leads to development. The openness of a system, however, does not rule out its stability and even if most dynamic systems behave in an unstable way open systems can sometimes be 'far from equilibrium,' but still remain stable (Prigogine & Stengers, 1985; Thelen & Smith, 1994). The stability of a fixed point means that the trajectories of other points will tend to move closer to it while full equilibrium involves a state where there is "a point attractor that nothing ever changes" (Byrne, 1998, p. 27). The main difference between stability and equilibrium lies in the distance from the attractor and thus in the ability to change. Closed or isolated systems reach the attractor and do not change, i.e. they achieve equilibrium. Open dynamic systems are stable when the trajectories of their elements approach the attractor but do not reach it. They cannot do so because they are subject to perturbation due to the constant inflow of energy. The 'far-from-equilibrium' state is thus maintained by a continuous exchange of energy and matter.

The openness of dynamic systems and the inflow of energy into them result in their self-organisation. The concept of self-organisation was developed by Ashby (1962). He distinguished between two different meanings of self-organizing system. The first involves the establishment of an interconnection between parts of systems that have become separated, which can be viewed as a transition from, as Ashby called it, "parts separated" to "parts joined" (Ashby, 1962, p. 266). The other meaning of a self-organizing system involves an automatic, qualitative change in the system as a result of feedback from the outside, or, in dynamic terms, as a result of an external action and an inflow of energy. Ashby saw this kind of self-organization as a transition from a "bad" to a "good" organization, i.e. a specialization or a process of adapting to the system's own environment. A "good" organisation keeps the system alive (Ashby, 1962). However, a quantitative change in the system should not be understood in the absolute sense. A positive change, for example, can occur even in constellations that are negative, in our everyday understanding of what is good or bad. Self-organisation occurs even in systems based on criminality or terrorism, and 'order' and 'co-operation' even increase in systems whose aims are negative in an ethical sense (Larsen-Freeman & Cameron, 2008). Self-organisation not only enables the maintenance of a system but even its coherence.

Dynamic systems theory describes systems that are complex. The first definition that comes to mind when we think of complexity is that this concept differs from simplicity in the number and heterogeneity of its constituting elements as well as in the degree of interconnectedness between the parts of the system. A simple system contains a small set of components whose behaviour is pre-defined and predictable. In our everyday lives we often come across such systems, for example in the case of household appliances like a vacuum cleaner, a food processor or a kettle. Even if they consist of hundreds of parts their functions have been precisely programmed and the triggering of an action leads to specific, fixed behaviour. Moreover, such simple systems behave in a linear fashion because they react proportionally to the strength of the input. If we change the level of the motor rotation, for example, the tool will work proportionally faster or slower. This is not the case with complex systems, which change dynamically. The changes can proceed in both discrete and continuous time, which can be illustrated as curves or iterative maps. The dynamics of complex systems should neither be understood analytically, with regard to particular parts of the systems, nor considered holistically. As Byrne points out, the key property of complex systems is their interconnectedness and they should thus be investigated in terms of the interaction between several parts of the system, and between the parts and the system as a whole (Byrne, 2002). Briggs and Peat even point out that due to their complexity, systems cannot be ultimately analysed and reduced into smaller parts "...because the parts are constantly being folded into each other by iterations and feedback (...). Any interaction takes place in the larger system and the system as a whole is constantly changing, bifurcating, iterating" (Briggs & Peat, 1989, p. 147).

2.1. Development of complex dynamic systems

The main characteristic of dynamic systems is change in time and this is a perfect condition for using DST in developmental studies. Development also entails change in time and this transition, due to the complexity of such systems, can hardly be supposed to proceed linearly, because we never know how the entire subsystem interacts with other parts of the system and what variable has more influence on the process at a particular time. There is, however, no consensus among researchers with regard to whether DST-research should focus on long or short-term development. Balibrea (2006, p. 1) claims that "the main goal when considering dynamic systems is to understand the long-term behaviour of evolving states according to the flow". Developmental psychologists, on the other hand, believe that research should focus on collecting and analysing individual, dense data over a rather short span of time, which is the domain of microdevelopmental studies (Granott & Parziale, 2002). Microdevelopment is opposed to macrodevelopment not only in terms of the time variable involved. The paradigms have the same goal but different research designs, data collection strategies and data analysis. Siegler and Crowley compared macrodevelopmental methods to the taking of snapshots and microdevelopmental research to the making of a movie (Siegler & Crowley, 1991). In macrodevelopmental studies the focus is on common patterns of behaviour and researchers investigate the development of groups rather than the development of individuals. Such studies are often in fact not developmental studies per se but instead, as van Geert states critically, describe a collection of peer groups, ordered according to their age, and which is incapable of building a model of developmental processes (van Geert, 1994). Lee & Karmiloff-Smith point out that the main assumption of macrodevelopmental research is that individual characteristics are random errors and differences between subjects are random variations (Lee & Karmiloff-Smith, 2002, p. 246). Developmental psychologists are increasingly changing their point of view and claim that the dynamics of development cannot be investigated using macrodevelopmental methods alone. Moreover, they see both approaches as complementing, rather than competing with, one other (Kuhn, 1995; Lee & Karmiloff-Smith, 2002; Thelen & Smith, 1994). In microdevelopmental studies two methods are used: the microgenetic and the DST approaches. 'Microgenesis' was introduced by Werner (Werner, 1956) as a term for short-time development and since that time the terms 'microdevelopment' and 'microgenesis' have been used interchangeably. Nowadays, 'genetic' refers to phenomena that are related to genes. The 'Microgenetic method', on the other hand, is widely used in developmental psychology in studies on microdevelopment. In a microgenetic study the researcher follows a subject over a short time span, from the beginning of a process up until a stable stage has been reached. The observations are dense during times when changes occur and the aim of the analysis is to discover the processes that led to the observed changes. In the case of the microgenetic method the focus is on the phenomenon of change rather than on any long-term developmental trajectory.

In the last few years the dynamic systems approach has even been used to study child development. The basic assumption is that, according to the nonlinearity phenomenon, a specific individual – rather than a group of individuals – must be followed[1]. Sensitivity to initial conditions makes it necessary to track the development of a child from the very beginning of the process of change. The complexity of dynamic systems requires the use of multiple measures so as to pick up the interconnectedness between the subsystems involved in the development. Thelen and Ulrich (1991) employed the dynamic systems paradigm to study treadmill stepping performed by infants. They followed the development of motor skills in seven children over a period of six to nine months. The study showed that development occurs as a result of the self-organisation of many interacting elements and that systems tend to approach an attractor state. The stability of the systems, however, is lost at transition points. They argued that an appropriate, well defined developmental variable must be identified for further DST-conducted studies. Moreover, they focused on attractor states in the development process and on describing the developmental trajectory. The next important issue concerns the transition

[1] Lee and Karmiloff-Smith (2002, p. 260) even claim that grouping individuals could be a violation of the fundamental principles of a dynamic systems approach.

points, which signify the emergence of a new point in a learner's development (Thelen & Ulrich, 1991).

In studies on development conducted from the point of view of dynamic systems theory, variability is seen not as an error, a noise or an incident but as part of the self-organisation of a system and a characteristic developmental attribute that leads to progress in the development process. Increased instability and a longer recovery time after perturbation are the most identifiable indicators of change. In nonlinear dynamic systems such instabilities are a natural harbinger and a natural outcome of change. These reoccurring instabilities in the development process are a constituent element of variability, which researchers see as an enabling factor of development (Goldin-Meadow & Alibali, 2002; Siegler, 2002). A high level of intra-individual variability during a developmental period may be a sign of considerable developmental transition in an individual. Differences between individuals, i.e. variation between individual outcomes, on the other hand, suggest that these individuals are currently at several developmental levels. In traditional developmental studies such diversity and variability are treated as deviations from modal performances whereas in a DST-approach they play an important role in helping us understand changes. Individual differences reveal the possible state spaces of a system and possible developmental trajectories. Therefore, they should be treated as an inseparable part of developmental research and, as Thelen and Smith (1994, p. 342) desire, "the general ground for exploration and selection." To study variability in dynamic systems van Geert and van Dijk proposed several measures, such as moving min-max graphs or progmax-regmin graphs, and discussed the use of broadly adjusted variability measures, such as the standard deviation or the coefficient of variation (van Geert & van Dijk, 2002).

Development is a process of change resulting in a mature state. This process, as was mentioned above, proceeds nonlinearly and can be characterised by considerable variability. Such variability in development is reflected in fluctuating growth during a time span. Growth and development are often viewed as being identical with one another, but there are differences between the two. Growth is a mechanism of development. We often follow the development of a system by measuring the growth of one or more features. The development of language skills, among other things, can be traced through vocabulary growth. Changes in vocabulary used by children take the form of an S-curve. Around the age of 18 months considerable vocabulary growth takes place. This is called a vocabulary spurt and occurs after a silent period, when there is no progress in the child's lexicon. In the silent period a child's vocabulary does not increase. However, this cannot be interpreted as a halt in the development process. Even if no growth is observed it represents an active maturation period during which the child tests hypotheses and reorganizes its mental representations of words. During the silent period the system undergoes restructuring and the changes are of a qualitative nature. Growth, in turn, is a quantitative change which includes an increase or decrease, respectively. A decrease in performance means negative growth, a temporary regression. Van Geert enumerates four properties of growth: growth involves a quantitative change; growth is autocatalytic, which means that it is a process that triggers itself and causes the system to self-organise; growth is resource-absorbing, i.e. resources are limited, which limits the scale of the growth; finally, growth requires a pre-requisite in the form of a specific structural possibility in the system which enables changes to occur. In other words, growth can only proceed if there is an object, an entity that can grow, i.e. change its size or number (van Geert, 1991; 1994).

There are two kinds of growth: predictable growth and unpredictable growth. Examples of predictable growth include arithmetic growth, geometric growth, quadratic growth, cyclic growth and decay. In such patterns growth can be calculated using a constant value or a predefined mathematic formula. Unpredictable growth, on the other hand, means that we cannot use such formulae to describe how a certain feature will change over time. Unpredictable growth characterizes dynamic systems. One type of unpredictable growth is logistic growth, developed by Verhulst to calculate population growth. The population increases but the growth is limited because of the limited resources that the environment has and thus the growth of population depends on the so-called carrying capacity of the environment. As with population, so in the case of other complex dynamic systems we cannot predict the developmental trajectory. Therefore predictable growth models cannot be used for such systems. What we may assume is that the development will probably not take the form of linear (i.e. arithmetic), geometric or cyclic growth.

In his dynamic model of cognitive and language growth van Geert (1991) distinguished between the growth level and the growth rate. The former indicates the relative number of applications of a certain linguistic or cognitive feature, i.e. its cardinality of application, such as, for example, the number of inversions in questions divided by the total number of questions in a data set. When a second language learner uses the inversion rule in five questions out of a total of ten produced, his growth level in the case of this structural property is 50%. The growth level can even be expressed as a relative value, e.g. the number of words understood by a child. A set of growth levels builds a growth relation (G) that has the following property:

$$G: (S, t) \Rightarrow (L_{t1}, L_{t2}, L_{t3}, ..., L_{tn}).$$

The growth relation of a structural property (such as the inversion rule or passive vocabulary) during time span (*t*) is expressed as a sequence of growth levels $L_{t1,}$ $L_{t2,}$ $L_{t3,}$ and so on. The growth rate, in turn, indicates the strength of the growth, measured by mapping the current growth level onto another (preceding) growth level and can be calculated as follows:

$$r = L_{t2}/L_{t1.}$$

A growth rate of r=1.5 would indicate that at time *t*2 application of the structural property was 50% more frequent, while a growth rate of r = 0.5 should be interpreted as meaning that the occurrence of the investigated time property *t*2 was 50% less frequent, which may be seen as a regression. The growth rate formula implies that the initial growth level can never be 0, according to the basic mathematical assumption, that we cannot divide by zero. When considering growth the *minimal structural growth level* must be present, which means that the investigated property or element must occur at least once and the time when it emerges is called the *growth onset time* (van Geert, 1991).

The developmental process can sometimes translate into a regression in skills, followed by a new, reconstructed level. As Fischer, Yan & Stewart (2003) point out, development is even more complex and more dynamic in adults than in infants and children. They differentiate between two main meta-metaphors for adult development: ladders and a web. Developmental ladders categorize development as a simple, stepwise progression. They sketch developmental trends, but in fact they even simplify the complexity of developmental phenomena, and at the same time eclipse the variability of the development. Developmental webs, in turn, depict adult cognitive development as a complex process of dynamic construction, "within multiple ranges in multiple directions;" (Fischer, Yan & Stewart, 2003, p. 492). Developmental, constructed webs include three dynamic patterns in adult cognitive development: dynamic ranges, dynamic strands and networks, and dynamic constructions. Adults show a wide range of cognitive levels which result in much greater variability in performance than in children. They are able to think more contextually and flexibly, but sometimes they still make errors and behave primitively. Adults can solve more abstract tasks and at the same time even use low-level skills in performance. They still move between optimal and functional levels. Individuals reach their optimal level of performance primarily when there is strong support from the environment, which does not happen often. This is the main reason why there is such a gap between the functional and optimal levels. Functional levels increase slowly, while optimal levels have an up-and-down developmental trajectory, even if the trend is upwards. With increasing age, the gap between functional and optimal levels becomes greater. Adults constantly expand and develop multiple cognitive skills and strands and networks in the developmental web reflect the breadth, complexity and interconnectedness of several skills. Cognitive development in adults is characterized by dynamic changes in all directions, both backward and forward (Fischer, Yan & Stewart, 2003).

As has been mentioned above, development is not just a form of growth, a quantitative change. It also means that the system changes qualitatively. It becomes more differentiated and integrated, while self-organization proceeds accordingly. The maturation process thus involves a transformation from a split formation into an increasingly integrated construct. One such developmental sequence has been proposed by Dahl who identified the following developmental stages for grammatical patterns: free, periphrastic, affixal, and, finally, fusional. Every subsequent stage involves a higher maturity level that builds on the previous one (Dahl, 2004, pp. 106–107). In this sample we see a developmental path beginning with great independence and unboundedness between morphemes and concluding in their full integration within a word. The system does not thus change quantitatively – the number of morphemes remains the same. But it re-organizes, which leads to a more mature (seeing qualitatively) stage, characterized by greater integration of items.

Dynamics in the case of development means a change in behaviour. Schöner compares behavioural patterns with attractor states that are stable and resist change. First, when stability is lost a change can occur and it is instability in the system that enables cognitive processes to emerge. Learning as a change in behaviour is thus seen as a change in the dynamic (Schöner, 2009), and the study of nonlinear behaviour is called nonlinear dynamics (Hilborn, 2010, p. 3). When considering learning or development as a dynamic process we cannot predict what it will look like or what form the developmental trajectory will take. This statement refers to one of the main properties of dynamic systems – their chaotic behaviour. In the case of development studies it means that a researcher cannot look at a potential future developmental trajectory or model it. To trace a development entails looking at it from the current state backwards, to look at the history of the development, or, in other words, to make retrodictions rather than predictions, as Byrne (2002) explains it.

2.2. Dynamic systems theory and second language development

Language is a system that changes: "language is motion" (Segalowitz, 2010, p. 4), "there is nothing static about language" (Larsen-Freeman & Cameron, 2008, p. 6) – these are just two of the claims that can be treated as basic pre-requisites for investigating language as a dynamic system. Language is also a complex system, consisting of a set of subsystems such as phonology, morphology, syntax or semantics and embodied in other systems, for example the external environment in which it is used or the system of its users, which itself is complex and dynamic. Following this reasoning dynamic systems theory can most certainly be applied to language studies, especially those focusing on the development of language. The area of second language acquisition is one such field where complexity and dynamics are inherent properties.

Adopting a developmental perspective of second language learning is not new. The fact that a second language unfolds in steps and does not involve a sudden spurt in skills and competence is nowadays regarded as obvious. The maturing process whereby a student develops linguistic skills in a new language should be understood within the framework of three fundamental questions concerning second language acquisition, i.e. who, where and how. The developmental aspect covers the "how" question, i.e. what are the stages involved in acquiring skills in a second language. The "who"-question focuses on the diversity of learners: their age, social and educational background or individual characteristics. Finally, the "where" question highlights the role played by environmental factors in second language learning. Complexity and variability are also included within these three questions: there are many different individuals and groups of learners who learn a second language in different frameworks:

in a classroom environment or in natural settings. Furthermore, they develop their skills differently, depending on many factors, such as, e.g., their language background, individual characteristics, quantity and quality of input etc. Each of these factors encloses a system, which, in turn, is open and interacts with the environment, and is complex, because it consists of a variety of parts that are interconnected with one other.

Nevertheless, second language development is not in itself a system, just as development is not a system. It would be a logical error to treat a set of parts and a change in time as cognitively equal entities. Second language development is a process that involves many nonlinear, dynamic and complex systems that are embedded in these systems and where such systems are interconnected with each other. One of these systems is the learner, who is him or herself a complex set of many variables and subsystems. The human brain is the most complex system that exists and it develops continuously over a human lifetime. The learner enters the world of second language with his or her prior experiences, aptitudes, motivations, intelligence, learning strategies, cultural background, social competences, and so on. And these subsystems change continuously during the process of second language learning. The new language that they discover is complex and changes not only in its role as the learner's interlanguage but even as an open system that is a living organism and thus evolves. The next most important system is the environment. A second language can be learned in a classroom environment or learning can unfold in natural situations, when the learner lives in a community where the new language is used in everyday situations. These kinds of environment are complex systems. There are several properties that can change, such as, e.g., the group dynamics in the classroom, the time when a lesson in a second language begins, or the teacher. All parts of the systems in question interact with one other and this makes it impossible to predict how the second language will develop. Of course, the aim is to master the second language in the best way possible and to achieve the best level. However, this "best" is relative and cannot be unambiguously defined. For some learners the end point may mean building understandable utterances, for others it is the ability to speak without a foreign accent, for yet others it may entail pursuing a native level in written and spoken forms. When all these systems meet there is interplay between them, with some of them more active than others at certain points.

This interplay between systems is reflected in the nonlinearity and variability of language development. A learner can display a very high level of second language mastery not only because of his or her personal characteristics, such as aptitude or intelligence, but even as a result of being highly motivated at that very moment, being in good physical condition or because of having a good sociometric status in a group that gives the learner strong support (for a discussion of group dynamic factors in second language acquisition see e.g. (Dörney & Murphey, 2009; Kowal, 2012). Furthermore, it cannot be ruled out that the learner was at his or her optimal level at the point when the data were collected. At any other time, no matter whether it is the following day or next month, the same learner, even after spending more time on learning the new language, may perform worse than in the previous experiment. And in this case the interplay of other subsystems may be involved, e.g. the learner was in a poor physical condition, focused on a specific property in second language that distracted him from other features, or the experiment was carried out in another room, which caused the learner to feel uneasy and distracted, and could only perform at his functional level.

Variability in second language acquisition is not a new approach. The idea of a new emerging language as a system that undergoes change has been a subject of research since Selinkers raised the issue of interlanguage. In his ground-breaking paper (Selinker, 1972) he described interlanguage as variable in the sense that even if a structure in the second language has been mastered its erroneous version can re-emerge in several situations, i.e. when there is a disturbance in the learner's environment or in him-/herself. In this statement we can also recognize a complexity that influences this variability, where the factors are, for example, a learner's emotional state, the influence of second language instruction or the influence of the first language (Selinker, 1972). While Selinker sees variability in interlanguage as a systematic feature, Bickerton (1975) distinguishes between free and socially motivated variation, where the former is random in character and the latter is motivated by the individual choices the language user makes. Ellis broadens this approach to include a distinction between free and systematic variability. Free variation can manifest itself in false starts or in the use of second language rules in a random manner. Systematic variability, on the other hand, can occur in three contexts. The irregular occurrence of a target language's structures can thus be connected with a linguistic context, where a learner chooses a particular form in one and another in a different context. Systematic variability in the interlanguage can have its roots in a situational context when the learner uses one (correct) form in a formal situation and another (incorrect) form in informal conditions. The psycholinguistic context, in turn, is connected with planning conditions. When a learner has the opportunity to plan his or her utterances in a second language, he or she will produce more correct utterances than when no such possibility is available (Ellis, 1997). However, Ellis sees variability as part of the regularity of the interlanguage and thus as its predictable feature.

Variability in interlanguage has mainly been discussed from the point of view of the correct use of second language rules. Seen psycholinguistically, the learner may vary in his or her production in the second language depending on how much attention he or she pays to these norms. From this point of view variability may occur either as a sign of an activated vs. inactivated Monitor, based on Krashen's theory (Krashen, 1981). On the other hand, Tarone, criticizes such a dichotomic approach and proposes a Chameleon Model to explain variability, which is more gradual in character and emphasizes the variety of environmental conditions that lead to multifarious production in the interlanguage. The learner thus varies in his or her production in the second language not because of how much attention is paid to the language form, but because he or she adjusts the correctness of his or her utterances to the situation or the environmental context (Tarone, 1989). In general, research on variability in the interlanguage conducted in the 1970s and 1980s focused on finding regularities in the different uses of the target language structures, seen from the viewpoint of accuracy.

Another view of variability in second language development emerges with the processability approach. Processability theory investigates the developmental hierarchy of morphology and syntax. It distinguishes between five processing procedures, beginning with the word/lemma level, where the learner uses uninflected words in the second language, which is an effect of cognitive access being restricted solely to the lexical category in the target language. The next step involves the emergence of the category procedure. When he is at this level the learner can process inflectional paradigms in the second language. This ability, in turn, is a prerequisite for processing phrases, i.e. exchanging grammatical information between words within a phrase. The fourth level implies the processing of grammatical information at the sentence level and is the stage preceding the fifth level, namely the subordinate clause procedure, which, however, must not be applicable to every language (Pienemann, 1998). What differentiates the Processability Theory from earlier issues concerned with interlanguage development is the emergence, and not the accuracy, criterion. And with this shift in perspective another aspect of variation in second language production comes into view. The PT approach to interlanguage variation aims to determine the range of variable features that can occur at a particular developmental level. This perspective, however, once more implies a predictive factor in second language development. In other words, based on a learner's current developmental level we can predict what grammatical features may appear in his or her second language production. And this predictability is an effect of the so called Hypothesis Space, which is seen as defining the scope of Processability Theory and setting the limits of possible grammatical structures that can occur within it. The processability approach, however, comes close to DST, because it sees second language development as a dynamic, nonlinear and variable process. Due to its focus on morphosyntactic structures, processability theory implies a degree of predictability in development and it does not investigate the interconnectedness and interplay between several systems in the developmental process, even if it does not exclude their presence and importance.

An explicit focus on DST became more remarkable in linguistics at the end of the 1990s. In the years following the pioneering paper of Larsen--Freeman (1997) interest in this area increased rapidly. The idea of viewing language as a dynamic nonlinear system is closely connected with the concept of complexity and chaos theory. In fact, all these paradigms are used, or at least mentioned, when the development of a second language is considered and they are also interconnected with other sciences, such as biology, sociology and economics. The acquisition of a new language is a process that involves many systems that are complex, behave chaotically and change dynamically. The new point of view has even led to a shift in the nomenclature, whereby the term *acquisition* is no longer used and has been substituted by *development*. The replacement of the widely used expression *Second Language Acquisition* with *Second Language Development* is explained by the fact that linguistic skills undergo continuous changes – they can improve or decline. Furthermore, there is no end point at which a language can be stated as completely acquired, as it is developing all the time. Finally, language cannot be acquired and then possessed forever. From a developmental perspective we can even conclude that a second language is never acquired (de Bot & Larsen-Freeman, 2011; Larsen-Freeman, 2002).

Since the beginning of the 21st Century dynamic systems/complexity theory has appeared more and more often in second language studies, both as a theoretical issue (de Bot, Lowie & Verspoor, 2005; 2007; de Bot,

2008; van Geert, 2007; Larsen-Freeman & Cameron, 2008) and in empirical studies (Verspoor, Lowie & van Dijk, 2008; Spoelman & Verspoor, 2010; Polat & Kim, 2013; Caspi, 2010). There is even a practical guide with methods and techniques that can be employed in DST-driven second language research (Verspoor, de Bot & Lowie, 2011), while a Dynamic Model of Multilingualism has been devised for multilingual development purposes (Herdina & Jessner, 2002).

In DST-conducted studies on second language development most research assumptions together with DST methodology have been adapted from developmental psychological studies. Such research has focused on the development of a small number of subjects, based on dense data collection, which corresponds to microgenetic studies in developmental psychology. A study devised in this way focuses thus not on general developmental patterns but rather on the development of an individual, or a few individuals over a certain period of time. Furthermore, the focus is on variability in development. However, due to the limited number of subjects involved, the primary goal is to investigate within-subject variability. Finally, owing to the complexity of the systems, the focus is on tracing interconnectedness between several subsystems during language development, which may make it possible to explain the nonlinearity, variability and unpredictability of such development.

Verspoor, Lowie & van Dijk (2008) analysed intra-individual variability in a Dutch advanced learner of English. In this longitudinal, three-year study, the authors studied 18 academic writing samples. Although it was not explicitly mentioned in the study, data collection probably took place twice a month. However, we do not know if the intervals between the experiments were equal, owing to, e.g., holidays (the subject was a university student). The study investigated the development of vocabulary use and sentence complexity. Inter-individual variability was presented in the form of min-max graphs. Although the emphasis was on variability, also the interplay between several variables was studied. The analysis showed that the average Nominal Phrase length and number of words per finite verb correlated with one another and that there was even a strong correlation between (detrended) sentence length and (detrended) number of words per finite verb. Even if an increase in all correlates over a three-year period could be observed, the development was far from linear (Verspoor, Lowie & van Dijk, 2008). The study not only shows how dynamically second language development can proceed, even in the case of an advanced learner, but also highlighted the variability that can occur at any stage of development. Spoelman and Verspoor (2010) studied the dynamics of the development of accuracy and complexity. As with the analysis above this was a longitudinal three-year case study of a Dutch university student (19 years old at the beginning of the experiments). In this case, however, the target language was Finnish and the learner had no previous knowledge of the Finnish language when she began her language course at university. A total of 54 writing samples were collected over a three-year period. As it was a DST-study it entailed dense data collection. An accuracy rate was taken to measure the accuracy of the overall case. Complexity was investigated at word, phrase and sentence level. In accordance with the principle of system interconnectedness the authors investigated the interaction between case errors and word complexity. In line with this approach a broad range of statistical tools was used to show how variability changed, how dynamically the language development proceeded and how the variables interacted with each other: min-max graphs, Progmax-Regmin graphs, row, and detrended correlations. The study not only revealed development in accuracy and complexity during this three-year period, but it also explored how this development proceeded. The variability in accuracy was greater at the beginning of the experiments, after which it almost stabilized. In the case of complexity the trend was similar, even if a little more variability occurred at later periods of development. However, the system appeared to achieve an attractor state and stabilized. On the other hand, the interaction between accuracy and complexity did not appear to stabilize and tended to be rather random (Spoelman & Verspoor, 2010).

A study by Polat and Kim (2013) had a similar focus and followed the development of an advanced untutored learner of English with Turkish as L1. The data were collected over the course of one year and at equal intervals – every two weeks - which resulted in 24 samples. In this case study the authors traced the development of accuracy, lexical diversity and syntactic complexity. It turned out that no clear developmental tendency could be determined and all the studied properties showed distinctive patterns. Neither accuracy nor complexity increased over the one-year period. Even variability, presented in the form of min-max graphs, fluctuated in all the investigated features (Polat & Kim, 2013). Apart from variability in development the study also showed that the process of second language learning cannot be predicted and even in longitudinally conducted experiments no unambiguous developmental trajectory can be reconstructed.

The most extensive study in this field is the doctoral dissertation of Caspi (2010). She investigated vocabulary knowledge, accuracy and complexity in four university students aged 23–28. The subjects had different L1s: Portugese, Mandarin Chinese, Indonesian and Vietnamese, and the author studied their development of English over a 36-week period, which makes her analysis rather more micro- than macrodevelopmental in character compared to the topics mentioned above. To assess the students' knowledge of vocabulary the author looked at their receptive and productive levels, including recognition, recall, controlled production and free production. The data were analysed primarily at the individual level, with some general conclusions also being drawn for all four participants as a whole. The general outcome of the study was that vocabulary knowledge developed at all levels, and that variability was common, especially in free production. The second part of the study concentrated on interaction between lexical and syntactic complexity and accuracy, as well as on creating a dynamic model based on these interactions. The author analysed data from one of the four participants that took part in the study – the Portuguese student – but the main findings were compared with three other learners which served as a basis for modelling the developmental trajectory. The interaction between lexical complexity and accuracy was a more competitive one compared to that between lexical accuracy and syntactic complexity. The interplay of syntactic complexity and syntactic accuracy, in turn, tended to be more supportive than competitive (Caspi, 2010).

Until now the dynamics of second language development have mainly been studied at the intra-individual level. What is still missing, however, are longitudinal studies involving more participants where even inter-individual variability can be traced and investigated. Such a study format makes it possible to create one or more developmental patterns which cannot be modelled in case studies. In longitudinal research that focuses on the development of a larger number of individuals more systems are involved and following the development of a group of individuals can shed some light not only on any conceivable similarities in individual trajectories, variability and interconnections between several subsystems, but even on the dynamics of inter-individual variability in development. Because such longitudinal, multi-individual studies take up more time and resources the consequence can be that data collection will not be as dense as in microdevelopmental or longitudinal case studies. They can thus serve as a complementing stream in DST-conducted second language research.

Dynamic systems theory investigates the behaviour of dynamic, nonlinear, complex and open systems. The basic condition for studying such systems is to define the (sub)systems and explore their interconnection during the course of development, which thus makes it possible to reconstruct the developmental trajectory and brings us closer to answering the question: "why did the development take this certain shape?" The formation of developmental patterns in second language learning is more likely in long-term longitudinal research continuing over at least several months, because in such a format there is a greater likelihood that many possible variables will occur and thus have the space in which to act. However, it must be stressed that even in such extended longitudinal studies no prediction can be made about what level a certain learner will achieve or when he or she will reach this particular level. In this sense drawing a possible developmental pattern should be seen as an estimate, not a prognosis or prediction. And it should always be followed by the assumption that no parameter will change in the meantime, which, in turn, contradicts the main property of complex and dynamic systems.

Dynamic systems theory in second language development is used as a tool for describing, analyzing and explaining how entire subsystems interact in a process. As a theory of nonlinear changes in complex systems DST provides a space in which we can follow the process of a specific change from the perspective of microdevelopmental studies. Moreover, it allows us to trace long-term development, i.e. make a retrodiction of developmental trajectories, study intra- and inter-individual variability as well as the interplay between the many variables making up the entire system. Dynamic systems theory does not pre-empt other developmental or SLA-theories and should thus not be treated as a competing paradigm. Rather it captures those aspects of second language development that other theories do not investigate because of the different underlying conceptual assumptions and/or methodological solutions. Van Geert (2008, p. 183) even claims that:

> dynamic systems is not a specific theory but [...] is a general view on change, change in complex systems, in particular, systems consisting of many interacting components, the properties of which can change over the course of time.

3

Complexity, Accuracy and Fluency in a Second Language

The question of how to determine a learner's proficiency in a language he or she is currently learning has been a subject of research for many years now. One measure that is widely used in studies on first language acquisition is the mean Length of Utterance (MLU), introduced by Brown (1973) in his pivotal work on the development of English in three children aged 18 to 44 months. However, this index cannot be applied to second language investigations, not only because the learner has already passed through the early phases of learning his or her first language[2] and thus has a prior, more or less conscious knowledge of a language system, but also due to the fact that the skills the learner has acquired in the first language open up space for exploring the world and gaining new experiences. A journey into the world of another, new language also entails entering into a wealth of new systems: the language system, the learning environment, or a new culture – and all this at a time when the learner is already equipped with his or her first-language background and prior experiences. Therefore, by the 1970s L2-researchers were already calling for another, objective (Hakuta, 1975; Larsen-Freeman, 1978) developmental index for measuring second language proficiency.

Around a half century ago Lado proposed a "skills-and-element" model of second language proficiency in which three elements of language knowledge (phonology, structure, lexicon) could be assessed separately in the context of four language skills: listening, reading, writing, and speaking (Lado, 1961). The model was expanded and fine-tuned by Carroll, who claimed that even more elements should be measured within the framework of skills, i.e. phonology and orthography, morphology and syntax,

[2] The question of simultaneous bilingualism, when a child acquires more than one language as his or her first language at the same time, is not discussed here.

and lexis (Carroll, 1968). About a decade later, Canale and Swain called for another, multi-component model of second language proficiency, with the focus on communicative competence, including grammatical, sociolinguistic, discourse and strategic competence (Canale & Swain, 1980). Ten years later Bachman (1990) pointed out that the earlier skills and competence models should be further enriched through research on how language is used to achieve communicative goals. Furthermore, he postulated that language use needs to be viewed as a dynamic process. He created a theoretical framework for communicative language ability (CLA), consisting in a knowledge of and the ability to implement CLA for "appropriate, contextualized communicative use" (Bachman, 1990, p. 84). The proposed framework consists of three components: language competence, strategic competence, and psychophysiological mechanisms. Language competence refers to that set of elements used in communication in which language is the main medium. Strategic competence, in turn, expresses the mental capacity to apply language competence in contextualized communicative language use. Finally, the psychophysiological mechanisms have their origins in the neurological and psychological processes that are activated in a particular use of language as a physical phenomenon, e.g., sound (Bachman, 1990).

Besides these approaches second language researchers have often focused on factors of overall proficiency, such as fluency, accuracy or complexity, which, however, have often been studied separately (cf. Chenoweth & Hayes, 2001; Towell, Howkins & Bazergui, 1996; Bardovi-Harlig & Bofman, 1989; Lennon, 1990; Casanave, 1994; Ishikawa, 1995). At the end of the 1990s Skehan (1996; 1998) proposed an integrated, three-dimensional model of complexity, accuracy and complexity and this has been treated as complementing the approach to second language proficiency. The CAF-triad, as it is called and broadly used, has been increasingly adopted as the main property of learners' L2-proficiency. Although there is no common definition of each of the fields the broadly accepted specifications refer to the heterogeneity, interconnectedness and sophistication of linguistic structures as the main characteristics of complexity, to the ability to produce error-free language as an attribute of accuracy, as well as to effortless, smooth and rapid language production, which together should characterize fluency (cf. Ellis, 2008; Lennon, 1990; Wolfe-Quintero, Inagaki & Kim, 1998).

The concept of complexity, accuracy and fluency has also been assimilated into the Common European Framework of Reference for Languages

(2001). However, only accuracy and fluency are named explicitly, while complexity has been included within the categories *range* and *coherence*. Within the three overall reference levels, i.e. Basic User, Independent User and Proficient User, which in turn correspond to the levels labeled as A1-A2, B1-B2 and C1-C2, fluency is mentioned explicitly no earlier than at level B2 and this level is also described as one where the learner can produce and understand complex utterances in a second language. Looking exclusively at the descriptors for proficiency in speaking and writing, a basic user has low level of complexity, with a limited range of words and constructions. Accuracy in a level A1 or A2 learner is low, and only "some simple structures" (CEFR, 2001, p. 28) are used correctly. Basic users cannot communicate fluently and they very often stop, reformulate or correct themselves. Independent users are characterized by higher complexity, meaning that they possess a "sufficient" vocabulary and the ability to link linguistic elements into longer chunks. Level B2 in particular is described as a stage with complex sentences and coherent utterances. Accuracy in independent users is expected to be limited to frequently used situations at level B1, and more controlled in other situations at level B2. Fluency, in turn, is mastered in the case of short and simple utterances, and at level B2 occurs even in longer text units. Proficient users can produce complex utterances in their second language by using many connectors and a broad range of lexical items. They make few errors and have considerable control over their free production in their second language. Their fluency is characterized by natural flow and a lack of effort in language use (CEFR, 2001)

The development, measurement validity and interconnectedness of particular dimensions have been broadly discussed in the literature, as is echoed in the report compiled by Wolfe-Quintero, Inagaki and Kim (1998), a special issue of *Applied Linguistics* (2009, Vol. 30(4)), and the monograph edited by Housen, Kuiken and Vedder (2012). For example, Skehan proposed a Trade-Off Hypothesis, suggesting that more attention paid to one of the above three dimensions would undermine the performance of the other two. This hypothesis and previous research he refers to lead to the conclusion that "simultaneously advantaging all three (CAF) performance areas is unusual" (Skehan, 2009, p. 512). However, as Skehan points out, research on this interplay is limited. Furthermore, he advocates the implementation of a fourth dimension – lexical performance – in SLA proficiency studies. Larsen-Freeman calls for an integrated, interrelated view of all three dimensions, which is a DST/CT perspective. This is because "if we examine the dimensions one by one we miss their interaction and the fact that the way that they interact changes with time as well" (Larsen-Freeman, 2009, p. 582). Housen and Kuiken (2009), and Housen, Kuiken & Vedder (2012) stress the multifaceted and multidimensional characteristics of these phenomena, which in turn affect the validity, reliability and efficacy of measurement. Using as their starting point an association with the word *calf,* which is biological in character, Norris and Ortega propose an organic understanding of these three dimensions, pointing both to the complexity of each of these and to their developmental character. This in turn led them to the claim that "... CAF as a whole represents a dynamic system of loosely related phenomena that interact in often unpredictable ways" (Norris & Ortega, 2009, p. 556). The complexity, dynamic character and unpredictability of development is thus an exceptional challenge that needs to be taken into consideration when devising appropriate measures that would cover all the aspects involved in each dimension of proficiency.

Wolfe-Quintero, Inagaki and Kim reported 39 studies in which more than one hundred measures were used. They focused on two main questions: how these measures evaluated development in writing, and what measures could be treated as the best indicator of developmental level. A comparison of the above studies and measures shows that in the case of fluency, the "best" measures corresponding to development were number of words per T-unit[3] (W/T), number of words per clause (W/C), and number of words per error-free T-unit (W/EFT). The most appropriate measures of grammatical complexity were number of clauses per T-unit (C/T), and the number of dependent clauses per clause (DC/C). In the case of lexical complexity, on other hand, the most valid developmental measures turned out to be the number of word types divided by the square root of two times the total number of words (WT/√2W) and the ratio of sophisticated word types to the overall number of word types (DWT/WT). Finally, the most valid measures of accuracy development were deemed to be the number of error-free T-units per T-unit (EFT/T) and the number of errors per T-unit (E/T) (Wolfe-Quintero, Inagaki & Kim, 1998).

From a developmental point of view the fundamental question is, however, how these three dimensions change over time and how they interact in the process of second language development. Besides the cited

[3] A T-unit refers to the 'minimal terminable unit' and was a term introduced by Hunt. A T-unit is defined as "one main clause plus any subordinate clause or nonclausal structure that is attached to or embedded in it" (Hunt, 1970, p. 4).

DST-studies on complexity and accuracy development (Caspi, 2010; Polat & Kim, 2013; Spoelman & Verspoor, 2010; Verspoor, Lowie & van Dijk, 2008) two other studies need to be mentioned here. The first study is that conducted by Larsen-Freeman, who was the first to look at the development of all three dimensions from a dynamic point of view. Five Chinese adult learners of English were observed over a six-month period. The fluency of their written output was measured as the average number of words per T-unit (W/T), their grammatical complexity as the average number of clauses per T-unit (C/T), their accuracy as the ratio of error-free T-units to T-unit (EFT/T) and their vocabulary complexity as the ratio of word types to the square root of two times the word (WT/√2W). In every dimension the average results showed progress in development, although with great variation between subjects. The development of particular learners was very dynamic and did not reflect the average path. Larsen-Freeman identified different learner profiles. One of the five learners, for example, focused more on vocabulary complexity while the others tended to concentrate on grammatical complexity. The same participant made the greatest progress in fluency compared with his fellow students, while another showed the most improvement in grammatical complexity. In general, however, the common and most pronounced change, measured in terms of the rate of change, was observed in the case of accuracy. The study showed that individual developmental patterns can differ from the average. Furthermore, Larsen-Freeman makes a very important point by emphasizing that "no particular subsystem of language has a priori priority, and no dimension of language proficiency has a priori privilege" (Larsen-Freeman, 2006, p. 615). She makes this observation in reference to Thelen and Bates' (Thelen & Bates, 2003) interpretation of system complexity. From a second language learner perspective, on the other hand, such an assumption may not apply, and, as Ellis assumes, "L2 learners may be content with less than target language competence and may also be more concerned with fluency than accuracy" (Ellis, 1994, p. 107), a fact which has even been explained by Skehan's above-mentioned Trade-Off Hypothesis, which views all three dimensions as receiving unequal treatment from second language learners.

Another study that should be mentioned here is that conducted by Gunnarsson, in which she reported on the development of complexity, accuracy and fluency in five Swedish high school students learning French. This study is interesting not only from the viewpoint of the language mode investigated – as in other research studies cited above the focus was on written production. Furthermore, the experimental tool used in the study was ScriptLog, which in turn meant that fluency was measured as the mean length of burst, i.e. the number of words between pauses or other interruptions. To measure complexity the number of clauses per T-unit was used (C/T). To measure accuracy four morpho-syntactic features were adapted: subject-verb agreement in the present, correct choice of past tense, accurate use of negation, and correct use of clitic object pronouns. In the present study, however, only fluency and complexity were analyzed from a developmental point of view, with first and the last of the four experimental sessions being compared. In turn, in the case of accuracy, due to a small number of occurrences, all data were taken together, which precluded the comparison of all results. The results for fluency show that the writers who were most fluent in the first session also made the greatest progress in fluency at the end of the study. The development of complexity, however, was characterized by a decline in a student's performance with the highest level of complexity at the beginning and growth observed in three other students. No general relationship was noted between the development of fluency and complexity. Gunnarsson even found that little interconnectedness was possible between fluency and accuracy, but due to the different data sets involved this conclusion should be treated rather cautiously (Gunnarsson, 2012).

A developmental view of complexity, accuracy and fluency was also adopted by Ferrari who investigated these dimensions in four L2-learners of Italian over a three-year period. The informants represented a heterogeneous group of different nationalities, L1s and language skills in the target language. The study was macrodevelopmental in character. Hence there were four data collection points, with four tasks each: two monologic and two interactive. The analysis focused on spoken texts in Italian so that the AS-unit[4] and not the T-unit was chosen as the reference measurement. Syntactic complexity was thus measured for subordination and length, using the average number of subordinate clauses per A-unit and the average number of words per clause, respectively. Accuracy has been investigated as the ratio of error free A-units and fluency, in turn, was measured as the average number of silent pauses per AS-unit and the av-

[4] AS-unit is defined as "a single speaker's utterance consisting of an independent clause, or sub-clausal unit, together with any subordinated clause(s) associated with either" (Foster, Tonkyn & Wigglesworth, 2000, p. 365).

erage number of hesitation phenomena per AS-unit. The study revealed a considerable (U-shaped) increase in accuracy, almost linear progress in fluency and increased syntactic complexity, although solely with regard to clause length. Furthermore, Ferrari suggested a trade-off effect in the case of one learner due to a decrease in accuracy accompanied by an increase in complexity. The development of complexity, accuracy and fluency in students was also interconnected with their level of proficiency in L2 at the beginning of the study. Variation between tasks was greater in less advanced students while it remained at the same level in more proficient learners. However, as Ferrari stressed, the limited number of participants ruled out more general interpretations of the study results (Ferrari, 2012).

The development of complexity, accuracy and complexity has been studied in many contexts and with many target languages. On the other hand, no general developmental sequence could be determined, first of all due to the small number of subjects investigated longitudinally and because of the fact that most studies examined learners who had already achieved at least an intermediate proficiency level at the beginning of their courses. However, by employing cognitive interpretations of the mechanisms involved in SLD some researchers have tried to find a way in which these three proficiency dimensions could emerge. Housen, Kuiken and Vedder, for example, assumed a certain developmental sequence, which can be illustrated as follows:

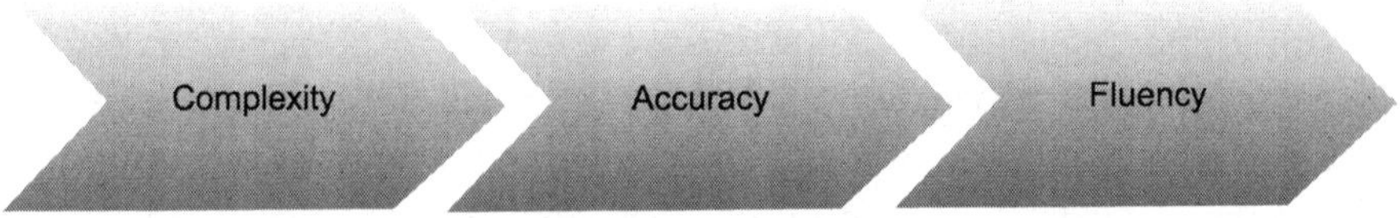

Figure 3.1. The suggested developmental sequence of Complexity, Accuracy and Fluency

The underlying assumption is that the learner first has to internalize new and complex structures in the new language, which leads to a growth in complexity. Once it has become more complex, the language increases steadily in accuracy. Only after achieving control over the performance and acquiring the target structures will the learner be able to produce fluent utterances in his or her second language. At the same time, the authors point out that the proposed sequence is only speculative and may even be simplistic (Housen, Kuiken & Vedder, 2012, p. 7). The same sequence, however, is also mentioned by Skehan and Foster (Skehan & Foster, 2012, p. 201). From the descriptors presented in CEFR (2001), however, another developmental sequence emerges. The learner begins with easy and incorrect language use and it is fluency that appears to develop earliest, based on simple and incorrect structures. Afterwards accuracy, although only in noncomplex and not sophisticated utterances, and not until learners at B2 level are able to express their thoughts in the second language in a more complex way.

3.1. Complexity

The diversity of definitions and approaches focusing on complexity can best be understood through a non-linguistic explanation of the phenomenon: "A criterion of the complexity of a phenomenon is the amount of information necessary to define it and the practical difficulty in obtaining that information" (Favre *et al.* 1988, p. 7). In other words, the deeper the insight the more elements we need in order to describe it accurately.

Complexity in second language development is considered to be the most difficult component to handle, both because of the ambiguous way it is defined in several studies and also owing to its multidimensional character. We can find more general definitions in the literature, which characterize complexity, such as "the extent to which learners produce elaborated language" (Ellis & Barkhuizen, 2005, p. 139), or more fine-grained descriptions, involving more definientia, and focusing on selected aspects of language, such as in the definition of linguistic complexity referring to "the intrinsic formal or semantic-functional properties of L2-elements (e.g. forms, meanings, and form-meaning mappings) or to properties of (sub-)systems of L2-elements" (Housen, Kuiken & Vedder, 2012, p. 4). The latter view understands complexity to be two-dimensional in character, being either cognitive or linguistic, where cognitive complexity, sometimes even called difficulty, expresses the relative difficulty a L2-learner has in processing second language elements. Such a view has been forwarded by DeKeyser (1998), Housen and Kuiken (2009), as well as by Williams and Evans (1998), and is paralleled by the taxonomy devised by Dahl (2004) and Miestamo (2008), consisting of absolute and relative complexity, where absolute complexity corresponds to linguistic complexity, and relative complexity to cognitive complexity.

It is not seldom the case that complexity is associated with difficulty, which we can see on the one hand in the view of cognitive complexity as being on a par with difficulty. A similar approach has also been adopted by Pallotti, who distinguishes between the complexity of tasks, which he identifies as difficulty in an objective sense, and the complexity of performance, which has a subjective character (Pallotti, 2009). The difficulty-factor of complexity seems to be one of its most distinctive features: Skehan, for example, juxtaposes it with "challenging language" (Skehan, 2009, p. 511), while Trudgill identifies it with "difficulty of learning for adults" (Trudgill, 2001, p. 371). However, Dahl suggests that complexity should not be treated as equivalent to difficulty. Beginning with the assumption that relative complexity can be associated with difficulty he argues that "what an individual finds difficult obviously depends not only on the complexity of the object of learning but also on the individual's previous knowledge" (Dahl, 2004, p. 282). Therefore, the subjective and objective aspects of complexity should be treated as two distinct entities so as to avoid any misunderstanding both in theoretical considerations and empirical investigations.

Pallotti distinguishes between three different meanings of complexity in linguistic research: structural, cognitive and developmental. The first reflects the formal range of linguistic elements and their relational patterns, the second is associated with the effort needed to process linguistic structures and the last, i.e. developmental complexity, refers to the process of mastering linguistic structures when the first or second language is being acquired (Pallotti, 2015). Structural complexity is very often treated as a representative of complex systems, where there are "many different elements each with a number of degrees of freedom" (Nichols, 2009, p. 111), "the number of discrete components that a language feature or a language system consists of, and the number of connections between the different components" (Bulté & Housen, 2012, p. 24) or "the number of different elements and their interconnections" (Pallotti, 2015, p. 120)

The most common classification proposed in most studies on structural complexity involves a distinction between lexical complexity, on the one hand, and grammatical complexity, on the other. Lexical complexity is often understood as the diversity of lexical items used in a text. The more the vocabulary varies the more complex the utterance is perceived to be. Lexical diversity can be measured using, for example, type/token ratios, the Giraud Index or the D-index, while the type/token ratio has very often been criticized due to its unreliability in view of its negative correlation with text length. Another way to investigate lexical complexity is to look inside the word-level, i.e. to measure the number of lexemes in a word or the number of derivational affixes, which, however, tends to illustrates grammatical rather than lexical complexity, as Bulté and Housen (2012) point out. Yet another view of lexical complexity, and one that has also been criticised, entails looking at the density of words, where lexical words should reveal themselves to be more complex than function words. Even this perspective, however, has no reasonable explanation when we base our reasoning on the assumption that complexity means diversity of items AND their interconnectedness. In investigations of lexical density the mutual interconnections of lexical items are completely ignored.

Grammatical complexity can be analysed as morphological or syntactic complexity. However, morphological complexity seen as, for example, the frequency of inflectional morphology of words, is not often the subject of SLA-research. Syntactic complexity, on the other hand, has attracted much more attention and appears in a variety of studies on complexity.

Norris and Ortega investigated syntactic complexity from the point of view of the reliability of the adopted measures and their correspondence with the multifaceted characteristics of this proficiency skill. They discussed the most commonly used measures, based on: (i) length, (ii) the amount of subordination and coordination, (iii) the variety, sophistication and acquisitional timing of grammatical forms and (iv) the frequency of certain grammatical structures treated as more sophisticated and (therefore) later acquired (modals, passives or infinitival phrases). On the one hand, they point out that some measures are redundant and should not be used together in one study – especially those concerned with subordination as the main indicator of syntactic complexity. On the other hand, they call for the use of complementary measures that can refer to other dimensions of complexity, such as, for example, the variety of grammatical constructions. In an analysis of 16 studies they severely criticized the incomplete view of complexity that emerges when applying only one measure, which turned out to be the most common practice among researchers. The most common measures either focused on global complexity, such as the mean length of T-unit, or, which was even more common, subordination, which Norris and Ortega treated as providing a too limited understanding of complexity. What they observed was the increasingly common view of syntactic complexity as a form of structural variety and sophistication. They thus argue that a reasonable way to investigate complexity is to analyse it both generally and more specifically, i.e. using length-based measures in combination with measures exploring subordination and phrasal elaboration (Norris & Ortega, 2009).

Following on from earlier approaches, Bulté and Housen presented a detailed overview of several aspects of L2-complexity that focused on grammatical and lexical complexity, and linked them together with different levels of construct specifications (theoretical, observational, and operational) and different measurements. They referred to forty studies on linguistic complexity, in which 40 measures were used. The most frequently employed measures turned out to be those that are general in character, such as the mean number of words per T-unit and the mean number of clauses per T-(c- or AS-, respectively) unit for grammatical complexity, and the number of different words per total number of words (TTR) or the Guiraud Index (WT/√W) for lexical complexity, rather than measures that take into account more specific features, such as the frequency of specific linguistic constructions, e.g., passive forms or infinitival phrases (Bulté & Housen, 2012).

If we view complexity as a property of complex, dynamic systems we can assume that the development of this dimension will involve the self-organisation of several subsystems, such as lexicon, morphology and syntax. This self-organisation can proceed in the form of "parts separated" to "parts joined" (see Ashby, 1962), which, for example, can be expressed in the broader use of extended, complex phrases instead of simple phrases, consisting only of the necessary constituting elements, or in the increasingly extended use of subordinated structures, such as subordinated clauses or clause-like constructions used in order to package information, instead of adding linguistic elements in the form of coordinate constructions. A complex and dynamic view of the development of lexical and syntactic complexity should thus cover more than one aspect of it. Based on the definition that complexity in general refers to a variety of elements and their mutual interconnection we will thus investigate lexical complexity as lexical diversity, on the one hand, and phrasal elaboration, on the other. Syntactic complexity, in turn, expresses itself not solely in subordination, but also in a variety of syntactic constructions. And all these features are in ongoing interplay with one another during the entire developmental process.

3.2. Accuracy

Accuracy is an inherent part of second language proficiency. The more correct an utterance the more the new language is assumed to have been mastered and internalized in the learner's mind. The reference to a learner's accuracy was one of the earliest issues in second language studies. However, what should be stressed in this context is the topsy-turvy effect that occurs in this context. Even if second language teachers and researchers use the word *accuracy* they very often focus on *inaccuracy*, i.e. the amount and gravity of errors. In analyses of a learner's performance in the second language his or her accuracy is in most contexts discussed from the point of view how many and what kind of errors have been committed. And even if the focal point tends nowadays to shift from error analysis to an analysis of accuracy, it appears almost automatic to begin with the "dark side of the force," i.e. with errors, and not with the light side.

Such an approach was very common at the beginning of SLA-research. As early as the 1960s Corder pointed out the significance of errors when he distinguished between mistakes that are nonsystematic and thus treated as errors of performance, and "real" errors, which are systematic in character and offer evidence of insufficient competence in second language. The significance of a learner's inaccuracy refers to the teacher, the learner and the researcher. For the teacher the analysis of his or her learners' errors can be an indicator of the learners' stage in the learning process. From the second language learner's point of view errors are on the one hand a sign that the learner is testing a hypothesis about the second language. On the other, they can be treated as a learning strategy. Finally, based on errors in second language production researchers can gain insights into the process of how a student learns a new language (Corder, 1967). Even though almost half a century has passed since the advent of error analysis, and forty years since the shift to performance analysis in the 1970s, when aquisitional stages rather than deviations from the target norm became the focus, accuracy has remained one of the main issues in second language research.

The first impression one might have when investigating accuracy is that this is the simplest dimension to define because it provides information on how correct the learner's performance is in the target language. Housen and Kuiken thus present it as the most transparent and most consistent of the three performance areas of Complexity, Accuracy and Fluency (Housen & Kuiken, 2009, p. 463). Foster and Skehan described it as "freedom from error" (Foster & Skehan, 1996, p. 305), but the difficulty begins when we try to define what an error means in the context of second language development. As in almost every investigation, the key question is where the cut-off point is and what should be taken as the reference: the normative account, native speaker/rater acceptance (native speakers/raters can differ from each other in this respect) or something else? In the context of second language learning Lennon describes error as "a linguistic form or combination of forms which, in the same context and under similar conditions of production, would, in all likelihood, not be produced by the speakers' native speaker counterpart" (Lennon, 1991, p. 182).

In her own investigations of accuracy Polio (1997) distinguished between three main rating approaches: holistic scales, accuracy of the T-unit/clause and error frequency. The holistic view of accuracy involves a general assessment of the learner's text, in which both lexical-grammatical accuracy and content are taken into consideration, but where accuracy is treated as one of many different aspects of the text quality. In a study conducted by Evans *et al.* (2010) 75% of the total score is based on accuracy and 25% on content, Lo and Hylan (2007), for example, also took text organization into account. Lundstrom and Baker adopted what is known as Essay Scored Rubric, which was devised by Paulus (1999) where six features were assessed on a scale of one to ten: organization, i.e. how effective the thesis were stated, development, expressed as, inter alia, an appropriate use of examples, and cohesion, which was scaled according to the mutual relationship of ideas expressed in the text. The feature evaluated next, i.e. structure, referred to syntax complexity and grammatical accuracy. Vocabulary, in turn, was rated high when words were used precisely and the meaning was clear. The final aspect, mechanics concerns the general formatting of the text and spelling accuracy (Lundstrom & Baker, 2009). The accuracy of a T-unit or a clause is on the one hand more objective than holistic scales and distinct from measures of complexity. The drawback of this measure is that it neglects the severity of errors and their frequency within one syntactic unit and as a consequence this measure tends to be a zero-one method when a clausal unit is evaluated, whether it be completely error-free or erroneous. This measure also has been criticized by Bardovi-Harlig and Bofman (1989), who stressed that such a measure does not allow us to differentiate between T-units containing only one error from those featuring many errors. The third method for rating accuracy encompasses a number of errors. This approach, however, is more susceptible to being treated as a measure of inaccuracy, rather than accuracy. Fischer used the ratio of the total number of errors occurring in a clause as the "error-to-clause measure of structural accuracy" (Fischer 1984, p. 15), while Ashwell (2000) analysed accuracy by dividing the total number of errors by the total number of words in text. Kuiken and Vedder took the total number of errors per T-unit and the number of several types of errors, graded as first-, second- and third-degree errors, into account and treated it as a means of coding accuracy (Kuiken & Vedder, 2008). All these studies, and many others, conducted in order to validate second language learners' accuracy, in actual fact, formally speaking, investigate the opposite, i.e. the level of inaccuracy. Thus, for example, if in a study the ratio of the total number of errors per T-unit is equal to 0.2 it means in fact that the accuracy of this unit was 0.8, which, however, has never been discussed from this perspective.

Similarly to studies measuring general accuracy at a particular point of second language learning, researchers tried to find a measure that could best estimate accuracy from a developmental point of view. In their report Wolfe-Quintero, Inagaki & Kim (1998) devised three measures that most reflect the development of second language writing: the number of error-free T-units (EFT), the number of error-free T-units per T-unit (EFT/T) and the number of errors per T-unit (E/T). However, as earlier mentioned, there was no standardised definition of what constituted an error. Larsen-Freeman and Strom took a more rigorous view and accepted only those T-units as error-free that did not contain any errors at all (Larsen-Freeman & Strom, 1978). On the other hand, Arthur (1979) took a more relaxed view, allowing for spelling, morphologic, grammatical, semantic and punctuation errors to be included in his analysis. Scott and Tucker (1974) analyzed only morphological and syntactic errors while Vann (1979), apart from deciding on the sense in a given context, counted lexical and syntactic errors. On the other hand, Homburg adopted the classification of Nas (1975), who differentiated between three degrees of spelling, lexical and grammatical errors, depending on how they influenced the comprehensibility of the text (Homburg, 1984). The seriousness of errors as an indicator of accuracy has, however, been criticized by Pallotti, who pointed out that accuracy and comprehensibility are different constructs and thus cannot be treated as one entity of different degrees (Pallotti, 2009).

Although EFT/T has been used in many studies and is rated as one of the "best" measures of accuracy it has some disadvantages, which has especially important repercussions for developmental studies. In the case of students who make errors particularly in the beginning phases development is barely noticeable in every T-unit, because in these cases the EFT/T equals zero. When this value remains unchanged at two subsequent data collection points it is not possible to observe any growth and calculate the growth rate, due to the main mathematical assumption that we cannot divide by zero. And a lack of error-free T-units is highly probable in the beginning phases of learning, especially in microdevelopmental studies, characterized by dense data collection. Furthermore, it is very likely that learners will have the same amount of error-free units during their development but that there will also be considerably fewer errors within each T-unit – and even if their accuracy has in fact increased it will not be shown in the calculated value. This in turn negatively influences the validity of the analysis of accuracy development and can also make it impossible to compare students who have the same EFT/T but differ in their amount of errors.

3.3. Fluency

As the third dimension in the triad fluency is defined intuitively as effortless, smooth and rapid text production. But even this quite spontaneous characterisation involves a degree of complexity. Firstly, complexity is already enclosed in all three definentia: effortlessness can refer to the ease with which language items are retrieved, or even to the automaticity in retrieving these items from long-term memory; smoothness is associated with the absence of disturbing interruptions such as long pauses and self-corrections, while rapidity, in turn, tends to mean a speaker's physical ability to deliver a large amount of information in a short period of time, which inseparably is connected with both automaticity in language and the distribution of pauses. Secondly, all these features are inseparably interconnected with one another. Doing something easily and without any effort triggers rapidity. The ability to think in longer chunks thanks to automaticity leads to the creation of longer text passages without any unintentional breaks. Therefore, as with the case of complexity and accuracy, we cannot treat fluency as a homogenous dimension, but rather as a complex system involving at least three facets: automaticity, smoothness and rapidity.

Fluency has already been proposed as a complex phenomenon in earlier studies. Fillmore counts not only automaticity as a distinctive component of fluency, but also coherence, complexity, appropriateness, and creativity in speech (Fillmore, 1979). Lennon sees it as a subjective impression from the listener's side, who perceives the psycholinguistic processes of speech planning and speech production in the speaker as "functioning easily and efficiently" (Lennon, 1990, p. 391). An even more complex view of fluency has been forwarded by Skehan, who claims "It is now increasingly accepted that finer grained analyses of fluency require separate measures for (a) silence (breakdown fluency), (b) reformulation, replacement, false starts, and repetition (repair fluency), (c) speech rate (e.g. words per syllables per minute), and (d) automatisation, through measures of the length of run" (Skehan, 2003, p. 7).

Fluency in a second language can even be seen as the result of a transition from declarative to procedural knowledge. Fluent speakers use procedural knowledge, which costs them less time to activate their memory, as a consequence of which they are able to produce longer chunks of texts (Towell, Howkins, & Bazergui, 1996). The cognitive processes underlying fluency are thus complex. In light of this, Segalowitz distinguishes between three meanings of fluency, which he defines as cognitive fluency, utterance fluency and perceived fluency. Cognitive fluency requires the mobilisation, coordination and then integration of several cognitive processes activated for text production, such as e.g. conceptual preparation, grammatical and morpho-phonological encoding or articulation. Utterance fluency refers to general features that characterise an utterance, such as the time of speech, the repairs or the pauses the speaker makes and it thus focuses on utterance as a product. In turn, perceived fluency can be understood to mean the listener's impression of the text that the interlocutor has produced. Based on the utterance the speaker can also infer how cognitive and utterance fluency are interconnected (Segalowitz, 2010). Housen, Kuiken & Vedder (2012) calls for a three-dimensional view of fluency, i.e. speed fluency (rate and density of linguistic units in production), breakdown fluency (number, length and location of pauses) and repair fluency (false starts, misformulations, self-corrections and repetitions). These factors have been explored in a number of studies that examined a variety of fluency-related variables, such as hesitations, repairs and the rate and amount of speech or interactivity (Ellis & Yuan, 2004; Freed, 1995; Kormos & Dénes, 2004; Riggenbach, 1991).

The concept of fluency refers above all to fluency in speaking, although, even fluency in writing is become increasingly an object of study. However, we cannot overlook the fact that a one-to-one comparison between fluency in writing and fluency in speaking is still not possible due to the diverging conditions in which texts are formed. A spoken text emerges and disappears from the speaker's mind much faster than a written one. The writer can still see what he or she has produced even if his or her thoughts are on another topic. Therefore, divergence is also between a second language learner's fluency in writing and speaking, and a fluent second language speaker can be less fluent in producing a written text. Fluency in a second language is interconnected not only with a student's general proficiency but also with their metalinguistic knowledge, which in turn can have an effect on fluency. The more a student knows about how the acquired language is constructed the more attention they will pay to achieving an error-free text, which in turn can lead to an increase in self-revisions. Even if these are evidence of increased proficiency and metalinguistic knowledge they result in disruptions in the text flow and slow down the writing tempo and thus have a negative influence on the general smoothness of text production. Therefore, Gelderen and Oostdam point out that written texts can be treated as an indirect indication of writing fluency because linguistic fluency facilitates the writer not only in writing down his or her ideas but also in quickly reviewing them before they are transcribed (van Gelderen & Oostadam, 2005).

Due to different definitions of fluency several measures have been adopted. The common measures used to analyse spoken texts are those employed by Möhle in her study of German students of French and French students of German. Möhle distinguished between speech rate (number of syllables per second), articulation rate (number of syllables per second of time of articulation), pause length and length of run (mean number of syllables between pauses) (Möhle, 1984). These measures have then been used by many researchers (de Jong & Perfetti, 2011; Lennon, 1990; Towell, 1987). A description and evaluation of different fluency measures in second language writing can be found in Wolfe-Quintero, Inagaki & Kim (1998), who concluded that the best measures of fluency are the number of words per T-unit, the number of words per error-free T-unit and the number of words per clause, because "these three measures consistently increased in a linear relationship with proficiency levels across studies, regardless of task, target language, significance of the results, or how proficiency has been defined" (Wolfe-Quintero, Inagaki & Kim, 1998, p. 29). The report compiled by Wolfe-Quintero, Inagaki, Kim did not include any studies that take into account disturbances in fluency. As a consequence, such approaches to measuring fluency do not correspond to those definitions of fluency where not only rapidity but also automaticity and smoothness, i.e. infrequent occurrence of pauses and false-starts, are inseparable factors of fluency.

In a study focusing on written composition Kaufer, Hayes & Flower (1986) adopted a new measure that covered both pauses and revisions in text production. The tool, called a "sentence part," was defined as a chunk of text between a pause of two or more seconds or a discontinuity regarding a revision. A comparison between expert L1-writers and novices showed that the more experienced writers wrote on average about 11 words between two disturbing elements while novices wrote on average 7 words. Instead of a "sentence part" as a unit of measurement other researchers have used the terms "burst" or "mean length of burst" in further studies on fluency in L1- and L2- writing (Chenoweth & Hayes, 2001; Gunnarsson, 2012; Kowal, 2014; Palviainen, Kalaja & Mäntylä, 2012; Spelman Miller, Lindgren & Sullivan, 2008).

In a longitudinal study on fluency development in second language writing, conducted from the point of view of Dynamic Systems Theory, Kowal used two of the above-mentioned measures, namely transition time and mean length of burst, and showed that there is a strong interconnection between typing speed and smoothness in writing. The less time the students needed for moving between keys the longer chunks they wrote until a revision or pause occurred. She also found that writers who were slower at the beginning of the second language learning period (in terms of longer transition time) made the greatest progress, compared with so called "quick starters," who already had a high writing tempo in their first period of learning a new language (Kowal, 2014). However, only two aspects of fluency have been investigated in this study, namely automaticity and smoothness. Therefore, it would be interesting to see how rapidity in text production develops over time and how all these three dimensions interact with one other.

A dynamic view of fluency in second language development should also explore on the one hand the entire complexity of the phenomenon, such as the rapidity in text production, the automaticity and smoothness. On the other, however, the interconnectedness of all these aspects and their interplay must not be neglected.

4

The project – the development of Swedish as a second language

The project presented in this book is a longitudinal multi-individual study of the development of Swedish as a second or, to be more precise, a third language. Research on third/next language acquisition is not new in linguistic studies. It has grown as a branch of second language studies due to the increasingly widespread view that multilingualism is at least as common as monolingualism (Aronin & Singleton, 2008; Cook, 1992; Grosjean, 1982) and in many cases studies referred to as 'second language investigations' actually explore the development and use of a third or fourth language. For example, we can with a high degree of probability assume that the Dutch learner of Finnish in the study of Spoelman and Verspoor (2010) described above knew at least one more language, due to the fact that English is a compulsory subject in Dutch schools and Finnish was thus at least his third language. The term *second language* most often occurs in monolingual communities in contexts where English is learned as a foreign language at school, in countries where there is an official language but in which co-official languages are also represented (e.g. as in Spain) or in the case of languages learned by uneducated immigrants originating from monolingual regions. In all other settings the learner in fact acquires a third, fourth or fifth language. The expression *third language* can mean an individual's third language, ordered chronologically, or a third and every subsequently acquired language, called L ≥ 3 (Fouser, 2001) or a "third or additional language" (de Angelis, 2007). In many studies, the following definition, devised by Hammarberg (2010, p. 97), is used:

> *third language (L3)* refers to a non-native language which is currently being used or acquired in a situation where the person already has knowledge of one or more L2s in addition to one or more L1s.

However, even if such a distinction (between second and third language) is made, researchers often use the term *second language* even in those contexts where it is actually the development of a subsequent, i.e. third, fourth and so on, language that is being investigated. The term *third language*, on the other hand, occurs in settings where the focus is on the phenomenon of multilingualism and the interplay of the learner's languages. In the present study the term *second language* is used due to the fact that no explicit reference is made to the interconnectedness between the already acquired languages and the new language (Swedish).

4.1. Participants

The learners of Swedish that participated in the study were fifteen students of Swedish Philology at Jagiellonian University in Krakow who were aged 19–21 at the beginning of the project. They comprised a fairly homogenous group, and not only with regard to their onset age. All of them had Polish as a first language and had grown up in monolingual families. They were all at the same level in Swedish when they began their undergraduate studies. None of them spoke Swedish or had been to Sweden before. They had the same number of Swedish lessons – ten hours a week in the first and second year, and eight in the third year. After three years they had completed around 840 hours in Swedish. Due to the specific character of the curriculum, during their three-year-long study the students also participated in other courses related to Swedish, such as Swedish Grammar, Swedish Phonetics and Swedish Literature. They only learned Swedish in a classroom environment and all of them used the same learning materials during their courses and had the same teachers, one of whom was a native speaker of Swedish. However, three students changed their learning environment during the project. They obtained scholarships in Sweden, at folk high schools, where they each spent one semester. Two learners resided in Sweden during their fifth semester, i.e. after their second year of learning Swedish, and one student came half a year later, i.e. during the sixth semester.

The study participants had the same language (English) as their (chronologically) second language, which is an obligatory subject in primary and secondary school in Poland. Furthermore, the students also learned an additional language, German, which they had chosen as their main foreign language and which they learned more intensively than English at secondary school level. All of them had passed their matriculation exam in German at a very high level (at least 80%). The Polish education system offers students the possibility to choose between a basic and an advanced level of the examination for the exam. Both levels consist of a written and a spoken part. The written part at the advanced level takes about three hours[5] and includes writing a 200–250 word text (a narrative, a description, an argumentative or a review – a choice of subjects), listening and reading comprehension. All the study participants passed their matriculation exam in German at an advanced level. The language skills recognised by the certificate are assumed to be equivalent to level B2, according to the Common European Framework of Reference for Languages. Possession of Maturity Certification in German is one of the compulsory requirements for those applying to study Swedish Philology and only those candidates with the best results can be admitted. Due to the popularity of Sweden and Swedish language, literature, and culture in Poland there are approximately ten candidates per place. Although Swedish is the main language studied within the framework of the Swedish Philology programme, the students must also complete an obligatory course in German. They have six hours of classes a week at bachelor level (three years) and four hours a week at MA level (two years).

This fact is of great importance for learning Swedish as a subsequent language. German and Swedish are typologically close languages. Both are Germanic languages; German belongs to the western branch of this language family and Swedish to its northern branch. They are closer to each other than to the students' first language (Polish), which forms part of the Slavic family of languages. Polish differs from German and Swedish in many aspects: the morphology of the nominal word classes is more complex – there are seven cases in Polish, compared with four in German and two in Swedish; the word order in Polish is freer than in the other two languages; Polish has no grammatical category for marking the definiteness of noun phrases, whereas both Swedish and German have quite

[5] This was the examination time when the study participants ended their secondary school education. Nowadays, however, the written part of the matriculation exam has been shortened and lasts 150 minutes.

complex article systems with indefinite and definite articles, and Swedish even has double definiteness. These are only a few of the many structural differences that can play an important role in the development of Swedish as an L2/L3.

However, typology is not the only factor that should be mentioned here. Recency of use is the next important variable. German can influence the development of Swedish because it is still being learned. The students can have both Swedish and German classes on the same day, even directly following each other, and even if the focus of learning is on Swedish and there are more hours of Swedish than of German per week, the influence of German cannot be ignored.

Age, language background, learning environment and prior knowledge of Swedish are the most important characteristics the study participants have in common. They were, however, not homogenous in terms of gender: twelve of the fifteen participants were females, which is a typical ratio in university language programmes. Currently, only 10% of Swedish Philology students at Jagiellonian University are males.

4.2. Study design

During the three-year study period a total of six experimental sessions were conducted. The first took place after the first semester of study, i.e. after approximately 150 hours of Swedish. The subsequent data collections took place at equal intervals, i.e. following each semester. The end of the experimental part of the project coincided with the completion of the undergraduate programme in Swedish Philology. Participation was voluntary and the students received no financial compensation for their involvement in the project. A total of 32 students took part in the first experimental sessions. Due to the longitudinal character of the project and the general mobility of students, there was a considerable drop off in numbers over the three years. Many of the students obtained scholarships to study in other European countries, while some interrupted their studies or took Dean's leave, and thus were unable to continue to be involved in the project – only fifteen were able to take part in the whole study.

Written samples were collected during the experiments. The task was to write a narrative text that referred to the students' personal although not necessarily true experiences. Hence, the subjects could even make up a fictional story. The topics were as follows:

Experiment 1: *Jag ska aldrig glömma det*! [I will never forget it]
Experiment 2: *Vilken dröm det var*! [What a dream I had!]
Experiment 3: *Jag har aldrig tidigare varit så rädd* [I had never been so afraid]
Experiment 4: *Ett äventyr på semester* [An adventure on my holidays]
Experiment 5: *Min största lögn/Mitt största brott* [My greatest lie/my greatest crime]
Experiment 6: *Jag ska aldrig glömma det* [I will never forget it]

The topics in the first and the final experiment were the same; however no student retold the same story. The project was preceded by a shorter, one-year pilot study, in which the topics were the same (*Jag ska aldrig glömma det* [I will never forget it]). It turned out that even if the participants received the explicit instruction that they could write a new story, some of them tried to reconstruct their previous texts, which made the data incomparable. This led to the decision that different topics should be given in the current project. The purpose of repeating the same task in the first and the last experiment, however, was that if the students described the same experience it would be possible to compare similar texts written at the beginning and at the end of the three-year course. As was mentioned above, none of the students retold their story from the first experimental session.

The texts were written on a laptop computer. The students often used computers. Both in secondary school and during their courses in the first semester, i.e. before the experimental sessions began, they had often written their homework on a laptop or a computer. They also used computers every day for internet surfing or chats. However, they were accustomed to a Polish keyboard and in the experiments a laptop with a Swedish keyboard was used. This means that the students only had to deal with a Swedish keyboard in the experiment sessions, i.e. twice a year. Even when this is a QWERTY-keyboard (see Figures 4.1a and 4.1b) there are many differences in the placement of, e.g., the diacritics (Swedish *ä*, *ö* and *å* do not appear on Polish keyboards) or punctuation marks (such as, e.g., the colon, the question mark and the quotation mark) which in turn can influence learners' fluency in text production and lead to increased concentration on typing.

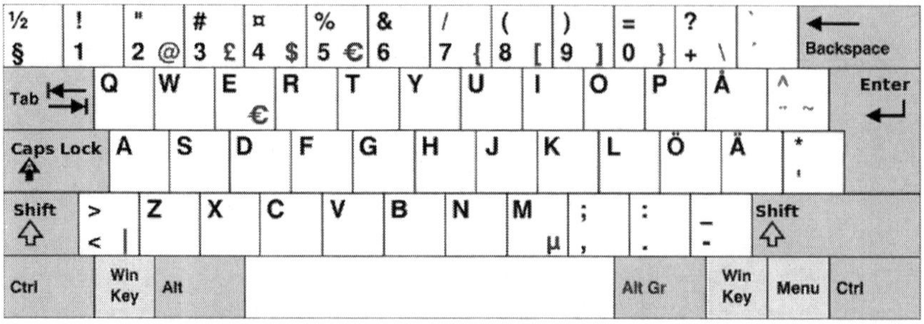

Figure 4.1a. Swedish PC-keyboard (https://sv.wikipedia.org/wiki/Tangentbord#/media/File:KB_Sweden.svg)

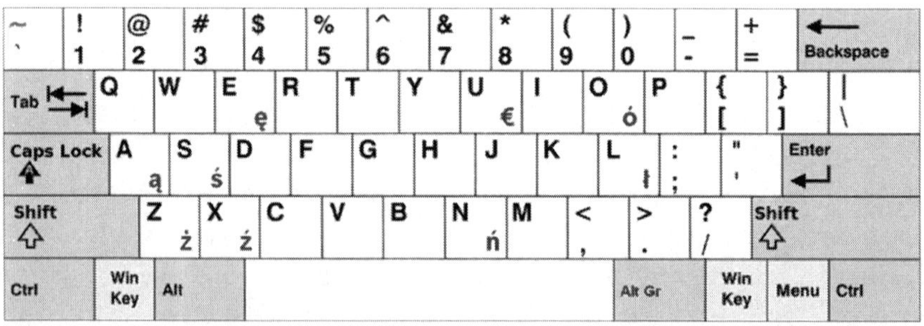

Figure 4.1b. Polish PC-keyboard (https://commons.wikimedia.org/wiki/File:Polish_programmer's_layout.PNG)

The experimental sessions took place before or after the compulsory courses. Because there was only one laptop at their disposal, the participants wrote separately. No time limit was set for the writing task and the students had no dictionaries or internet connection, so they could not search for words or expressions in external sources, or check spelling. The writing sessions were recorded using ScriptLog (Strömqvist & Malmsten, 1998). This is a tool that enables the user to follow every writing activity: not only the pressing of keys but also the movements of the mouse, pauses and deletions. The writer only sees the final text. The operations are, however, saved in a logbook from which they can be uploaded and analysed. Furthermore, the application offers numerous tools that facilitate data editing. ScriptLog has been widely used in writing research, both in studies on L1-writing (Johansson, 2009; Strömqvist, 1996; Uppstad & Solheim, 2007; Wengelin, 2002) and on L2-writing (Gunarsson, 2012; Kowal, 2008; 2011; Palviainen, Kalaja & Mäntylä, 2012).

The data logged in ScriptLog on student writing tasks can be analysed both as an end product and as a process. Below is an excerpt from one of the texts, which may illustrate what information the application can provide the researcher. The first text represents the first two sentences of a narrative in the final version and only this text was available to the writer. As in subsequent parts of the book every writing sample is presented in the original version, i.e. with occurring errors. The second excerpt is the same section, but in the logged version:

> *Jag kan inte komma ihåg om jag hade en något lögn i sista tiden. Vanligen ljuger jag när gäller prisen av mina kläder för min pappa blir inte arg på mig.* [5-S2][6]
> (I can't remember if I have told a lie recently. Generally, I used to lie about the price of my clothes so that my father wouldn't be upset with me)
>
> <START><jag<BACKSPACE4>Ja <BACKSPACE>g kan inte komma ihåg v<0.06.820><BACKSPACE>om jag hade en någon <0.02.443><BACKSPACE2>t lögn i sista tiden. Vanlige<0.02.554>n<0.02.313> ljuger jag när gå<BACKSPACE>äller prisen av mn<BACKSPACE>ina <BACKSPACE>kl<BACKSPACE2> kläder för min mm<BACKSPACE2>pappa <0.02.183>blir inte arg på mig.

After starting the program (marked in brackets as START) the student wrote the word *jag* (I), but after realising that she had begun with a lower instead of an upper case, she deleted it, using the backspace key and began once more with the upper case. However, after writing the first two letters of the word (*Ja*) she entered a space and then went back in order to complete the word with the last letter 'g'. She then continued to write the passage *kan inte komma ihåg* (can't remember). Afterwards, she wrote the letter *v*, which probably would have introduced the pronoun *vilken* (what), but she then paused for nearly seven seconds, deleted it, wrote *om jag hade en någon* (if I had a some*), reflected on this for about two seconds, after which she deleted the last letter (n), which in turn indicated the common gender of the pronoun *någon* and replaced it with the neuter ending *t*. Following this action she ended the sentence by writing *lögn i sista tiden* ("a recent lie"). In the following sentence she made five deletions and three pauses. It took one minute and forty one seconds to write these two sentences and without looking at the logged text the information regarding what had been changed and where the student had stopped could not be provided.

Besides the possibility of tracking the entire writing process ScriptLog also provides a lot of statistical data. Presented below is information describing the text of the above cited participant:

---

[6] AS-unit is defined as "a single speaker's utterance consisting of *an independent clause, or sub-clausal unit*, together with any *subordinated clause(s)* associated with either" (Foster, Tonkyn & Wigglesworth, 2000, p. 365).

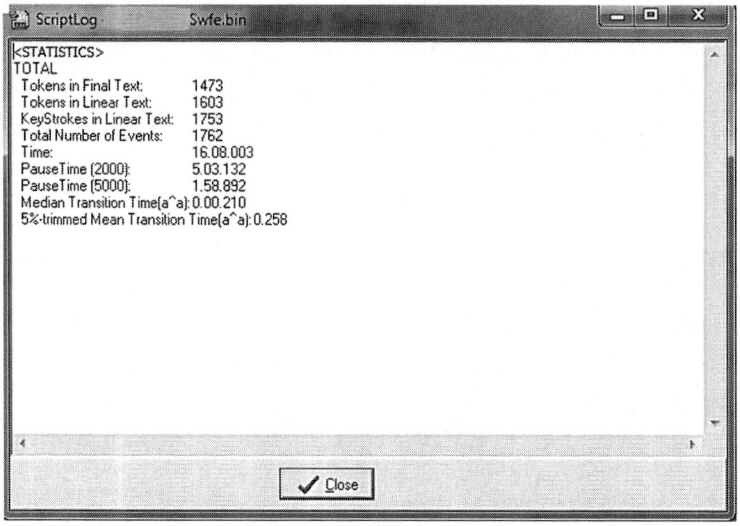

Figure 4.2. ScriptLog – statistical data of a text

The statistics inform us of the number of characters both in the final text, after all revisions (1473 tokens) have been taken into account, and in the linear text (1603 tokens), including deleted tokens. The ScriptLog does not calculate the number of words. This can be done after the text has been copied to a word or excel application. Furthermore, even the number of all the keystrokes during text production was calculated (1753), which provides a picture of all keystrokes made, including, e.g., the backspace key. The total number of events often does not differ very much from the number of keystrokes, because it includes such activities as pressing the Start or End key or moving the mouse during writing. In this particular writing sample the difference between the number of keystrokes and the total number of events is only nine, which indicates that the writer pressed the Start key when she began to write, the End key when she decided to finish, and she moved the mouse seven times during writing. In total, it took about sixteen minutes to write the text and 30% of the time (5 minutes) was spent pausing. As a default setting, the application calculates pauses with a minimum duration of two seconds. It is, however, possible to set a shorter time span for pauses. Additionally, information about pauses longer than five seconds is included. In this case, a total of about two minutes was spent thinking for longer than five seconds during the production of the text. When the data was examined in more detail it turned out that the writer made 15 pauses of fairly equal length (between five and six seconds) and one longer, thirty--second-pause after finishing the writing task and during the pause the writer probably concentrated on reading the whole text.

The last two rows in the statistics file provide information on how fast the writer types. The median transition time reflects how much time (in seconds) on average it took for him or her to move between two letters within a word. For fast writers the value will thus be lower than for slow typists. The S2 learner in our sample had a transition time of 21 milliseconds. As with the previous measure the last post in the data, called "5%-trimmed Mean Transition Time," is an indicator of typing speed. In the case of this feature, however, 5% of the shortest and 5% of the longest pauses between letters within a word are excluded.

All data in ScriptLog can be analyzed separately using other programs, such as Excel or SPSS. The compressed data in the statistical file can even be extracted in more fine-grained files, where particular features can be presented – the location of the pauses, or lists of deletions. It is even possible to display the entire writing process or trace a selected string of the text.

4.3. Aim of the study

The objective of the present study is to follow the process of second language development in young adults during a three-year-period of intensive language study. Special attention is paid to individual developmental trajectories, the dynamics of development at the individual level, and to variation between individuals. Even if there are many longitudinal studies on second language development, they either explore groups of learners at different levels and/or age, or they describe the individual development of one or a few learners during a longer period (ranging from weeks up to a few years). What is missing, however, are longitudinal data with more subjects involved, which would allow the researcher to follow the development of the same learners over a longer period. On the other hand, it can provide sufficient material for modelling developmental patterns in groups of learners, and may even make it possible to identify several learner profiles. The hypothesis is that a learner's development will not involve any linear growth of language skills, but rather will show irregularities during the learning period, and that substantial individual differences will occur. Furthermore, the assumption is that even if such divergences between individuals exist there are some types of learners that show similar patterns in their development.

When a larger group of learners is studied the number of interacting systems increases, which enables researchers to obtain deeper insights into the dynamics of the entire learning process. It also opens up the possibility of creating a more general developmental pattern than in case studies or longitudinal multi-group studies. Dynamic systems theory appears to be an appropriate paradigm for studying these complex systems of learners and languages, especially with respect to the estimated variability, or nonlinear and unpredictable behaviour of the systems involved in the interaction.

The present study is meant to fill the gap between existing case studies and multi-group comparative studies. By following the development of fifteen learners who can be identified as a homogenous group that started to learn a new language at the same level, had similar initial conditions and in most cases had the same learning environment all the time, we can gain a broader, more general insight into second language development.

The analysis will cover the interaction of several subsystems. First, there will be a presentation of the development of (lexical and syntactic) complexity, accuracy and fluency, and this will be followed by an exploration of the interconnectedness and correlation between all these phenomena over a three-year developmental period. While the constantly repeated question is that of how development of a second language proceeds (both in individuals and at group level), a parallel and perhaps even more important issue is what causes the development to take that particular shape? In other words, how do systems interact and what influence does this exert on the entire process of second language development?

5

Development of Complexity

In previous studies on complexity one of aspects that are taken into consideration was text length. Being an extern indicator of the amount of words used in a text produced by the second language learner we can consider it as an output condition for complexity, thus the longer the text the more interconnectedness between its units is expected to occur.

As might have been expected, the texts produced by the students got longer over the three-year observation period, although the average growth path was nonlinear (Figure 5.1). The greatest progress could be observed in the first three semesters, in particular in the first half of the second year. After achieving an average length of about 280 words the length of the texts appears to approach an attractor state, with slight, average variability in the second half of the experimental sessions.

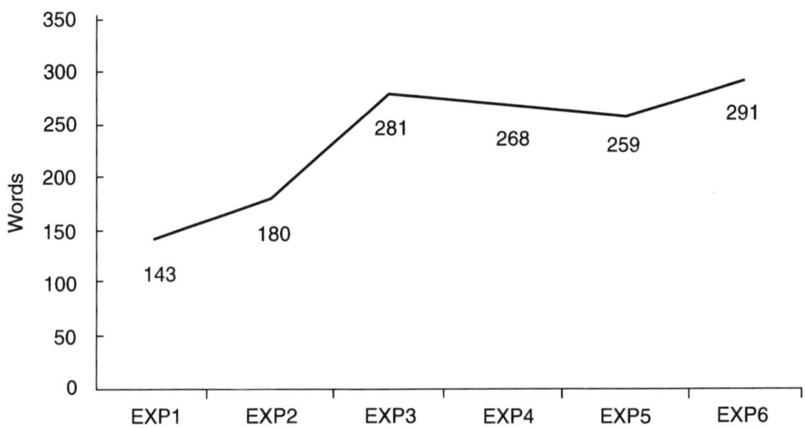

Figure 5.1. Mean length of texts

This overall impression from the above diagram, i.e. that the most significant growth in text length was achieved at the beginning of the learning period, is clearly confirmed by observing the degree of growth measured on the basis of the growth rate. The index informs us of how much higher or lower a subsequent value is in relation to its predecessor. The growth rate has been used, for example, by van Geert (1994), and Kowal (2009; 2011). It is a relative indicator of change that, instead of showing language development in the form of absolute numbers, reflects the relationship between adjacent values. The formula for growth rate, proposed by van Geert (1994) and presented in previous chapter, has been slightly modified in order to make it more transparent and easier to interpret. The proposed formula for the growth rate (*R*) is:

$$R = (V_{t1} - V_{t0})/V_{t0} \cdot 100$$

where V_{t1} stands for the value in time 1 and V_{t0} for the value obtained in the preceding time. From the illustration above (Figure 5.1) we can also calculate the growth rate between the first and the second experimental sessions, where the average text lengths amounted to 143 and 180 words, respectively. The growth rate during the first year of learning Swedish will be:

$$R = (180–143)/143 \cdot 100 = 26$$

Based on the modified growth rate formula, the change in the average text length between the first and the second experiment equals 26. In other words, the texts in the second experiment were on average 26% longer than in the first. A value equal to zero should be interpreted as meaning no change has taken place, while a negative value, on the other hand, will reflect a decline in length. The solution to the equation can be directly referred to as a percentage value, which makes the results more transparent and readable. To determine what can be treated as a considerable change or a slight development a cut-off point of 20 has been taken. Growth within the range of $-20 \geq +20$ will thus be interpreted as a minor change, while values lower than –20 and higher than +20 will represent a substantial, dynamic change – a decline or growth, respectively.

The average growth rate, measuring the development of text length in all participants of the study (Figure 5.2), is clearly nonlinear in character, with the most dramatic change occurring in the first three semesters of learning Swedish and with almost no change taking place in later periods.

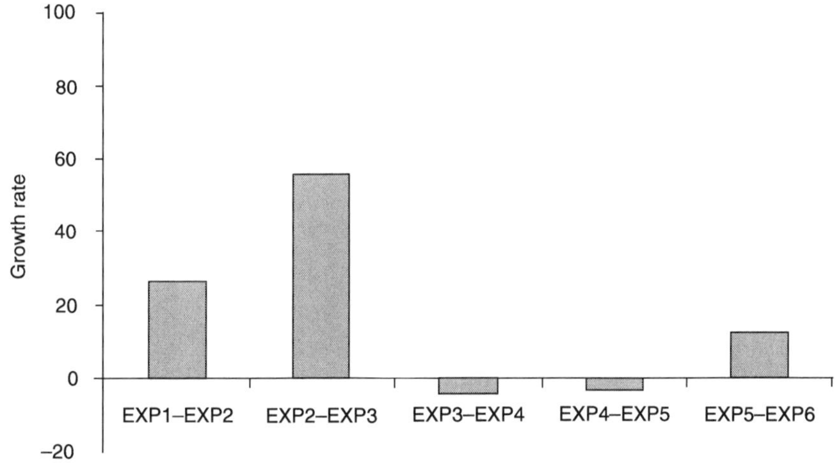

Figure 5.2. Growth rate in the case of average text length

A dynamic view of language development treats variability within and variation between individuals as an inseparable part of the developmental process. As earlier DST-research has shown, the average results do not reflect individual development, which also the present study confirms. As presented in the illustration below (Figure 5.3) the length of the texts produced by particular students changes very dynamically and does not fit the average development path.

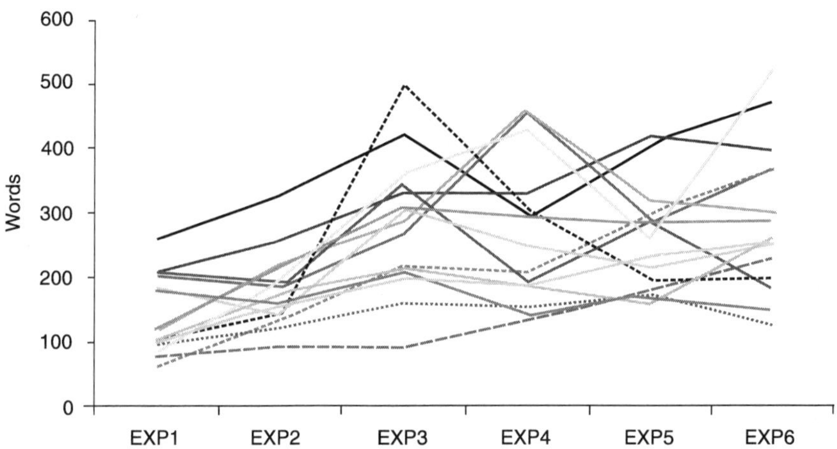

Figure 5.3. Text length in individuals

In fifteen subjects such a cumulated presentation barely readable. Therefore, it is more reasonable to divide the results into smaller groups that exhibit similar developmental patterns. The development of text length may be regarded as similar to the average in only two of the learners (S6 and S10) (Figure 5.4a), and even in these cases only with regard to the shape of the developmental path. As with the average, there is substantial growth during the first three semesters, followed by stability in the second part of the study. The most striking difference is in the number of words produced. Both subjects generally wrote considerably shorter essays than the (virtually) "average" student in this group. The difference between the mean path and these students can be seen in the outcome of the final experimental session, when the text produced by S10 is shorter, while the average shows progress being made in text length. The production of the other student, on the other hand, increased at a much stronger growth rate (R = 61) than the average (R = 12) and thus cannot be characterized as being stable.

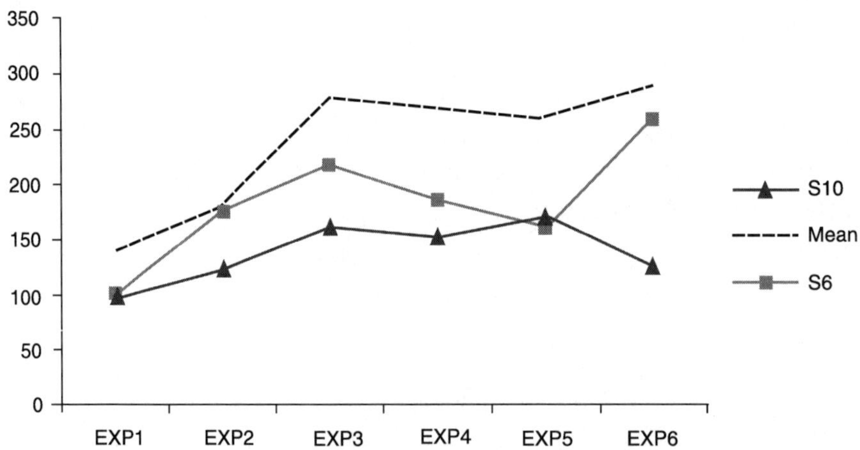

Figure 5.4a. Near-average developmental path in the case of text length

In the next group of students (Figure 5.4b) almost continuous progression can be observed in text length over the course of the entire study, although their development cannot be regarded as linear. However, even this group is not homogeneous. These learners included writers whose texts were very short at the beginning, but who made considerable progress to later become long-essay-writers (S11, S15), a writer who composed long texts from the very beginning and went on to produce even longer texts later on (S1) and a writer who tended to write generally shorter texts (S12).

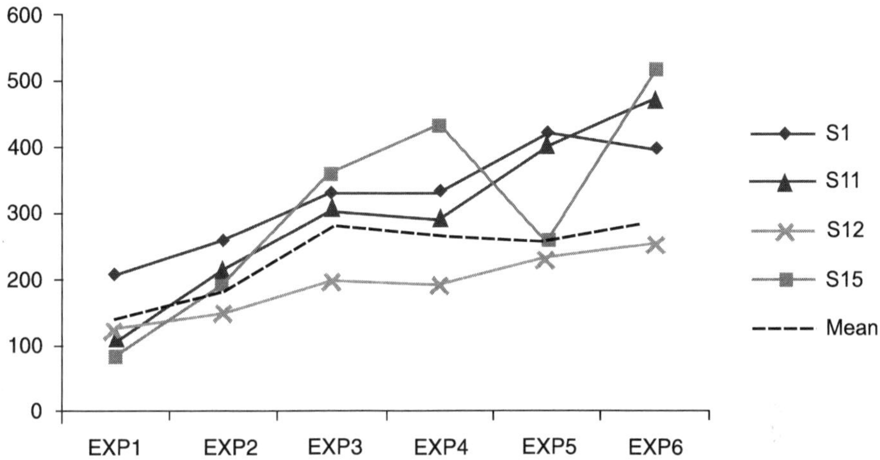

Figure 5.4b. Continuing progress in text length

The third group (Figure 5.4c, Figure 5.4d and Figure 5.4e) can be described as comprising writers with one peak length – either during the third (Figure 5.4c), the fourth (Figure 5.4d) or the fifth (Figure 5.4e) semester. These students showed steady progress culminating in a considerable spurt in one period, ranging from R = 28% to R = 254% (!). In later phases, however, they produced texts of similar length. This may suggest that their functional level lies at the same level as the result they achieved in the time preceding the peak, when the system appeared to stabilize, while the outranging length might be a sign the students were

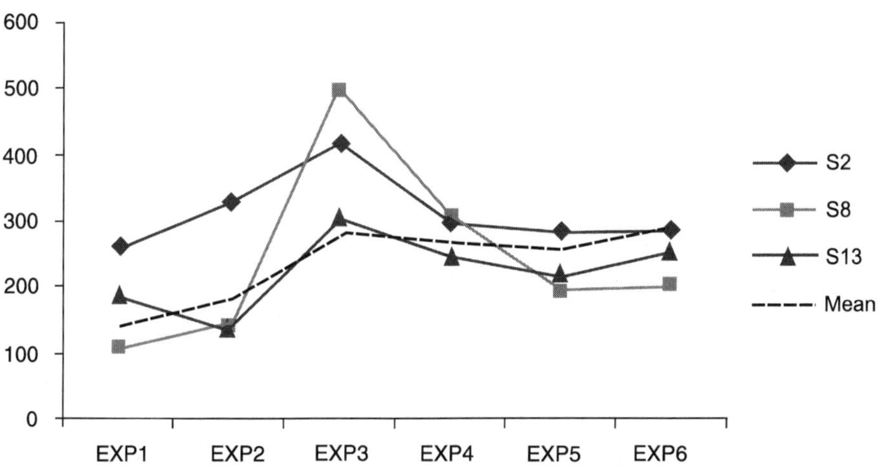

Figure 5.4c. Peak in text length in the third experiment

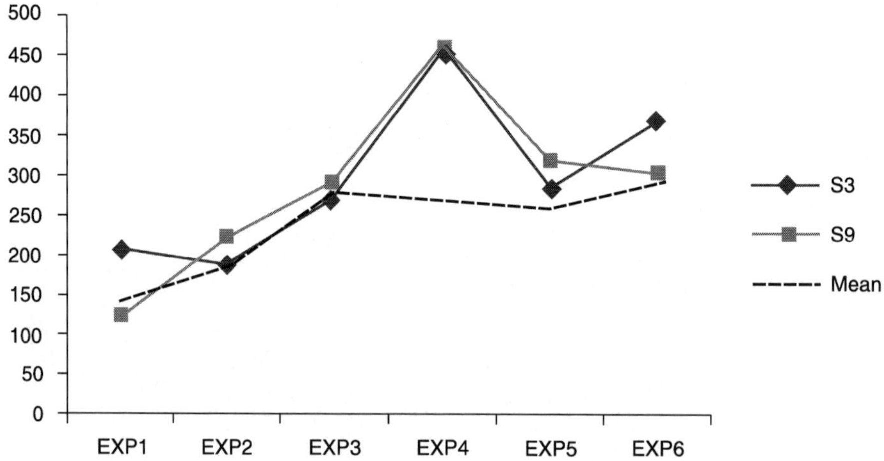

Figure 5.4d. Peak in text length after the fourth semester

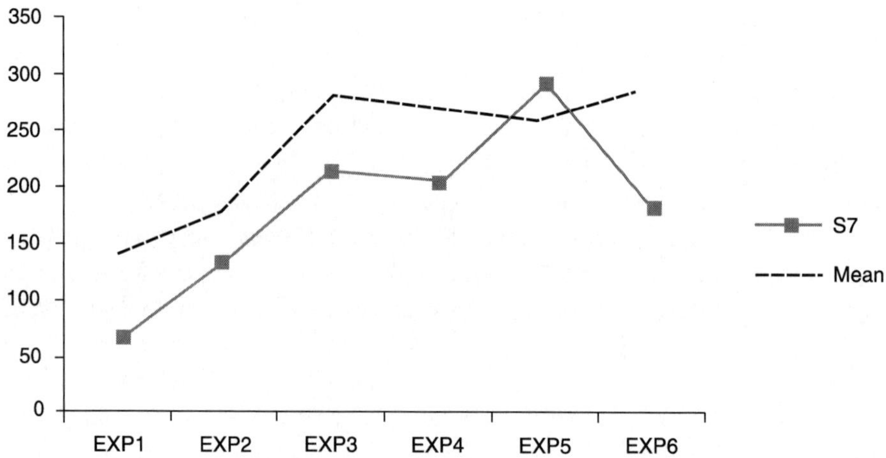

Figure 5.4e. Peak in text length after the fifth semester

at the optimal developmental level during the experimental time, or, to use Verhult's meaning, the learners achieved their carrying capacity at that particular point of data collection.

One student in the group (S4), progressed along a unique developmental path (Figure 5.4f). Her development appeared to proceed more slowly than her fellow students. In the case of this writer no change in text length could be observed in the first three experimental sessions. However, beginning from the fourth semester the student subsequently wrote longer and longer texts. What should be stressed in this context is that this subject wrote the shortest narratives, which might give rise to the preliminary speculation that it may probably take her longer to develop skills in a new language.

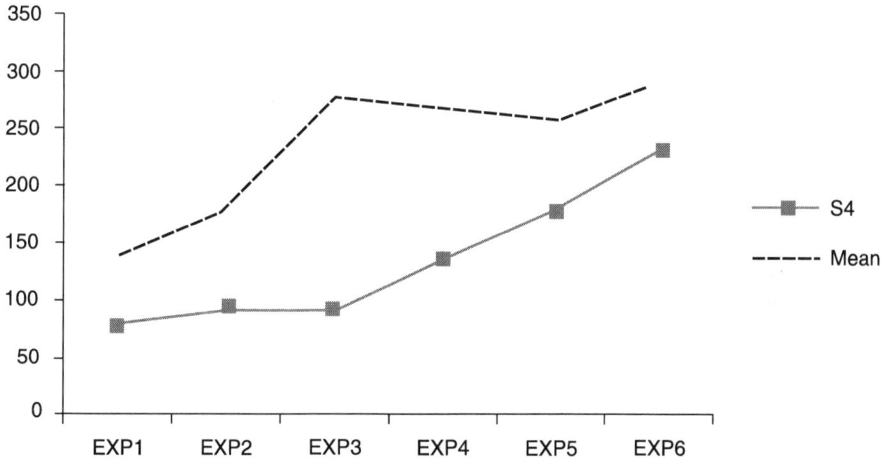

Figure 5.4f. Progress in text length only achieved in the second part of the study

The length of text produced by the two remaining participants of the study (S5, S14) varied from one experiment to another, such that their development paths do not fit into any of the above described scenarios. Figure 5.4g shows that the development of text length was similar for both students almost the whole time – from the first up to the fifth experiment the developmental path takes the shape of a sine wave. At the end of the three-year period, however, the curves diverge and one of the students (S5) kept writing longer and longer texts, while the other continues to vary. Apart from a similar developmental path the general dynamics of these two writers diverge considerably, especially with regard to overall intra-individual variability. The Monte Carlo Analysis of resampled data from both students showed that S5 is much more variable in text production than S14 (p-value = 0.008).[7] Common to both writers, however, is the fact that even their texts are longer in the third experiment, which partially corresponds to the average tendency.

A deeper examination of the individual data confirms the conclusions of the previous outcomes that calculating the mean value cannot serve

[7] For a detailed explanation of how to compare variability in the development of two learners see van Dijk, Verspoor & Lowie (2011), Versporr *et al.* (2011).

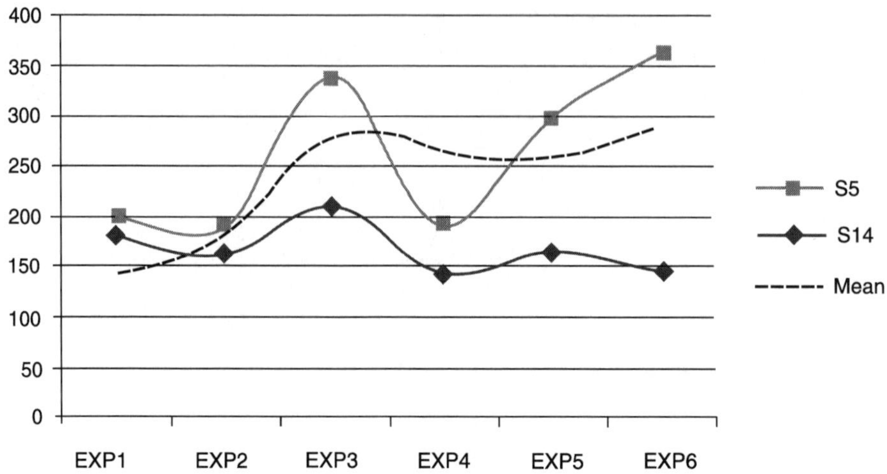

Figure 5.4g. Sinusoid-like change in text length

as a general indicator of development. However, what can be stated is that the length of most students' texts does in fact increase considerably in the first period of learning, in most cases up to the third semester. In the context of increasing length it is interesting to determine if the purely numerical increase in words used corresponds with the development of complexity. In other words, does a longer text mean that it is more elaborate and contains more heterogenic words and constructions? The underlying assumption is that growth in text length will be paralleled by self-organisation of the lexical system in the sense that words will not only be repeated in a near-echographic way but may even create a network of interconnections.

5.1. Lexical complexity

Lexical complexity is here understood to mean the diversity of lexical items and the degree of their interconnectedness. Such a view should, in my opinion, encompass the two most specific properties of complexity, namely the heterogeneity of elements and their interrelated organisation. For this reason two measures have been used here: the Guiraud Index and the ratio of words included in complex phrases to the total number of words (WCP/W). Although another measurement of lexical complexity, the number of different words per total number of words (TTR, even called Type/Token Ratio), has been used in most cited studies, it has been criticized as a developmental measure in many contexts, due to its strong correlation with text length (Johansson, 2009; Malvern *et. al.* 2004; Vermeer, 2000). An increased ability to produce long utterances negatively influences the use of different words, which could lead to the conclusion that learners who produce longer texts in fact use a less varied vocabulary. The correlation between TTR and text length has, however, been measured also in the present study purely for control purposes. The average Pearson's coefficient for the fifteen subjects participating in the study was very strong ($r = -.74$), which confirms the outcomes of previous research.

5.1.1. Development of lexical diversity

As was mentioned above, lexical complexity reflects the diversity of lexical items and the degree of their interconnection. However, due to the lack of a uniform, covering measure, a combination of several instruments is needed, each of which corresponds with one of the two properties.

Lexical diversity was measured according to the Guiraud Index (Guiraud, 1954), which has also been widely used in studies exploring lexical complexity (Gilabert, 2007; Kuiken, Mos & Vedder, 2005; Kuiken & Vedder, 2007; Michel, Kuiken & Vedder, 2007). The Index is a ratio and expresses the number of different words (Types) divided by the root square of the total number of words (Tokens), which can be presented in the form of the following formula: $WT/\sqrt{W}$.

The average tendency in lexical diversity development is almost constant growth throughout the entire period, with a slight dip in the first half of the third year of language learning (Figure 5.5). Even if the general developmental path shows progress, vocabulary diversity does not increase dynamically, with the average growth rate being $R = 6\%$.

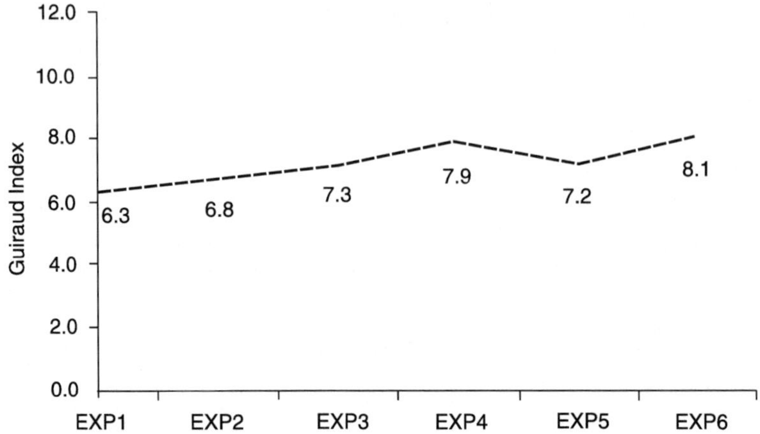

Figure 5.5. Development of mean lexical diversity

The development of individuals does not differ greatly from the mean pattern (Figure 5.6). In about one half of the students there was continuous (gentle) growth in vocabulary diversity up to the end of the second year, followed by a fall in the next experimental session, and a return to the previous level of diversity after the final semester.

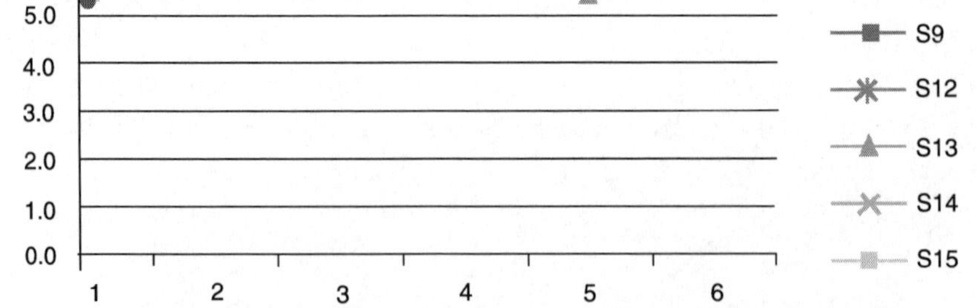

Figure 5.6. Near-average developmental path of lexical diversity

In some of the students lexical diversity increased very dynamically at the beginning – during the second semester (Figure 5.7), when the growth rate exceeded 20%. Afterwards they achieved an attractor state, without fluctuating changes, except for one learner (S11) who made further considerable progress in complexity at the end of the study.

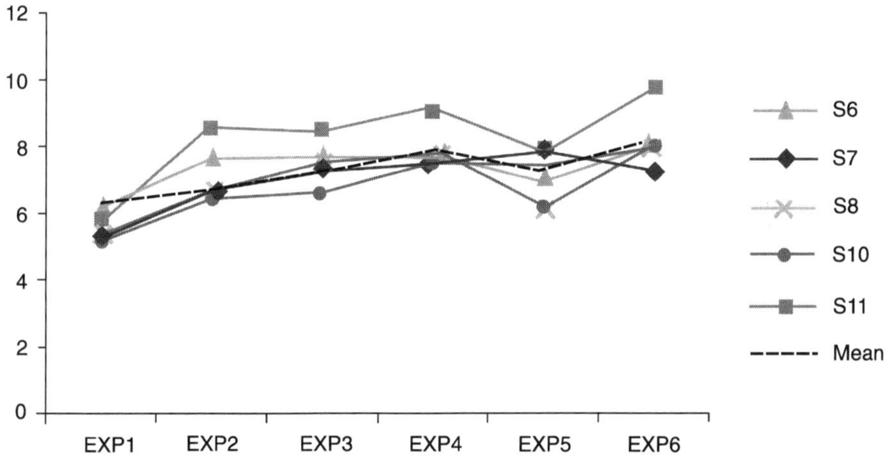

Figure 5.7. Dynamic development at the beginning

Two of the learners differ from their fellow students in terms of the development of their lexical diversity (Figure 5.8). The first conclusion to be drawn from the illustration below is that they do not seem to have made much progress until the end of the study. However, the lexical diversity of student S4 steadily increased during the last year (R = 19%) and far exceeded the average growth in this period. It should be pointed out that this is the same learner who produced the shortest texts and who did not begin to write longer pieces until the fifth experiment. She thus seemed to develop more slowly than her fellow students. The other student developed very rapidly at the beginning – he had the highest level of lexical diversity of all the students at the end of the first semester. After this, he scarcely made any progress until the final semester, which leads to the assumption that he probably developed other aspects of his language skills during this period, such as syntactic complexity or accuracy.

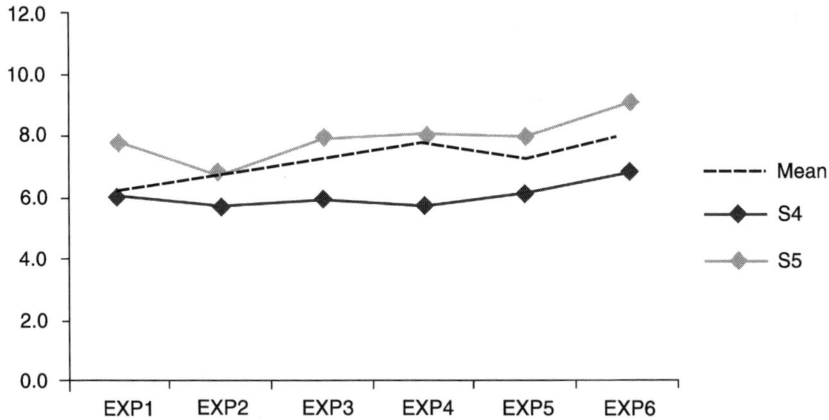

Figure 5.8. Growth in lexical diversity in the second part of the study

Regardless of the developmental paths the patterns of lexical diversity are similar and connected with text length. The average correlation between both properties is very positive ($r = .89$), which may confirm the assumption that an increased ability to write longer texts is in fact a result of vocabulary growth. This relationship, calculated for each participant separately, can also be observed in almost all the students. Only in one participant (S2) was no such interconnection present, while in another (S14) the growth in text length meant a decrease in lexical diversity.

Table 5.1. Correlation between text length and lexical diversity (GI)

Subject	*r*
S1	.64
S2	.02
S3	.65
S4	.77
S5	.69
S6	.91
S7	.93
S8	.59
S9	.81
S10	.56
S11	.75
S12	.82
S13	.40
S14	–.57
S15	.73

In terms of the average values in each experiment there were students whose texts were generally longer and lexically also more diversified throughout almost the entire learning period, while there were writers who preferred to produce short texts and use less elaborate vocabulary (see Figure 5.9a, b and Figure 5.10a, b, respectively). The illustrations below present such different groups of learners, with data relating to the mean, expressed on the Y-axis as 1. The values above 1 refer to longer vs. more lexically complex production than the average while values less than 1 mirror shorter vs. less complex texts than the mean for the entire group. We can conclude from the diagrams below that both groups are more polarised in terms of text length, where the most outstanding values exceeded the mean by 70% or 80%, respectively. In the case of lexical diversity the differences deviated from the average by no more than (+/–) 30%.

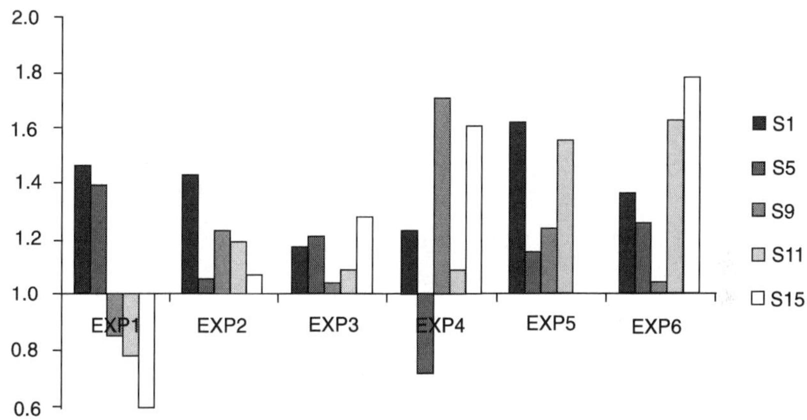

Figure 5.9a. Writers with above-average text length (Mean expressed as 1)

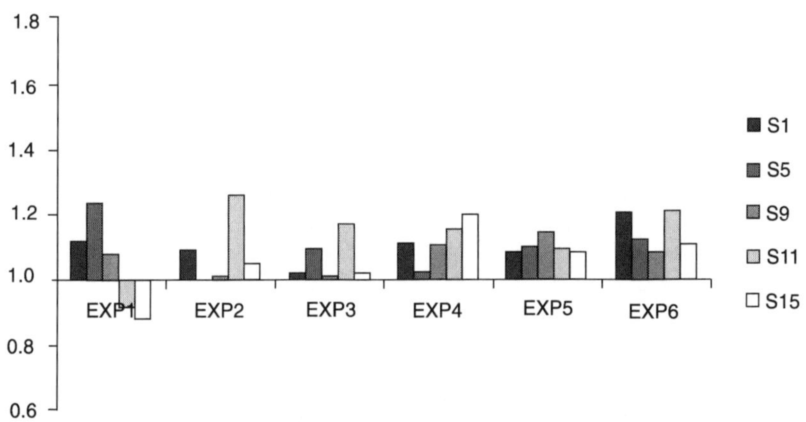

Figure 5.9b. Writers with above-average lexical diversity (Mean expressed as 1)

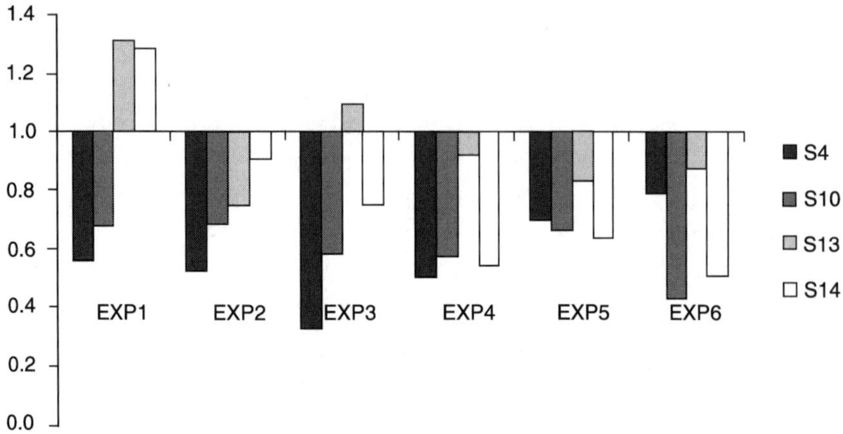

Figure 5.10a. Writers with below-average text length (Mean expressed as 1)

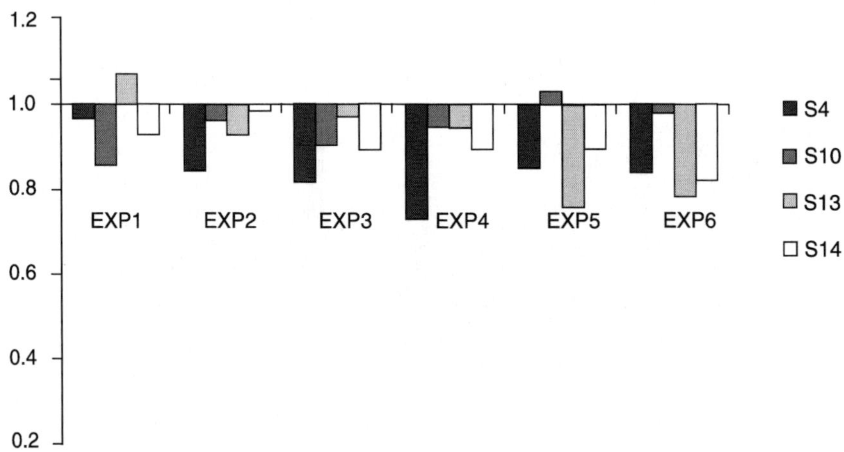

Figure 5.10b. Writers with below-average lexical diversity (Mean expressed as 1)

The values for the remaining five participants in the study lie somewhere in between, with no patterns in terms of text length and/or lexical diversity predominating. What the diagrams above not only show a general tendency to write long and complex texts or short and not elaborate texts but also indirectly inform us of variations both between and variability within subjects and unpredictability in development. It may appear surprising, but the variation between participants remained stable during the three-year-period, both with regard to text length (*cv* = 0.3–0.4 in all experiments) and lexical diversity (*cv* = 0.1 in all experiments). Differences between students at every data collection point do not change in scope. However, this cannot be observed in the case of within-subject variability. Among the above-average writers, for example, there were two (S11, S15) who after the first semester wrote considerably shorter texts than the "average" learners while using less diversified vocabulary. After three years, however, they became the best in the entire group in both these properties. On the other hand, one learner with above-average text length and lexical complexity at the beginning (S13) became one of the short- and simple-text writers during almost all later phases of learning Swedish.

While inter-subject variation reveals differences between students and emphasizes the degree to which they are spread around the mean value, intra-individual variability reflects the dynamics of development. The stronger the changes between reference time points the greater the individual variability. Furthermore, these changes can go either in one direction – for example, progress continues at varying rates, at all times – or they can include many ups and downs to create a kind of sinusoid-shaped development path. However, in these divergent cases the coefficient of variation would often give the same value, because it always refers to the mean, regardless of whether progress is continuous or we have a wave-shaped developmental path. Moreover, variability in individual development does not necessarily mean deviation from the average, but above all else indicates variable directions of growth and changing growth rates. Therefore, when measuring intra-individual variability the focus should be on the extent and the direction of change over time and not exclusively on any deviation from the average. From this point of view another measure should be used to emphasize diversification and heterogeneity in development. The proposed tool is the mean absolute growth rate between subsequent points:

$$\textit{Intra-individual variability} = \textit{Mean}\ \left|R_{x_{t+2}} - R_{x_t}\right|.$$

where x stands for the investigated variable.

This measure ensures that even substantial spurts or dips in progress will be picked up that might be overlooked by the coefficient of variation. However, this does not illustrate the direction of change: the absolute value is always positive so we can only state how dynamic the changes were and not the directions they took.

For a better visualization of the validation of the measure a comparison will be made between variability within subjects using the coefficient of variation on the one hand and the proposed tool on the other. As a representative sample two participants will be presented, characterized by several levels of variability, depending on what measure is used (Figure 5.11).

Learner S3 has a CV of 0.07, which is 37% under the mean (CV = 0.11), as a consequence of which she has one of the lowest levels of variability in the group. From the diagram above we can see that her development resembles a sine wave: first her lexical diversity decreases, then it increases and reaches its previous level, after which we can ascertain a slight increase, and in the fifth experiment her diversity is once again lower, such that the Giraud Index increases again at the end of the study. Such a developmental path tends to be interpreted as a variable process. However, both the spread between the lowest and the highest values of lexical diversity and the divergence from the mean are not so great as to classify her as a non-variable student. Our impression that an amplitude-like trajectory translates into variability does not correspond with the calculated coefficient of variation.

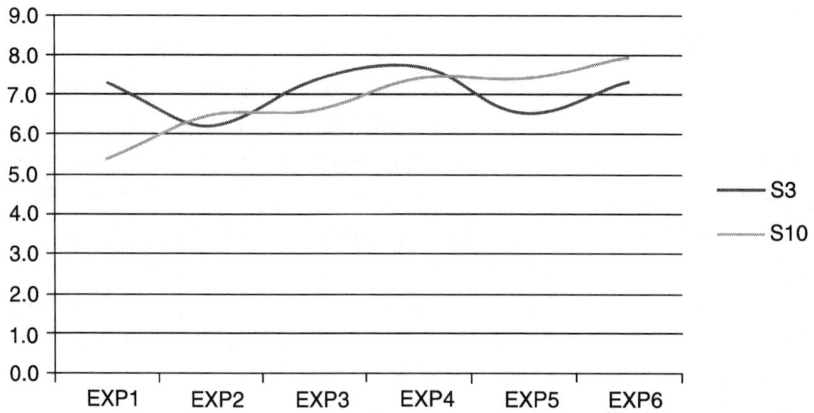

Figure 5.11. Development of lexical diversity in learners with different degrees of variability

On the other hand, when we look at the development of S10 we would assume that this learner is not variable, because her development proceeds almost linearly: her vocabulary became steadily and increasingly more varied. However, when we look at the degree of variability based on the coefficient of variation, she turns out to be one of the most variable of the learners. And this could be formulated in relation to the deviation from the mean, which is considerable in this student because of her considerable progress. On the other hand, the absolute mean growth rate suggests that she belongs to learners characterized by low variability, i.e. 30% below the average for the group as a whole.

In my opinion the proposed measure can provide a better reflection of the dynamics of development than the coefficient of variation and also enables us to make comparisons between individual levels of variability, which, for example, is only partially possible when using other tools, such as, for example, min-max graphs.

When the above-described measure is used to gauge within-subject variability we recognize that in the investigated group the development of lexical diversity varies greatly between three learners (S8, S11, S15) and is around 50% higher than the mean variability (represented in the Figure 5.12 by value 1 on the Y-axis). On the other hand, the development of four other learners (S4, S9, S10, S14) was not dynamic while the development of the other half of the participants in the study can be described as moderately variable.

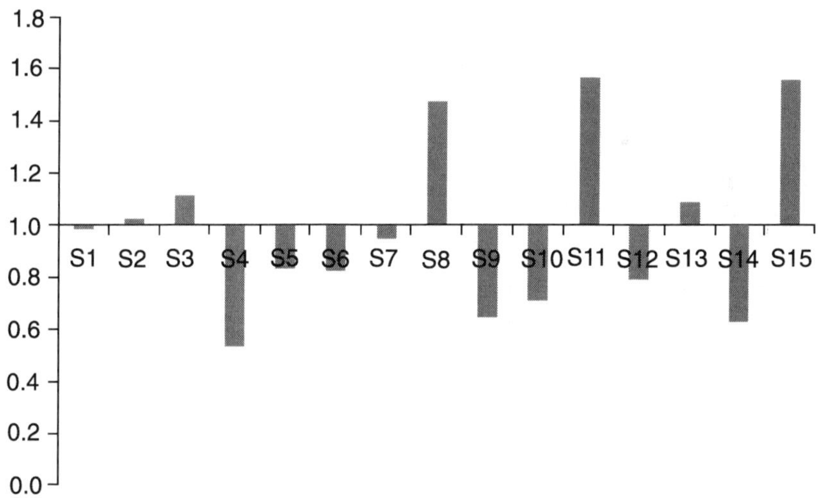

Figure 5.12. Within-subject variability in lexical diversity (Mean expressed as 1 on the Y-axis)

On the other hand, the degree of variability cannot serve as an indicator of any improvement in development or as a harbinger of a high level of language skills in the future. Among those students with average variability there were both those who write with a high level of lexical diversity (S1), and those whose texts were characterised by a low level of complexity (S13). In turn, learners who vary very little during the development, do not necessarily have to be classified as poor learners. On the contrary, they can be viewed as "quick starters" who are faster than others in acquiring and using new words, and even if they continue to develop their language skills, the dynamics of their development is lower than in other students. In this study learner S9 represented such a developmental profile. His variability was very low, with an $M|R|$ equal to 0.08 (35% below the average for the group as a whole), and yet during the entire study he outperformed the majority of his fellow students in terms of lexical diversity.

5.1.2. Development of lexical interconnectedness

Complexity not only involves a large set of different elements but is also characterized by mutual interconnection between them. Lexical diversity covers only a part of this property and even if the assumption is that increasing richness of vocabulary will lead to self-organization of the lexical system by creating a network of mutual connections, an instrument is needed that could confirm this hypothesis. Therefore, in order to gauge how strong the interrelationship is between lexical items a new measure will be used. The formula is expressed as the ratio of words included in complex phrases to the total number of words (WCP/W). At this point it is important to explain what is mean by a "complex phrase." In this study I use this term when referring to a (noun, verb, adjective, adverbial or prepositional) phrase consisting of more than its obligatory constituents. In this approach the following count as complex phrases:

1) Noun phrases containing more elements than simply the head noun:
   Jag hade ***möjlighet***^{NOUN} ***att göra detta*** [5-S12] – noun and a postmodifier (infinitival phrase)
   (I had (the) **possibility to do it**)
   Mitt stora rum^{NOUN} *var schönt och mysigt* [2-S6] – noun and a premodifier (possessive pronoun and adjective)
   (**My big room** was beautiful and snug)
2) Verb phrases – understood in a narrow sense, i.e. as the main verb and auxiliary verbs, participle constructions, or particles included in phrasal verbs, but without complements and adjuncts:
   Läkaren ***började***^{FV} ***att dra ut*** *min tand* [2-S1] – a finite verb and an infinitive

(The doctor **began to pull out** my tooth)
*En stor del av min läxa **var**^{FV} **tagen** från Annas uppsats* [5-S5] – a finite verb and a participle
(A large part of my homework **was taken** from Anna's essay)

3) Adjective phrases – containing more than the constituting adjective; most often an adverb
Jag bemärkte att den där vägen var **mycket lång**^{ADJ}* [2-S3] – an adjective and a premodifier (adverb)
(I noticed that that way was **very long**)
*...det tog också så mycket tid för hon är **så pratsjuk**^{ADJ}!* [3-S2] – an adjective and a premodifier (adverb)
(...it also took such a long time because she was **so garrulous!**)
4) Adverbial phrases – a complex adverbial phrase consists of an adverb an at least one additional modifier – in most cases another adverb
*Vi har en riktig bra kontakt så pratade vi **väldigt mycket**^{ADV}* [4-S10] – an adverb and a premodifier (adverb)
(We have a really good relationship so we talked **a great deal**)
*Jag var förberedd **ganska bra**^{ADV} för resan* [6-S14] – an adverb and a premodifier (adverb)
(I was prepared **quite well** for the trip)
5) Prepositional phrases – to be complex, a prepositional phrase must have a complex noun phrase as its complementing element
*Jag, som barn, hade rädslan **för**^{PREP} **djupt vatten** och var avvisande **mot**^{PREP} **mannens proposition*** [4-S11] – a preposition and a complex noun phrase (with a noun in the genitive as a premodifier)
(I, like (all) children, was afraid **of the deep water** and was averse **to the man's proposal**)
*Det var de svåraste sekunder **i**^{PREP} **hela mitt liv*** [3-S9] – a preposition and a complex noun phrase (with an adjective and a possessive pronoun as premodifiers)
(It was the most difficult moment **in my entire life**)

According to such a classification, the following sentence includes three simple phrases (*Jag*^{NP}, *var*^{VP}, *på semester*^{PP}) and two complex phrases (*på en liten by i Polen*^{PP}, *för två år sedan*^{PP})

*Jag var på semestern **på**^{PREP} **en liten by i Polen för**^{PREP} **två år sedan*** [4-S7]
(I was on holiday **in a small village in Poland two years ago**)

The sentence consists of 14 words, of which 10 are parts of complex phrases and four build simple constructions. The ratio of the number of words included in complex phrases to the total number of words in this sentence would be as follows: WCP/W = 0.71. The opposite is observed in the following sample, consisting of the same number of words (14):

Han såg mycket ***om sitt livet*** *och jag tänkte att han* ***behövde prata*** *mycket* [1-S2]

(He told (us) a lot **about his life** and I thought that he **needed to talk** a lot)

The WCP/W-ratio would in this case be 0.36, because only five words were organized in complex phrases.

The ratio serves, in my opinion, as a valid indicator of lexical complexity because it reflects the degree to which lexical items are interconnected. Moreover, indirectly it even provides information on lexical diversity, because the words included in a phrase most likely represent different lemmas.

The average developmental path for lexical complexity measured with this new tool is one of continuous progress, with more dynamic growth (R = 21) occurring at the end of the experiments (Figure 5.13).

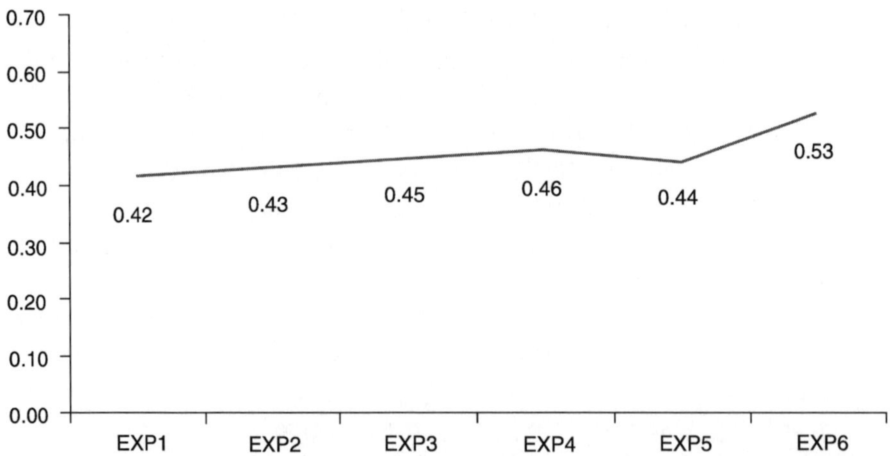

Figure 5.13. Average development of lexical interconnectedness (WCP/W)

The mean does not represent a group tendency, but rather the average lexical complexity at the particular time of the data collection. However, it in no way corresponds with the development of any participant. The only statement that can be made is that there was a general increase in complexity, which, however, would be expected after three years of foreign language instruction. On the other hand, the mean can be used as a reference point because it reflects the results of this particular group and not those of other groups of learners or native speakers. Again, however, as in the case of the previous considerations, individual data provide a true and reliable picture of the development, and they even uncover similarities between learners and the average serves as a reference point for each data collection point.

Firstly, lexical complexity develops very dynamically in most students, with a clear spurt in complexity greater than $R = 20$ (see Figures 5.14a–c). In most cases, the peak there is followed by a slight dip, but afterwards the system achieves an attractor state situated very often at a level similar to that before the spurt. In one student (S2), however, after a period of stability, there was an extremely sharp increase in complexity at the end of the study ($R = 89$). The question in this case is whether the spurt in complexity is a sign of her reaching her optimal level at this particular time or a signal of dynamic progress in lexical complexity at the end of her third year of learning. The answer to this question lies in the interplay of the systems included. This participant spent one semester (the sixth) in Sweden – so the last experiment took place directly after her return from her scholarship. The learning environment has in this case undoubtedly triggered considerable growth in terms of both vocabulary diversity and complexity.

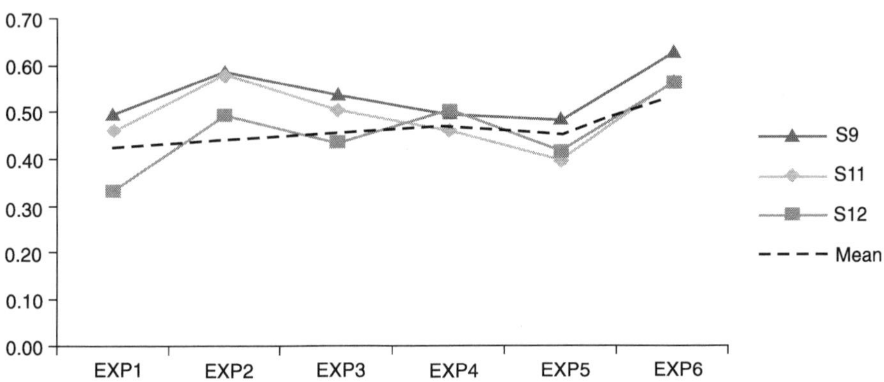

Figure 5.14a. Spurt in lexical complexity ($R > 20$) during the second semester

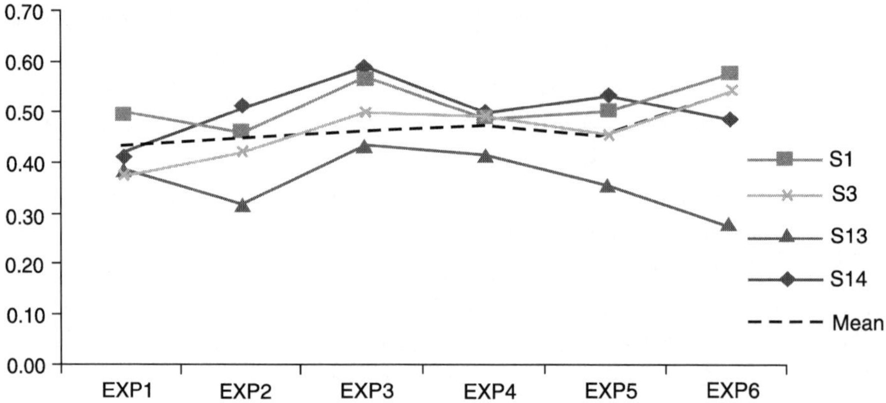

Figure 5.14b. Spurt in lexical complexity ($R > 20$) during the third semester

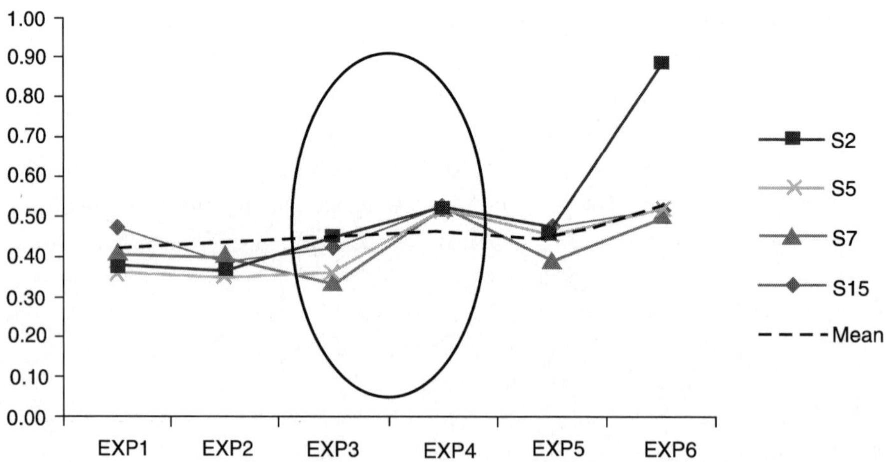

Figure 5.14c. Spurt in lexical complexity ($R > 20$) during the fourth semester

Three participants, however, do not share the same pattern. What they have in common is that they had already built lexically very complex texts after the first semester – all being the most complex in the entire group. Furthermore, students S6 and S8 were characterised by the least variability in development throughout the entire period, compared with the rest of the group. And although S10 produced a very simple text in the fourth experiment, this should not be interpreted as a reverse in development, but rather as an accidentally less complex performance at that specific point. In other experiments the texts did not differ significantly in their lexical complexity and like the other two learners her texts exhibited a rather stable and high level of complexity. Moreover, she wrote very short texts in all the experiments – she was the leading short-text-writer (after the above mentioned S4). Based on these two features we can build up a learner profile for this student – she seemed to have a tendency to write short and complex texts. All these three learners (S6, S8, S10) developed lexical complexity much earlier than their fellow students – doing so already during the first semester (see Figure 5.15).

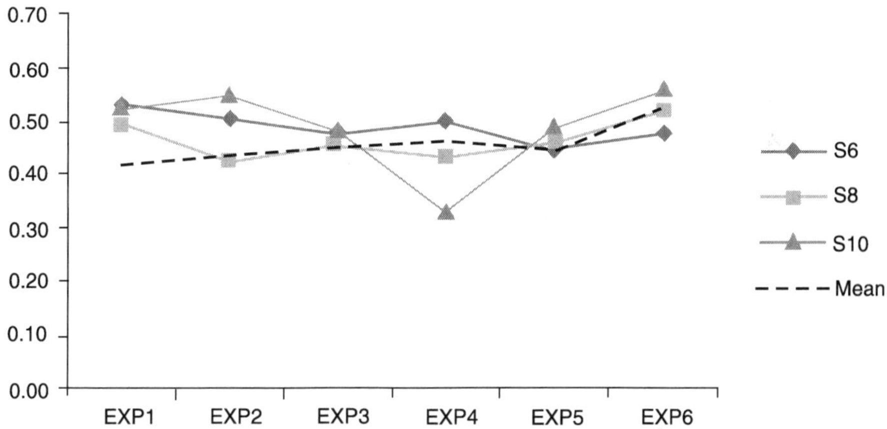

Figure 5.15. Early development of lexical complexity

One of the learners exhibited a different developmental pattern and cannot be described using any of the above-mentioned characteristics (Figure 5.16). In general, her lexical complexity was very low during the entire learning period. Slight progress can be observed no earlier than after the end of the second year (in the fourth experiment). This student also produced the shortest texts, had the lowest level of lexical diversity, and at the same time developed the slowest compared with all the other study participants. Neither can we identify a clear spurt in lexical complexity. Her development was rather slight, but even if it took longer for her to write more complex texts in Swedish and even if her texts were generally not lexically complex, she still made progress.

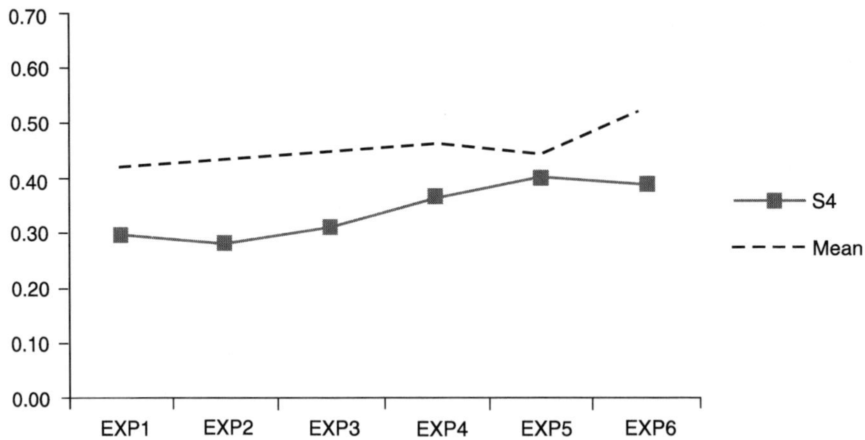

Figure 5.16. Later development of lexical complexity

In the case of lexical complexity the interplay with text length is again very strong (*r* = .72), but not as unambiguously so for the majority of students as in the case of lexical diversity. As the table below shows (Table 5.2) a major split can be observed between the participants. In about half of them the correlation between text length and lexical complexity is moderate or very positive. In the case of two of the participants the increase in text length resulted in a decrease in lexical complexity and in nearly half of the students the development of both dimensions proceeded independently. This outcome clearly deviates from the mean, which is evidence that the average value does not reflect development in individuals.

A similar pattern emerges in the interplay between lexical diversity and lexical complexity. There is a strong positive correlation between these two properties at an average level (*r* = .87), but this pattern is not so unambiguous when we look at correlations in individuals. The development of lexical diversity admittedly went hand in hand with lexical complexity in the majority of students, but in five participants no such interconnection existed.

As the above results show we cannot say that the development of lexical complexity proceeds in accordance with the mean for the entire group. What can be concluded is that this property of linguistic proficiency develops at different points in students and that it is often interconnected with the development of both text length and lexical diversity. In some students it develops earlier, i.e. during the first year of instruction, and at the same time does not correspond with the development of text length and/or its lexical diversity. On the other hand, in learners who need more time to organize new words in mutually connected units, the development of diversity and the development of complexity complement one another.

Table 5.2. Correlation between lexical complexity, text length, and lexical diversity

Student	Text length/ lexical complexity (*r*)	Lexical complexity/ lexical diversity (*r*)
S1	.57	.35
S2	−.20	.67
S3	.73	.41
S4	.89	.53
S5	.29	.73
S6	−.50	−.34
S7	−.03	.16
S8	−.24	−.03
S9	−.14	.06
S10	−.50	−.23
S11	.02	.47
S12	.58	.76
S13	.46	.60
S14	.35	.46
S15	.63	.67

5.2. Syntactic complexity

According to the adopted definition of complexity, syntactic complexity reflects the heterogeneity of syntactic constructions and the degree of their interconnection. In most common measurements complexity is associated with subordination or the length of clausal or sentence units. Norris and Ortega (2009), however, argue in favour of multidimensional measurements, according to Halliday and Matthiessen's (1999) systemic functional linguistics, where at the beginning the learners express their ideas most often using coordination or sequences of unconnected linguistic items such as words, clauses or sentences. In the next phase subordinated constructions occur and in the last step we see the emergence of grammatical metaphors, expressed by means of nominalizations or other structures of high lexical density (Norris & Ortega, 2009).

As in the case of lexical complexity one measure cannot express all the properties of syntactic complexity. Therefore, two measures will be used and discussed in more depth in this study. The first is the subordination ratio, expressed as the number of clauses per T-unit, and the other is a new measure: the ratio of different types of clauses to the number of sentences (DC/S). The latter tool should, in my opinion, mirror the heterogeneity of syntactic construction and, at the same time, also express their mutual interconnection. Furthermore, it takes a broader view of complexity, focusing on more types of syntactic structures than subordinated clauses alone.

5.2.1. Development of subordination

The transition from expressing ideas by means of simple clauses to doing so in the form of subordinations generally proceeded slowly and only began to speed up in the third year of learning, when the growth rate reached 20% (Figure 5.17) – we can get such an impression when we look at the average developmental curve below. When thinking in terms of average-related outcomes a rather strong positive correlation can be observed with the mean text length (r = .55), and a weak positive correlation with mean lexical diversity (r = .33) or lexical complexity (r = .29), which could lead to the conclusion that when texts become longer they become at the same time more syntactically complex – but tend to rarely do so at the lexical level.

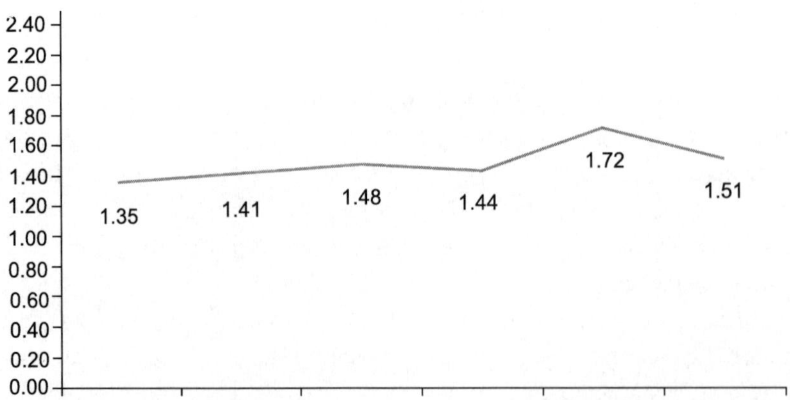

Figure 5.17. Development of the average subordination ratio (C/T)

Another picture emerges when we look at individual developmental trajectories. What the mean value mirrors is considerable growth in syntactic complexity in the fifth experiment, i.e. after the second year of language instruction, followed by a return to the prior value, which in fact may give the impression that syntactic complexity actually hardly progressed at all, except for one spurt (R = 21%). In the case of this specific experiment we can interpret this sudden, single growth event with task specificity (the topic was: "My greatest lie/my greatest offence"), which might have triggered more extensive use of subordinated clauses. Such an explanation could in fact be given if such growth had been observed in the majority or at least in half of the subjects. But there were only three students, in whom this peak only occurred in the fifth experiment, and with a growth rate of at least 38% (Figure 5.18), which undoubtedly had an impact on the overall mean growth. Apart from one learner (S11), in whom syntactic complexity continued to develop later on, i.e. up to the sixth experiment, the other writers experienced an exceptional spurt in complexity when they wrote about their greatest lie. And for these students it might have been the specificity of the topic that influenced the degree of their syntactic complexity, because in the next experiment they achieved a similar degree of complexity to that recorded at the end of the fourth semester, i.e. before the spurt occurred.

It is very difficult to identify any developmental patterns in syntactic complexity, because almost every learner developed in his or her own way. What could be observed was a growth in this property in about one half of the participants (Figure 5.19), which in fact goes against the developmental path presented in the average curve. The progress in these students proceeds not linearly, but smoothed results, established by means of the moving averages for each of them, clearly show a developmental upward trend.

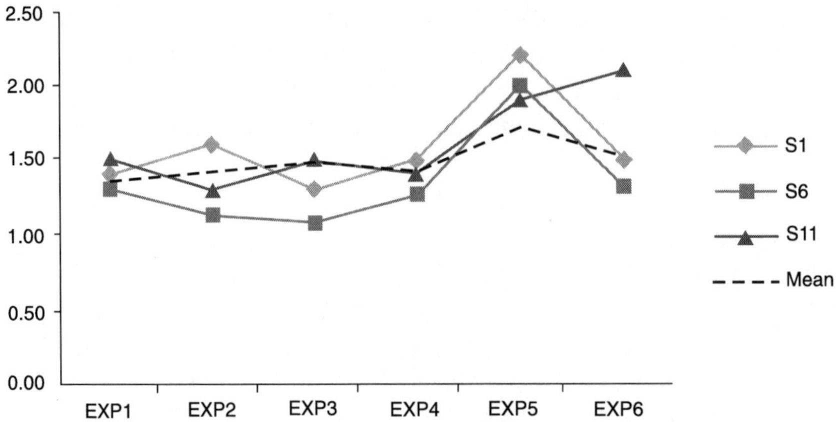

Figure 5.18. Peak of syntactic complexity in the fifth experiment

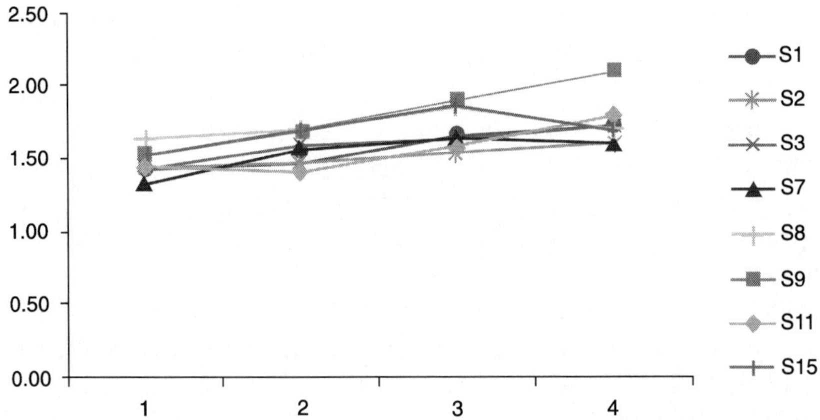

Figure 5.19. Progress in syntactic complexity (C/T-unit)

In turn, the other half of the participants did not show any progress in subordination after three years of learning (Figure 5.20). Apart from a few single spurts reported earlier in this chapter syntactic complexity appears to be a rather stable property in these students. And this appears to be the case regardless of the degree of subordination at the time of the first experiment. The question is what these results mean. They do not actually comply with the view that an increase in proficiency implies a greater ability to build syntactically advanced utterances. And because it concerns so many of the learners it cannot be interpreted as an error of measurement or an isolated case.

The answer to this question can be found in the overall tendency of each individual to use many subordinated clauses or not to do so.

Similarly to the development of text length and lexical diversity, some learners built syntactically complex texts throughout the entire period of the study. The majority of them were writers with generally high levels of complexity, regardless of whether they were already using a large number of subordinated clauses from the very beginning or first began to write more complex texts in later periods. Figure 5.21 below presents the data for this particular group, illustrating their complexity in relation to the mean (expressed as 1). All these participants achieved above-average syntactic complexity in at least four of the six experimental sessions.

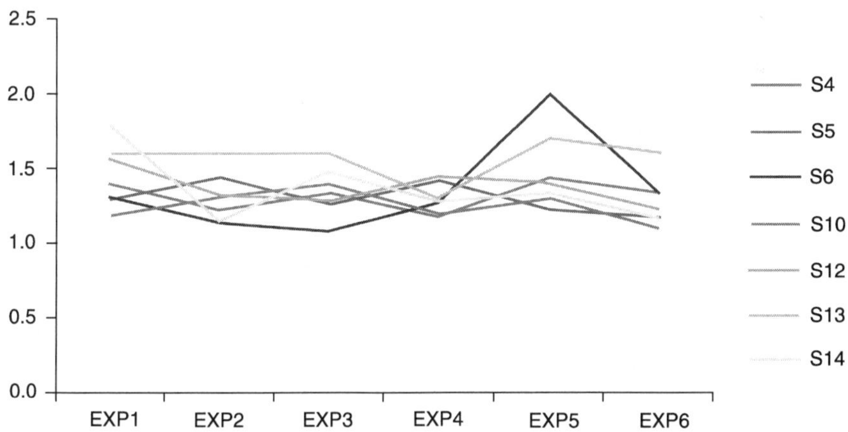

Figure 5.20. Learners achieving no progress in syntactic complexity

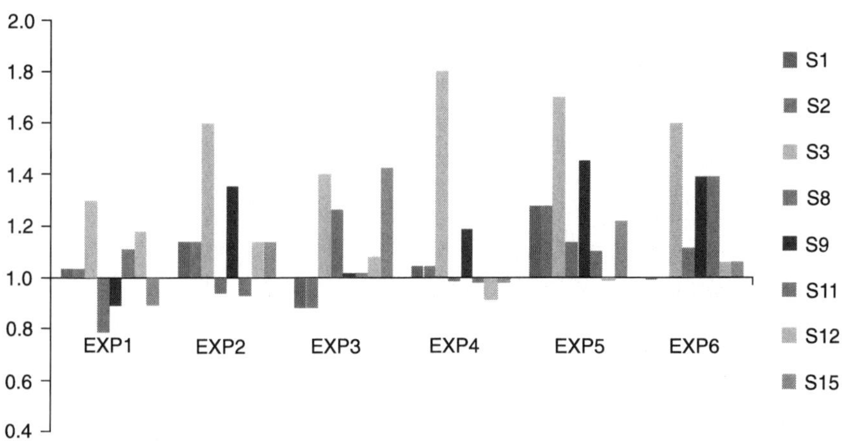

Figure 5.21. Learners with a high level of syntactic complexity (Mean for the entire group Y = 1)

Other learners displayed the opposite tendency (Figure 5.22) and generally wrote syntactically less complex texts. Two of the students in this group, however, diverged significantly from the general pattern. Their first texts consisted of many subordinated clauses, between 20 and 30% above the average. This was especially the case with student S14, whose syntactic complexity after the first semester was the highest of all the 15 students in the group. Afterwards, however, a considerable decline in complexity was noted in both cases, followed by a continuing low level of subordination in all subsequent periods. What is interesting is that these are the same students whose texts were also very long in the first experiment and which decreased afterwards and remained low.

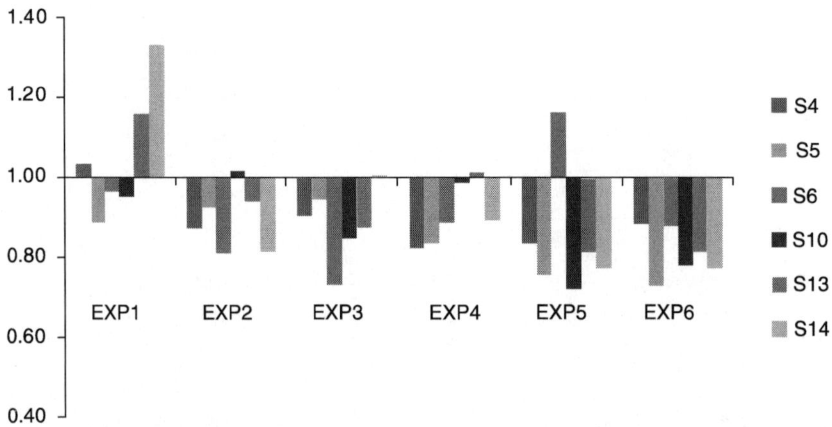

Figure 5.22. Learners with low syntactic complexity (Mean as Y = 1)

Another striking observation is that this group of learners with low syntactic complexity consists exclusively of writers whose subordination rate did not progress during the study, which may lead to the general conclusion that in some learners syntactic complexity is generally low. On the other hand, nor was any progress in the subordination rate observed in two other learners (S1 and S12) who, however, belong to the former group, i.e. those learners characterised by a high level of syntactic complexity. From these results two possible explanations emerge. The first one relates to the propensity of an individual to use few complex constructions, which, for example, could apply not only to the language that is actually learned, but even to the first language. This assumption, however, should be explored separately, by comparing writing samples in both languages. The other explanation is connected with the specificity of the measure. The ratio of subordinated clauses to a T-unit only informs us about how many clauses the writer used. What we do not know is how heterogeneous they were, i.e. if only the same constructions were involved, such as declarative content clauses (a), relative clauses (b) or temporal clauses (c) (conjunctions in bold):

a. *Jag drömde* ***att*** *jag åkte till Sverige med mina kompisar* [2-S2]
   (I had a dream that I went to Sweden with my friends)
b. *Då kom polisen* ***som*** *skrev en raporrt om det* ***som*** *hade hänt* [3-S9]
   (Then the police came and wrote a report about what had happened)
c. **När** *jag var liten tyckte jag väldigt mycket om godis* [5-S12]
   (When I was little I liked sweets very much)

What we can assume is that increased lexical diversity will result in greater diversity of syntactic constructions. This assumption, however, could be confirmed by measuring the correlation coefficient for syntactic complexity and lexical diversity (GI), which on average was moderately positive (r = .33). However, only in three students (S2, S3, S11) was the relationship between both dimensions very positive (r > .50). No such interconnection was observed in the other subjects or the correlation was rather negative.

The outcome of the analysis suggests that the C/T ratio might not give the whole picture when it comes to the development of syntactic complexity. The predominant lack of growth in so many learners (fully half of the participants) may suggest that the development of this aspect of proficiency may involve other variables than simply the degree of subordination, which in turn would require the implementation of other measures.

The fact that the learners are polarized into groups with low and high degrees of syntactic complexity, respectively, should not be interpreted as a natural outcome of the relation to the mean. We may conclude that the mean value by definition takes into account results that are below the average and above it. In general, the arithmetic mean encompasses such a logical conclusion. However, what should be stressed here is that this claim could be tenable if the same or at least some of the learners sometimes produced above average texts, and sometimes below average texts. And this is not the case. In the present study only one student (S7) could be called "an average learner," with syntactic complexity around the mean, and who did not display a tendency to write more or less complex texts. As Figures 5.15 and 5.16 above show, a clear pattern can be observed in all the other learners: they can be classified either as students with high or with low levels of syntactic complexity. Without such an individualised approach we would never be able to recognize this characteristic. This individualised approach to the data even revealed that four subjects (S4, S10, S13, S14) could be tentatively described as learners writing short texts, with low lexical diversity and syntactic complexity. At the same time, the interconnection between these different aspects is very clear: The longer the texts the less elaborate they are, both at a lexical and a syntactic level. These students appeared to have difficulties processing longer text units, and thus chose a way (perhaps unconsciously) to write simply.

The general absence of any growth in the subordination ratio in so many students, the splitting into groups characterised by low vs. high levels of complexity, as well as the lack of any correlation between lexical diversity and the number of clauses per T-unit suggest that the development of syntactic complexity cannot be reduced to a numerical account of subordinated clauses in a syntactic unit. This conclusion is in line with the previous findings cited above, which in turn suggests the need to take a broader view of the connectedness of syntactic structures.

5.2.2. Development of syntactic diversity

One suggested way of exploring the elaborateness of syntactic structures in foreign language learners is to look at the heterogeneity of clauses and clause-like constructions, which at the same time could provide an insight into their different interconnections and thus reflect the degree of syntactic complexity achieved. The newly adopted measure is a ratio expressing the number of different clauses and clause-like constructions per sentence (abbreviated as DC/S). This measure should, in my opinion, fit into developmental studies, because the development of language skills not only includes the ability to use more differentiated clauses but also other linguistic means that help to package information, such as infinitival constructions, nominalizations and participles, which cannot be classified as clauses. On the other hand, it focuses not only on subordinated clauses as the main indicator of syntactic complexity but also takes into account other syntactic relations, such as syndetic and asyndetic parataxis.

I classify the following structures as clause-like constructions:

1) infinitival constructions

   Jag hade alltid drömt om en sådan klocka för jag tyckte att det var kul ***att ha****$^{INF.}$* ***någonting fint på handen*** [5-S11]

   (I had always dreamt about such a watch, because I thought that it would be great **to have something beautiful on my hand**)

2) participle constructions
   Jag var i ett vackert gård ***fullt***[PART.] ***med många färiga blommor och gröna träder*** [2-S8]
   (I was in a beautiful garden full of colourful flowers and green trees)

As in previous analyses the exploration of syntactic diversity will begin with a presentation of the students' mean development, which was characterised by slight but continuous progress in the first three semesters, after which an attractor state was achieved. As in the case of the subordination ratio (C/T) there was a peak in the fifth experiment, followed by a return to the previous state (Figure 5.23). The average trend corresponds to the development of subordination, with a very strong positive correlation evident between both complexity dimensions (r = .92). This may lead to the preliminary conclusion that syntactic complexity in fact means both subordination and diversity of syntactic construction. The question is if the spurt in the fifth experiment is a general developmental pattern in all or in the majority of participants or whether it is once again an arithmetic outcome of the considerable growth achieved by a few students, as in the case of the subordination ratio.

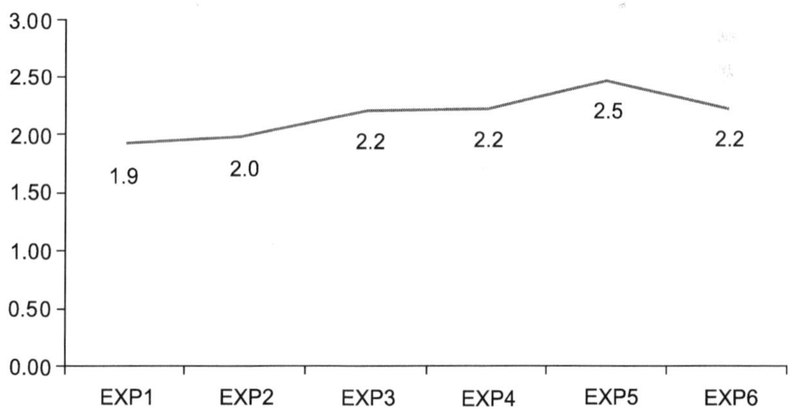

Figure 5.23. Mean development of syntactic diversity (DC/S)

Analysis of data at the individual level clearly shows that in half of the participants syntactic complexity increased up to the end of the fifth semester, when it achieved its highest level; except for one learner (S11), who made continuous progresses during the entire three-year study period (Figure 5.24). However, we can hardly speak of a spurt when looking at this experimental session alone, due the nonlinearity and variability of the development. There were in fact only two students who clearly peaked only in the fifth experiment (S6, S11). Their growth rates at this point were $R = 46\%$ and $R = 49\%$, respectively. Moreover, they are the same learners whose subordination ratios (C/T-unit) increased the most in the fifth experiment. In general, their development differed from other learners from this group. As was mentioned earlier, S11 made further progress in syntactic complexity also in the next experiment, while S6 only experienced a single spurt, which stands out against the nearly constant value of approximately 1.7 achieved in all other experiments.

In other learners this represents their highest level of complexity, but was achieved as a result of a steady growth in their ability to use ever more elaborate language.

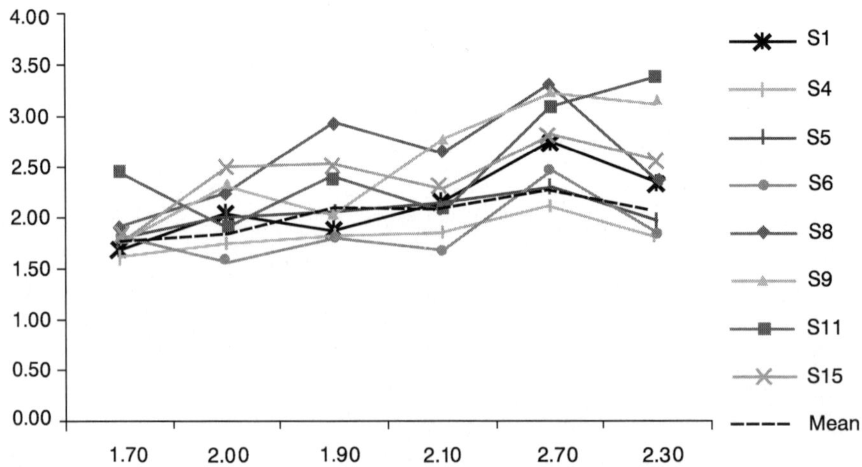

Figure 5.24. Development of syntactic diversity (DC/S) up to the fifth semester

A progressive tendency was also observed in three other students who, in turn, achieved their highest level half a year earlier (Figure 5.25). In general, most of the learners made substantial progress until they achieved an attractor state and even when the stability of the syntactic system was occasionally disturbed by dynamic change, it should be rather understood as a time when L2's development had reached its optimal level.

The attractor state can lie at different levels and may be interpreted as a time of low growth at more than one subsequent data collection point, which often occurs after a period of greater variability and a higher (both positive and negative) growth rate. The smoothed data show that many of the students achieved their attractor state. Most of them did so in the second part of the learning period (Figure 5.26).

The other learners who achieved growth in syntactic complexity had not reached an attractor state after three years, but are still developing their syntactic complexity (Figure 5.27).

Four learners (S10, S12, S13, S14) developed completely differently. Two of them (S10, S14) drafted their most complex texts in the first experiment, but afterwards used fewer and fewer differentiated syntactic constructions, which resulted in their having the lowest levels of complexity in the entire group after three years of learning. The other two students developed very rapidly, without displaying any clear trend

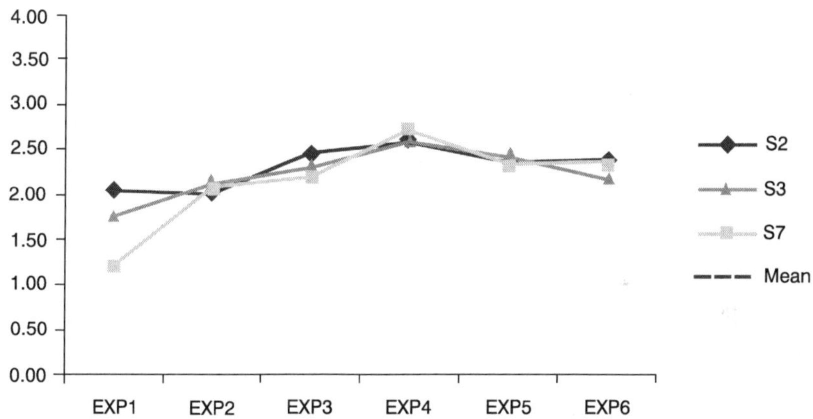

Figure 5.25. Growth in syntactic diversity up to the fourth semester

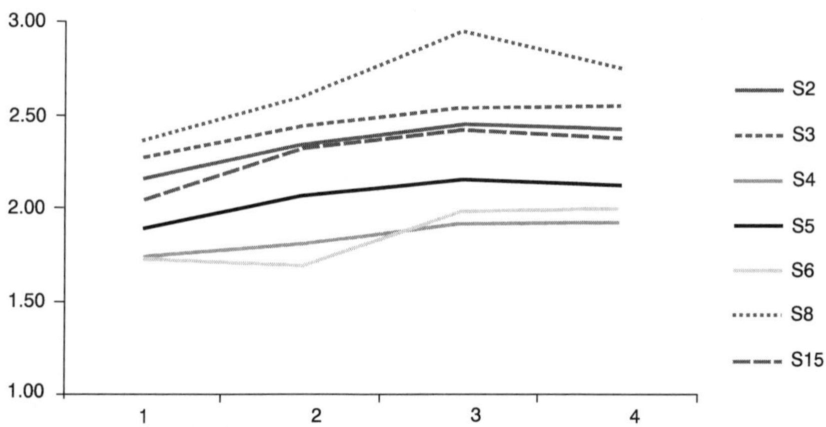

Figure 5.26. Learners with an attractor state in the second part of the study

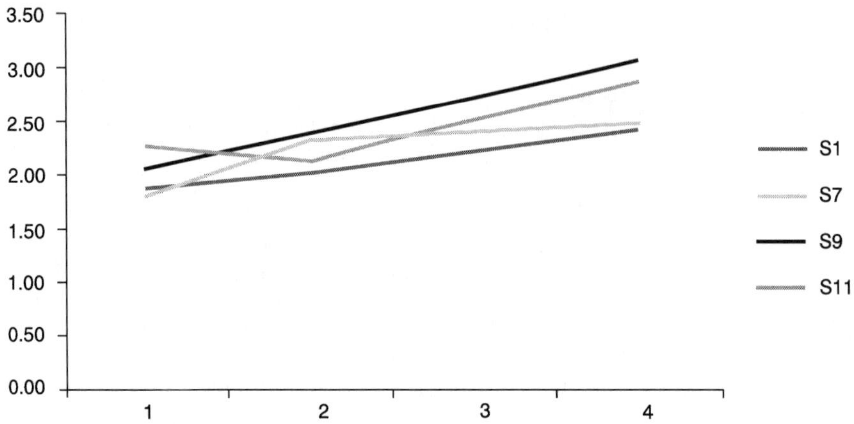

Figure 5.27. Learners who made steady progress (smoothed data)

(Figure 5.28). In the first and the last periods their syntactic complexity hardly changed at all, with growth rates ranging from –5% to +1%. In the middle of the three-year-period, however, their development was characterised by a high degree of variability, and their growth rates varied between –44% and +55%. It is very difficult to find an explanation for both types of learning curve. However, we can find a similar trend in the development of the subordination ratio, where no progress was observed in these writers' development. The group of non-progressing learners in subordination consisted of an additional four students (S1, S4, S5, S6), whose syntactic complexity, however, understood to mean the diversity of their syntactic structures, increased.

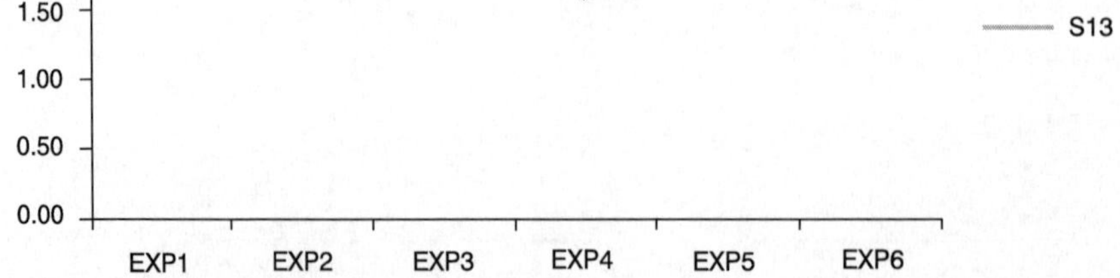

Figure 5.28. Dynamic development in the middle of the learning period

Furthermore, a lack of progress or even a decline in complexity during three years of language instruction characterised almost exclusively only those learners with generally low levels of complexity. It seems that these students did not focus on this particular aspect of proficiency and perhaps were more concerned with being fluent or accurate. On the other hand, we should not neglect the fact that all of them were capable of using elaborate, complex syntactic constructions in Swedish, because at least at one of their experimental sessions was characterised by an above-average level of syntactic complexity, with a value of 40% above the mean. The same can be said of the only student who made no progress, but displayed a high level of complexity throughout the whole study (S12). A lack of growth should not be treated as a lack of development. This student, for example, did not make any progress in syntactic complexity, measured as the subordination ratio and the diversity of syntactic constructions used per sentence, above all because she developed these skills earlier than many of her fellow students – already during the first semester. Afterwards, she improved other aspects of complexity, such as the overall variety of her syntactic repertoire, expressed in the total number of different syntactic constructions appearing in her texts. As presented in the table below (Table 5.3) her growth in this dimension was one of the highest in the entire group. This means that even if the number of different clauses or clause-like structures used in a sentence, or the number of subordinated clauses per T-unit did not change, she had more syntactic tools at her disposal, which she could combine together.

As a measure of frequency, the total number of different clauses or clause-like constructions strongly correlates with text length (r = .90). However, this relationship is absent in those two students who only produced complex texts in the first experimental session (S10, S14) and whose complexity steadily declined during the study. In these learners it was not only the subordination ratio or the diversity of syntactic constructions per sentence that decreased. They were also the only participants in the study in whom there was no or little increase in the overall enrichment of syntactic constructions (R = –5% and 2%, respectively – see Table 5.3 below). In the case of the other students the diversity of the syntactic means used to connect clauses increased. However, the least growth was observed once more in S4 (9%) whose lexical and syntactic complexity generally developed more slowly, as well as in S2 and S13, who, on the other hand, had already achieved a high level of complexity in the first experiment.

Table 5.3. Mean growth rate for total number of different syntactic constructions per text

Subject	R
S1	19
S2	9
S3	20
S4	7
S5	31
S6	15
S7	63
S8	37
S9	14
S10	-5
S11	23
S12	36
S13	9
S14	2
S15	25

Learner S7 (63%) made the most considerable progress in terms of the diversity of her syntactic construction. In fact S7 was one of the students characterised by an overall low level of complexity. After one semester of learning Swedish, S7's texts consisted only of simple clauses and two additional types: one coordinated clause connected with '*och*' (and) and one subordinated clause with '*att*' (that). After three years she was also using other coordinate clauses, expressing contrast ('*men*', '*utan*'), infinitival constructions as well as relative (introduced with the pronoun '*som*'), comparative (introduced with '*som om*') and content clauses (with '*hur*' and '*varför*'):

Different clauses (introducing connectors)		
	Jag glömma aldrig det.	I will never forget it.
	Jag var på semestern i bergen med mina kompisar igår.	I was on holiday in the mountains with my friends yesterday.

	Vädret har varit fint.	The weather was beautiful.
	Det har regnarit inte.	There was no rain.
och	Vi promenerade mycket i skogen **och** prattade.	We walked a lot in the woods **and** talked.
	Vi bodde hos mina vänern, i Zakopane.	We stayed with my friends in Zakopane.
	Vi har gått på theater och museen tre gånger.	We went to the theatre and museums three times.
	Jag hade dessuttom mycket tid för min själv.	I also had a lot of time for myself.
	Jag hade varit glad.	I was happy.
att[SUBJ]	Jag tycker **att** jag det var trevligt semastern.	I think **that** it was a nice holiday.

[1-S7]

Different connectors		
	Det var en gång för tre år sedan.	It was three years ago.
varför men hur	Jag kommer inte ihåg, **varför** det allt hade hänt **men** jag kan förtfarande inte komma underfud med **hur** det överhuvudtaget var möjligt.	I don't remember **why** it had all happened **but** I still can't fathom **how** it was possible.
som	Jag vill självklart berätta om en hemsk dröm, **som** jag hade drömt.	I will of course describe a horrible dream **that** I had.
	På natten hade sett jag en konstig film, **och** efter filmen funderade jag mycket om den.	That night I saw a strange movie, **and** after the movie I thought a lot about it.
	Mina alla tankar var riktade mo filmen.	My thoughts were focused on the movie.
	Den var insplelad i en postmodernistisk kovention.	It was made in a postmodern style.
	I min dröm spelade jag en huvudroll, **och** jag var i fara.	In my dream I had the main role, **and** I was in danger.

utan$^{ADEVRS.}$ att^{SUBJ} att^{INF}	Men min motståndare var inte någon vanlig människa **utan** en omateriell ande, **som** flög kring min gestalt **och** det verkade **att** dennes mål var **att hämta** min själ.	But my enemy wasn't a normal human being **but** rather a supernatural ghost **who** flew around my body **and** I got the impression **that** his goal was **to take** my soul.
	Jag kände mig hjälplöst **och** visste **att** ingen kommer med hlälp.	I felt helpless **and** knew **that** nobody would come to my aid.
	Den hela situationen var obegriplig för en vanlig människa **och** jag fick en känsla, **att** jag skulle komma utom mig själv.	The whole situation was incomprehensible to a normal human being **and** I had the impression **that** I would leave myself.
	Plötsligt fösvann anden **och** jag stannade ensam i rummet.	Suddenly the ghost disappeared **and** I was left alone in my room.
som om^{COMP}	Jag beto mig **som om** jag skulle vara en sinnesjuk person.	I behave **as if** I was mentally ill.
	Ingen ville tro på min brätelse **och** min familji bestämde sig för **att skicka** mig till mentaljukhuset.	No one wanted to believe my story **and** my family decided **to send** me to a mental hospital.
	Då vacknade jag.	Then I woke up.

[6–S7]

The difficulty in finding a general developmental pattern for syntactic complexity is closely linked to the dynamic behaviour of complex systems. Even though a progressive tendency was observed in many of the participants, some of the students did not develop in the same, expected direction. The explanation for this lies in one of the properties of complex, dynamic systems: their chaotic behaviour. These systems are sensitive to initial conditions. Even a slight change in parameters at the beginning can lead to unexpected outcomes in later phases. Such a slight variation can result in considerable growth, which, in turn can trigger a bifurcation in a learner's development. As described in the previous chapter, bifurcation in mathematics can, e.g., occur when the growth rate exceeds the value of three. This level, however, was a limit value for population growth (in Verhulst's study), and cannot be compared with language growth, which is a much faster process.

In the present study some of the students made considerable progress at the beginning of their learning period, i.e. during the first semester. Unfortunately, it is not possible to calculate the precise growth rate for this initial period, because we cannot assume that all the participants started with zero degree complexity. Therefore, the mean for all participants has been used as the reference value. Those students who far exceeded the mean level of syntactic complexity in the first experiment (by at least 20%) are assumed to have achieved a remarkable growth rate at the beginning of their learning period, which went beyond the level of development achieved by the majority of the students. In the case of those participants who stood out in terms of their development paths a clear bifurcation could be observed (Figure 5.29), when exceeding a certain growth rate may lead to unexpected results in later phases of development: both further growth (S11), no growth (S12) or a decline (S10, S14). Even if we cannot say what initial parameter lay behind such growth in the students' learning during their first semester we should not overlook the chaotic behaviour of the syntactic system in their language development. And this leads to the preliminary conclusion that the higher the growth rate at the beginning the more unexpected the later development can be. Such rapid progress in one language feature does not translate into an overall high level of language skills. The interconnectedness of systems calls for greater caution not only when predicting later development, but above all else when classifying or even labelling learners as good or poor, based exclusively on the initial phases of learning a new language.

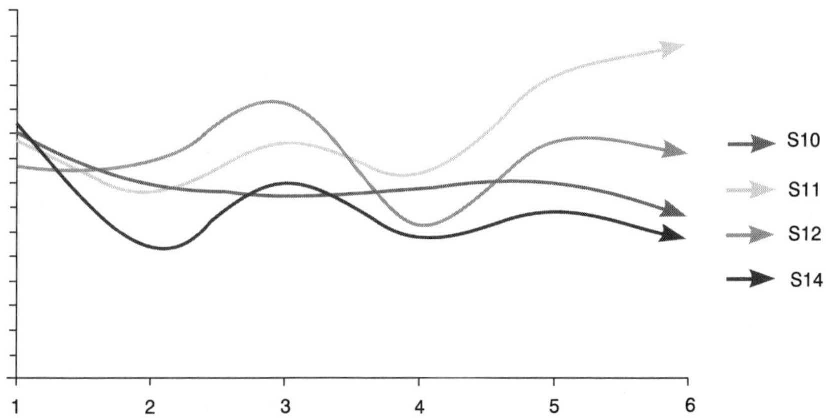

Figure 5.29. Bifurcation in the development of syntactic diversity (DC/S)

This factor is confirmed not only in relation to other complexity measures (C/T and the total number of different constructions), where considerable growth at the beginning led to different outcomes at the end of the three-year-period, but also when making comparisons with other students who did not produce such complex utterances in the first experiment (Figure 5.30). All learners with low levels of complexity in the first experiment made progress, even if they differed in their overall growth rate. Predictability in development goes hand in hand with the degree of progress made at the beginning of the learning process: the greater the improvement the less predictable the outcome. The butterfly effect appears to work even in foreign language development.

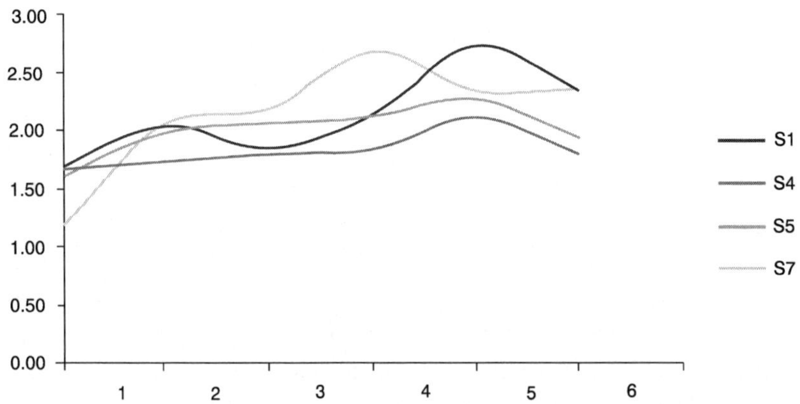

Figure 5.30. Development of syntactic diversity (DC/S) in learners with low growth rates before the first experiment

Syntactic complexity is a dimension of proficiency that not only includes many interacting language subsystems, but also learners' cognitive systems that enable them to process connections between mental representations. The ability to embed linguistic units within larger chunks increases when the learner not only has mentally internalized the mutual connections between thought strings, but also when he has learned the necessary vocabulary used for connecting clauses in sentences, and syntactic operations used for building phrases (such as, e.g., the use of prepositions or adverbs for Swedish). Therefore, the measures used for exploring complexity tend to complement one another and offer a deeper insight into the "complex system of complexity." This even appears confirmed by the high value of the correlation coefficient between all measures of syntactic complexity (subordination ratio (C/T), number of different clauses per sentence (CD/S), and total number of different clauses (DC)), both at the average level (*r* ranging from .74 to .91) and in individuals: with the exception of four learners (S10, S12, S13, S14) the correlation between all three aspects of syntactic complexity was at least moderately positive, and in most cases even strongly positive. The four subjects with other patterns differ from their fellow students only with regard to the type of interconnectedness involved: the relationship between lexical and syntactic complexity was in their case either strongly positive or strongly negative: some features compete and some complement each other during a learner's development.

The development of syntactic complexity involves the self-organization of many systems, during which variability can occur – the more unstable the system the more changes are ongoing and vice versa: the stronger the change the more variable the systems become. There are interesting differences between lexical and syntactic complexity when it comes to the variability of the systems. As was mentioned earlier in the chapter, inter-subject variability in lexical diversity was slight and remained unchanged during the entire three-year-period. A comparison of variation between individuals (Figures 5.31a and 5.31b) in lexical and syntactic complexity revealed that differences between learners in general did not exceed *cv* = .25. In general, variability between students is greater in the case of lexical complexity, measured as the complex phrase ratio (WCP/W) and syntactic diversity, expressed as the number of different syntactic clauses per sentence (DC/S), than for the other two properties (lexical diversity and subordination ratio). On the other hand, while differences between learners in lexical complexity did not increase after three years, the syntactic complexity shows a slight but clear upward trend (see the trend lines in Figures 5.31a and 5.31b)

A similar conclusion emerges when within-subject variability is considered. Here again we are dealing with syntactic complexity where greater individual variability was observed in almost all the students. However, intra-individual variability, expressed as the absolute mean growth rate, should in this study not be treated as an indicator of a system's instability. It could be a valid tool for dense longitudinal data, where the moment of change can be picked up. In uncompressed studies like the present analysis it should rather be explored in a relative sense, for example when comparing variability in development between different systems – in this case lexical and syntactic complexity.

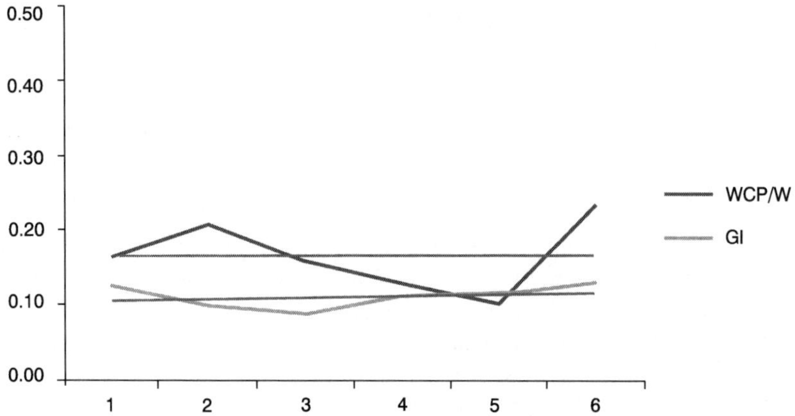

Figure 5.31a. Variation between individuals – lexical complexity

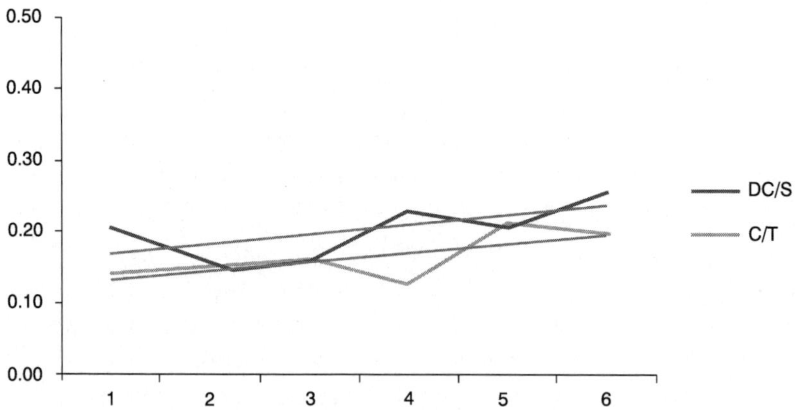

Figure 5.31b. Variation between individuals – syntactic complexity

As the above presented analysis shows, a substantial change in complexity occurs at some time points during the development path, but there are two kinds of these peaks or falls, respectively: the first occurs at the beginning of the learning period and is connected with a rapid growth in (lexical or syntactic) complexity, after which a stable period ensues. The latter is represented as a spurt or a decline between two rather stable periods, after a certain level of complexity has been achieved. Such single, rapid changes tend to be a sign that the learner has reached his or her optimal level at the time of data collection (the topic was especially interesting, and the motivation to participate in the experiment was exceptionally high) or, in the case of a significant, one-off decline the subject was in a bad shape, less interested in the topic or simply the story he

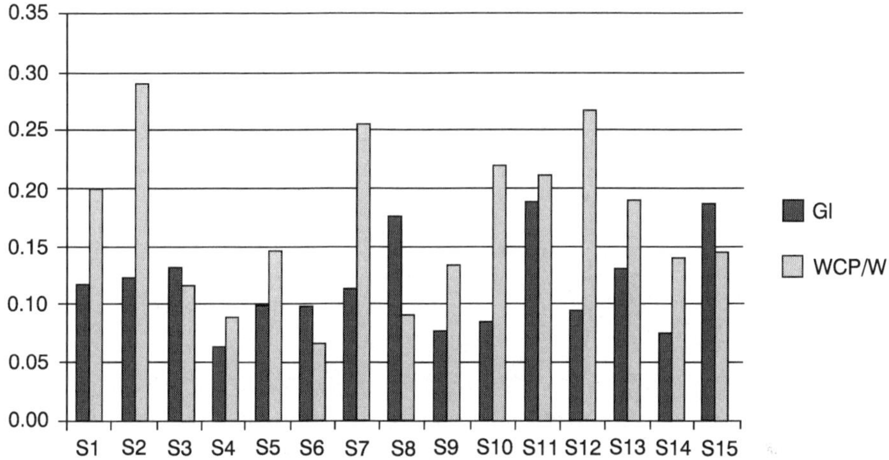

Figure 5.32a. Intra-individual variability – lexical complexity

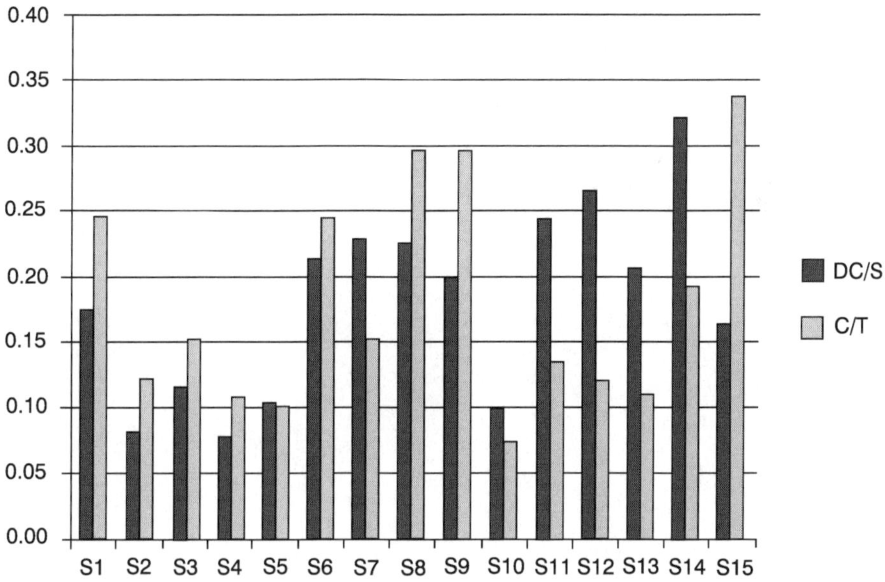

Figure 5.32b. Intra-individual variability – syntactic complexity

or she described did not trigger a high level of complexity. Furthermore, a rate of 15–20% in variability in six-month-intervals may generally not be very high, which, however, requires relativization through, e.g., a comparison between different aspects of language proficiency, such as accuracy and fluency.

There is no one general developmental pattern that can describe lexical and syntactic complexity. Even if the data were collected over rather long intervals (half a year), compared with dense, longitudinal data, intra-individual variability is an inherent property of the learning process. The development of complexity proceeded slowly during the three-year period, with clear polarization occurring between learners, regardless of whether complexity increased at an early stage, i.e. already in the first year, or later on. In students characterized by a high level of complexity at the beginning, development was more unpredictable than it was in those who needed more time to connect linguistic items in a network of complex structures. The development of complexity undoubtedly shows all the features of complex, dynamic systems – changes take place that are nonlinear in character and there is variability both between and within students. The systems behave chaotically; initial conditions play a crucial role in the process – substantial progress at the beginning of the learning process triggers bifurcation. There is continuous interplay between the systems – the length of the texts correlates with the development of vocabulary diversity and syntactic complexity. All these properties provide a platform for looking at other dimensions of proficiency in order to study their mutual interconnection during the entire development process.

6

Development of Accuracy

In investigations of accuracy, both developmental and cross-sectional in character, most researchers point to the general weakness of the most commonly used measure of accuracy, namely the number of error-free T-units per T-unit. As has already been mentioned, the major drawbacks of this measure were that the frequency of errors within a T-unit was neglected and that errors were not differentiated. On the other hand, measures that looked at the number and gravity of errors often tended to focus more on inaccuracy than accuracy.

These drawbacks also came to light in the present study, where many learners had the same ratio of error-free T-units, but differed in terms of the amount of errors in every unit. For example, in two learners (S12 and S10) the EFT/T was the same (0.38) in the first and the second experiment, respectively. This result could have led to the conclusion that their accuracy was at the same level. Even the length of texts, measured as the number of words (123) and the number of T-units (13), was the same for both writers. However, an analysis of the number of errors in each T-unit showed considerable differences. Student S12 only produced around 0.7 errors per T-unit while S10 made about four times as many errors per T-unit (2.9).

Another sample presents a student with the same rate of error-free T-units in the first two experiments (Figure 6.1). After the first and the second semester this writer's EFT/T was zero, which could be interpreted as meaning that the student did not achieve any progress in accuracy during the first year of learning Swedish. It was only in the third experiment that she began to write with greater accuracy, which represents a clear spurt. However, it is not possible to calculate a reliable growth rate in relation to the previous data collection point due to the above mentioned limitation that we cannot divide by zero. In such cases the researcher would be forced to artificially raise the calculated value up to e.g. 0.01 in order to estimate the growth in accuracy.

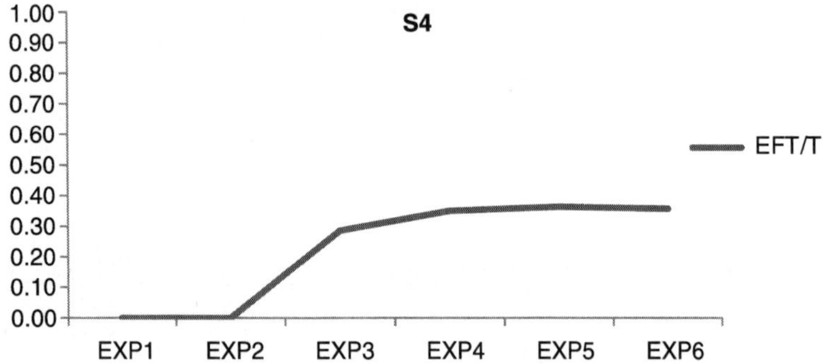

Figure 6.1. Development of accuracy in a student with no error-free T-unit during the first year of learning

However, an examination of her texts based on an analysis of the amount of errors in each T-unit (E/T) shows that she had in fact already been making progress from the very beginning of the study (Figure 6.2). The drop in error frequency is particularly strong in the third experiment, where a growth rate of $R = -54$ is noted, while other periods can be characterized as phases in which no dynamic changes occurred ($20 \geq R \geq -20$).

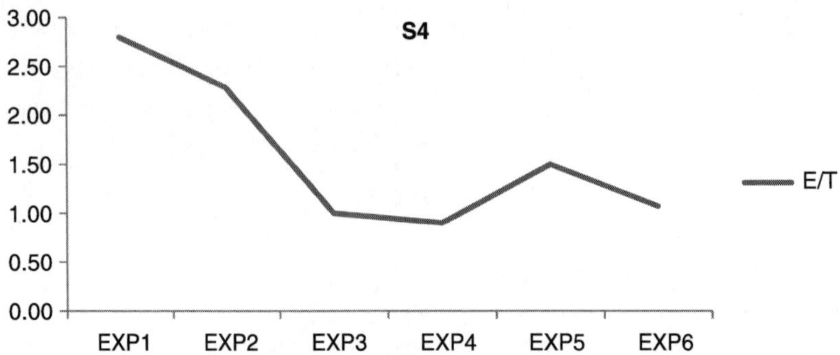

Figure 6.2. Errors per T-unit in S4

According to the above described situations, in those cases where different learners have the same EFT/T or the same learners have reached different points of development another more grained and more valid analysis of accuracy appears necessary. The present study makes use of a new tool called the Accuracy Index (referred to in its abbreviated form as AccInd). The index takes into account the number of errors in a T-unit and reflects the degree to which the performance is free of them. The formula for the index is as follows:

$$\text{AccInd} = \frac{1}{\sqrt{E/T}},$$

where E/T stands for the mean number of errors per T-unit.

The accuracy is inversely proportional to the error rate, calculated as the ratio E/T. The fewer errors in a T-unit, the greater the accuracy. For a more precise calculation the root of the ratio is, however, more valid than simple inverse proportionality. The validity of the index using the root of E/T can best be presented in graphic form (Figures 6.3a and 6.3b), where both measures in one student (S12) have been juxtaposed alongside each other.

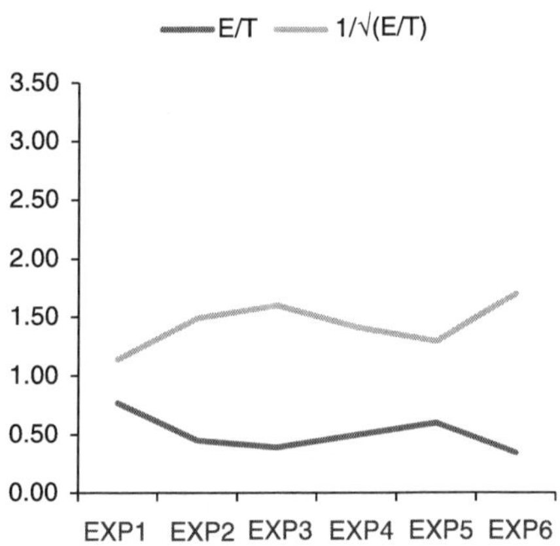

Figure 6.3a. Error rate and the reciprocal root of error rate

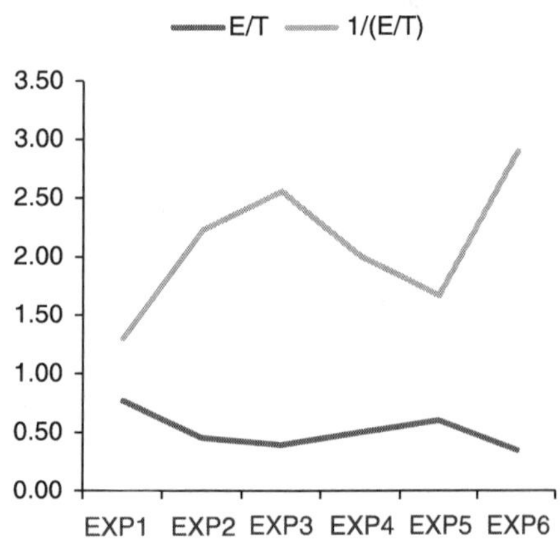

Fiure 6.3b. Error rate and the reciprocal of error rate (without root)

A comparison of the developmental curves of the error rate (E/T) and the accuracy measures, calculated as the reciprocal of the error rate and the reciprocal of its root, respectively, clearly reveals the almost symmetrical appearance of both trajectories in Figure 6.3a where the Accuracy Index was used, and different paths of development corresponding less to one another in Figure 6.3b.

The Index is of course not the first accuracy index to be used. In previous studies numerous features have been treated as accuracy indices. However, these tended to focus on single constructions, such as past tense marking in an obligatory context (Adamson *et al.* 1996) or erroneous words or tokens (Kaczmarek, 1980; Evola, Mamer & Lentz, 1980; Arnaud, 1992; Casanave, 1994; Engber, 1995; Ishikawa, 1995). The Accuracy Index proposed in this case does not focus on classifying errors, or measuring their severity, but instead treats them generally as a deviation from the norm. The following errors have been included in the analysis:

1) spelling errors – excluding typos,
2) morphological errors – errors in the inflection of words, such as plural marking, verb forms, comparison of adjectives etc., and errors in the morphological structure of words – i.e. derivational morphemes,
3) syntactic errors – errors in word order, lacking congruence in the nominal phrase or between subject and predicative, missing a subject in the obligatory context etc.,
4) lexical-semantic errors – incorrect word choice, wrong preposition, wrong article (error in gender), wrong tense use (but correctly inflected verb) etc.

Mean accuracy, expressed in the form of the Accuracy Index (Figure 6.4), develops in an almost linear way, with a slight attractor between the end of the second and the beginning of the third year of learning. The average growth in accuracy between experiments is not dynamic, with $R \in (-20, 20)$. However, the development between the first and the last experiment, compared with the mean results for the above-described dimensions, such as lexical and syntactic complexity, is characterized by a significantly more dynamic increase, where at the end of the study as a whole the texts were on average 64% more accurate (the corresponding growth rates for lexical and syntactic complexity were 28% and 15%, respectively). The clear progress achieved in accuracy after three years of learning a new language and more than 800 hours of instruction should not come as a surprise. The mean results are, however, insufficient to provide a dynamic view of language development. As was mentioned earlier the mean can only serve as a reference value at individual data collection points and should not be taken as an indicator of development.

According to the mean developmental trajectory, a similar path was only observed in two students (Figure 6.5), a fact that is confirmed by a very high coefficient of determination (R-squared above 0.9). However, their accuracy developed more dynamically than the mean and they differed considerably in terms of their level of performance correctness. While S15 achieved a high level of accuracy from the very beginning her fellow student S14 wrote texts with far more errors during the first two years of learning and a clear spurt in his accuracy was not noticeable until his third year of learning Swedish, such that by the end of the study he had even reached a higher level of accuracy than S15.

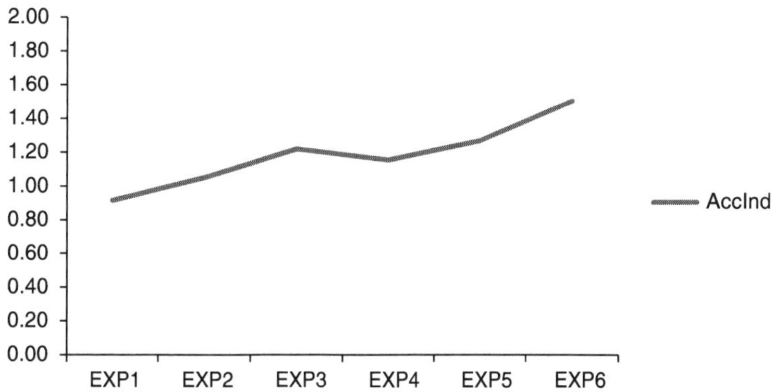

Figure 6.4. Development of mean Accuracy

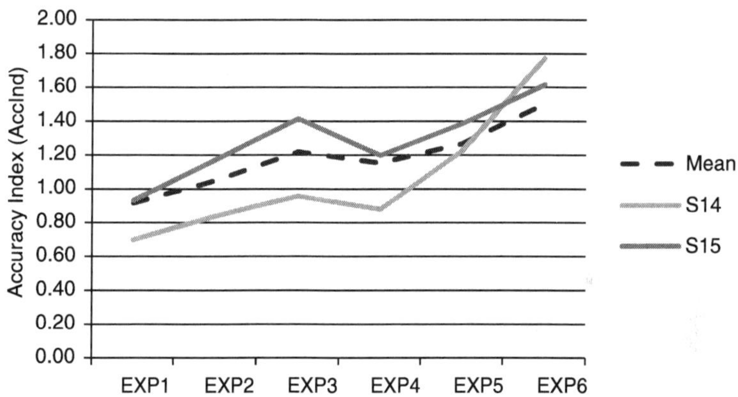

Figure 6.5. Average-near developmental trajectories for accuracy

Although learners develop in their own way and individual developmental trajectories differ considerably from each other, similar patterns could be identified in many students. However, these patterns do not correspond with the development presented by the mean. Almost all the participants (13 of the 15 who participated in the study) made the greatest and most dynamic progress in accuracy at the beginning of the learning process, i.e. during the first two or three semesters (Figures 6.6a and 6.6b). The growth rate in accuracy in all these students ranged between 20% and 51% in these periods, while the average R (for the entire group) remained at 15% and 16%, respectively. The results clearly show that the ability to create an accurate text in a new language develops in the early phases, during the first and at the beginning of the second year of learning. Afterwards the development reaches an attractor state, where the growth rate in most students does not exceed 20%.

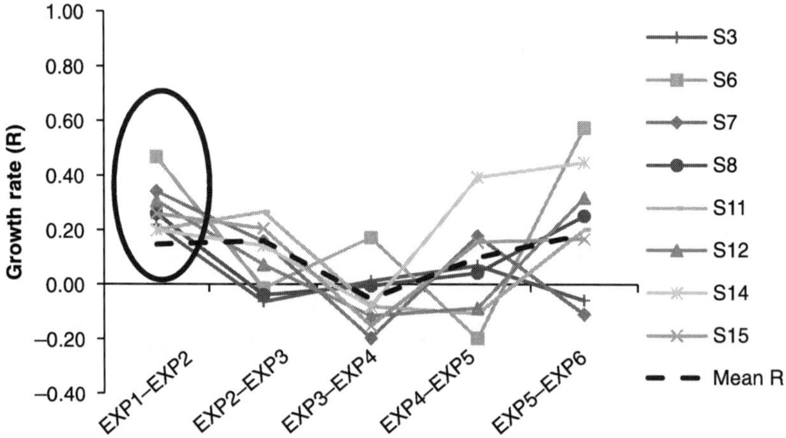

Figure 6.6a. Students achieving a considerable increase in accuracy during the second semester

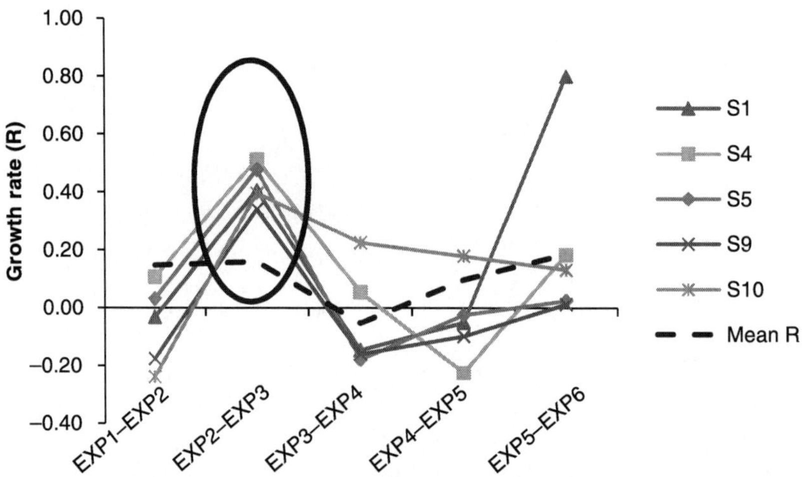

Figure 6.6b. Students achieving a considerable increase in accuracy during the third semester

One-third of the students managed to achieve a significant increase in accuracy one more time – during the sixth and final semester (Figure 6.7). It should be pointed out in this context that the change was very dynamic at this point and in all cases was greater than 35% according to the average growth rate. In one student it even reached the magical level of 165%. However, even these learners do not constitute a homogeneous group. While S6 and S12 are among those learners with the highest levels of accuracy in the entire experimental group and who during the three-year period outperformed other students, learner S1 can be described as an "average" student who only made considerable progress in accuracy at the end of the study. On the other hand, S2 represents an exceptional case of a learner who in all the earlier experiments had an almost constantly low level of accuracy and one of the two lowest mean growth rates. It took her longer to develop skills in producing correct essays in Swedish, but after a long period of ordering linguistic structures and creating mental representations of language she was able to write the most accurate text in the group. The question is, whether a dynamic change in accuracy can lead to a decline in, e.g., complexity in this student, which might be expected due to the interconnectedness of the systems and the Trade-Off Hypothesis. A detailed analysis of the mutual interplay of complexity, accuracy and fluency both for the group as a whole and for individual students will be described in the next chapter. However, a comparison of the development of lexical and syntactic complexity in this student shows that the growth in accuracy did not take place at the cost of complexity. In fact, in the last experiment she produced lexically and syntactically more complex texts than she did in the previous period. In the case of accuracy, the student outperformed her fellow students in terms of lexical complexity, where the complex phrase ratio (WCP/C) was about 67% higher than the average for the group as whole. In the case of this learner both performance dimensions complement but do not compete with each other.

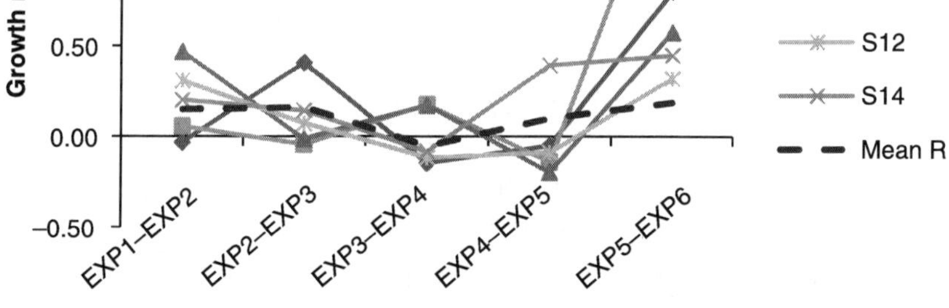

Figure 6.7. Spurt in accuracy at the end of the study

However, an exceptional spurt or decline in performance in one system is a clear sign of the influence of, and interplay with, another system. In the case of S2 the only reasonable explanation is the learning environment. As has been mentioned before, this student belonged to a group of three learners who spent one semester in Sweden on a scholarship at a folk high school and the experimental session took place directly after her return from Sweden. Hence, the ability to speak and learn Swedish and to live in Sweden has undoubtedly speeded up her language development.

The interconnection of systems is evident in another learner with a constantly low level of accuracy that hardly increased throughout the entire experiment, except for one occasion, when she achieved an accuracy of AccInd = 2.7, which was the highest value obtained by any of the students who participated in the study (Figure 6.8) – including the above-mentioned S2, who in the last experiment outperformed all the others with a score of AccInd = 2.2. Such a sudden increase cannot be interpreted simply as a later (compared to the other students) considerable growth in linguistic competence after five semesters due to the fact that afterwards, in the last experiment, she did not achieve a significantly higher level of accuracy compared with the period before the spurt. One explanation might be that she was at her optimal level on the day of data collection. However, such a huge change undoubtedly has other reasons, and in this case they can be found in the strong interconnectedness of accuracy and complexity. In the fifth experiment the student produced a very simple text with the lowest lexical diversity and complexity, compared with the entire group. The level of complexity corresponded with the lowest values noted in the first experiment. Even syntactic complexity was very low when accuracy was at its highest, but it did not stand out to such a degree as lexical complexity. The high level of accuracy at this point is the outcome of the simplicity of her text, both at the lexical and the syntactic levels.

In a group comprising many participants variation between learners is a natural phenomenon. However, every outstanding and unexpected result automatically leads to the search for a reason. In both the above-described cases the reason for exceptional accuracy could be found in a change in the learning environment or in its interconnectedness with complexity. However, another of the study participants also required more in-depth analysis. This learner attracts our attention because she was the only one in the whole group who did not make any progress in accuracy after three years of studying Swedish (Figure 6.9). This

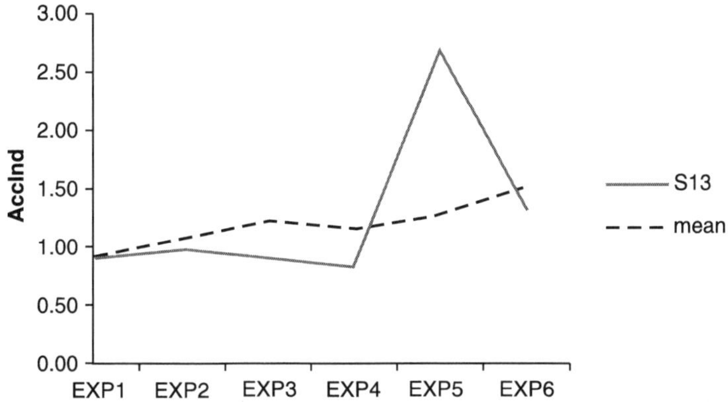

Figure 6.8. Huge spurt in accuracy in one experiment

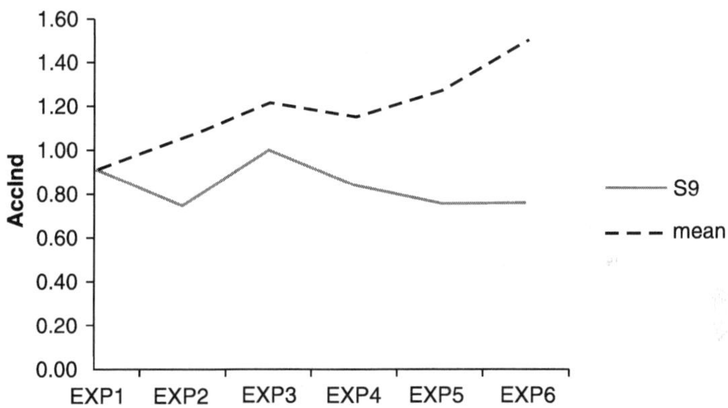

Figure 6.9. Student with no progress in accuracy

cannot be treated as a situation paralleling complexity, which in some learners remained at the same level or even decreased, because these students had already developed their complexity at the beginning of the learning period and thus did not make any progress in later phases. The same pattern is not evident in the objective student in whom no growth in accuracy was observed. After her first semester of learning Swedish her accuracy was at the mean level, so a decline in accuracy may be a surprise and it clearly goes against expectations. The answer to this situation can be found in the syntactic complexity of her texts. In this performance area she clearly outperformed her fellow students in almost all the experiments. In particular, this learners' subordination ratio was very high. The development of complexity clearly came at the cost of accuracy.

The three samples involving distinctive development paths in terms of accuracy – either in the form of an outstanding spurt or a lack of progress in this area – point to a need to look at such development as a complex phenomenon where all systems are interconnected with each other and where such interconnectedness varies solely in the degree of its intensity. The point is not whether they are in interaction, but rather which of these systems is more active in the actual interplay.

The striking results are an essential condition and cornerstone of variation between and within subjects. The more outstanding the values the greater the variability and the interconnection between systems. Due to the continuing interplay in a learner's development also variation is expected to change. Differences between learners' accuracy were evident throughout the entire study. As Figure 6.10 shows, inter-subject variation, expressed as the coefficient of variation, only slightly increased in the three-year period. Considerable growth (R = 37%) could be observed after the first semester, which went hand in hand with the spurt in accuracy observed in half of the participants. At this time polarization can clearly be observed among the participants. Some learners still had a low level of accuracy while other participants had significantly improved their ability to write Swedish correctly. This discrepancy remains at almost the same level during the entire study with one exception: another increase in variation occurred in the fifth experiment.

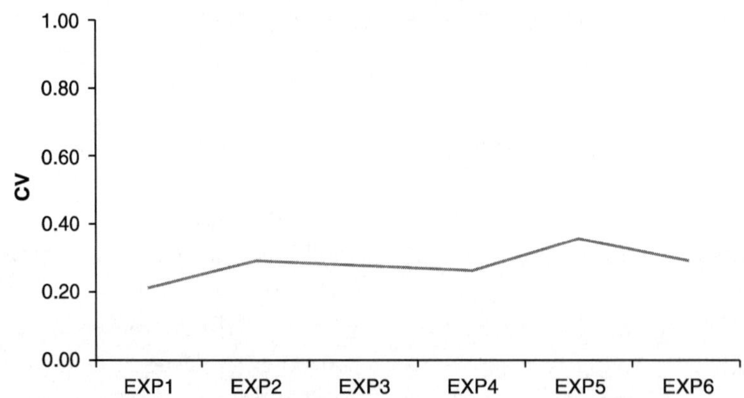

Figure 6.10. Between-subject variation in accuracy

At this point one might ask to what degree the extremely high peaks in accuracy in students S2 and S13 described above influenced this trajectory. As can be seen in Figure 6.52 below subject S2's result in the fifth experiment did not affect development in between-subject variation. On the other hand, the spurt in variability in the fifth experiment was a natural outcome of the extremely high level of accuracy achieved by learner S13, who produced a very simple and correct text at that time. Excluding this participant would clearly change the shape of the developmental trajectory and the variation between learners would remain at almost the same level from the second semester of language learning.

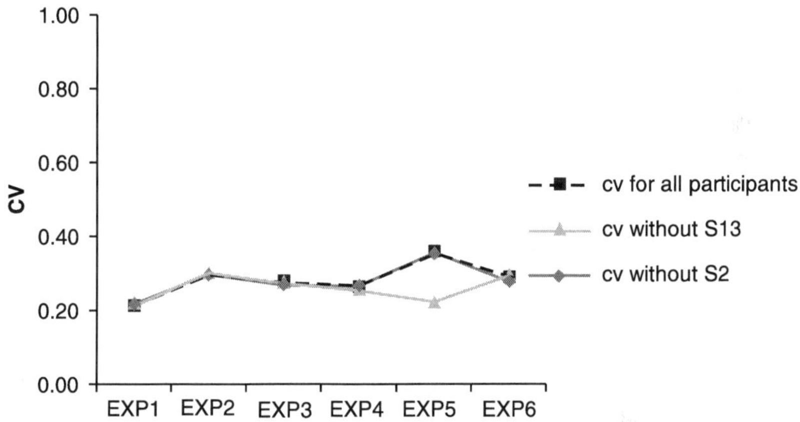

Figure 6.11. Between-subject variation excluding extremely outstanding participants

Regardless of whether we take into account results that stand out or not, the general developmental trend does not change: differences in text accuracy are less pronounced at the beginning and greater at the end of the three-year period of second language learning.

Peaks and troughs in development are inherent features of the learning process. The more instable the system the greater the variability, which is especially apparent in microdevelopmental studies. As the analysis of complexity shows, even intra-individual variability in longitudinal, macrodevelopmental studies varies a great deal between students. However, in such a design this could be more a sign of the continuous interconnection of systems than of the instability of language systems in the learner. In the case of variability, the results can also indirectly provide information about the extent of growth, because it is calculated on the basis of periodic growth rates. This assumption may be confirmed in the present study. As was presented in Figure 49 a strong correlation (Spearman's coefficient $\rho = .65$) exists between within-subject variability and the mean growth of accuracy in individuals. The greater the variability the more the students improved in accuracy after three years of learning. The outstanding subject, marked with an arrow, is the above-described S13, whose accuracy peaked in the fifth experiment, and this interconnected with a decrease in complexity. When the relationship between both features is calculated and this learner is excluded a much stronger correlation appears (ρ = .83). However, the same interconnection between development and variability was not observed in any of the other investigated dimensions. A moderately strong correlation (ρ = .60, p = 0.017) only occurs in the case of syntactic complexity, expressed as the subordination ratio (C/T) and lexical complexity (GI, WCP/W) (ρ = .38 and .34, respectively), while variability and growth do not correlate at all for syntactic diversity (DSC/C), where ρ = –.01.

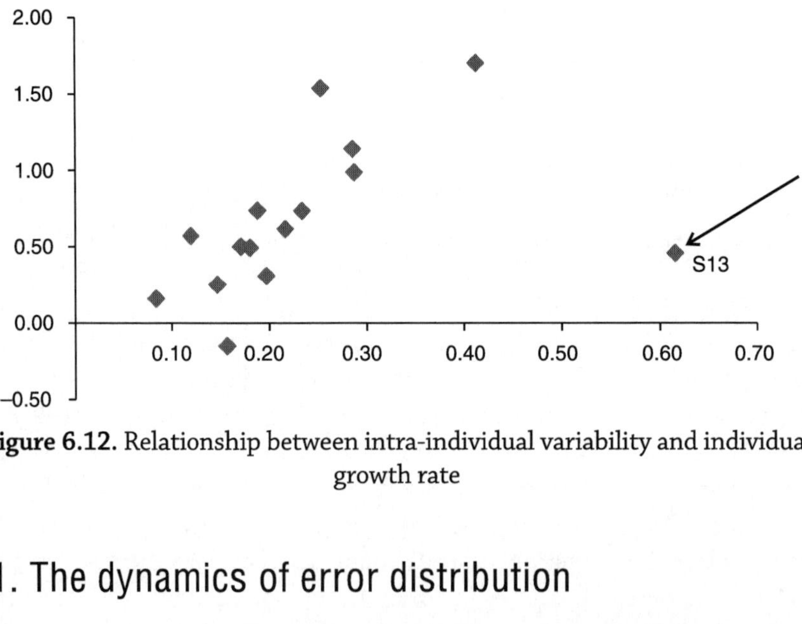

Figure 6.12. Relationship between intra-individual variability and individual growth rate

6.1. The dynamics of error distribution

Accuracy is not a uniform phenomenon but a complex system, consisting of smaller subsystems and interconnected with them. The inseparable counterpart of accuracy is the frequency of errors. When investigating accuracy we in fact always derive it from its mirror image: we look first at the reflection (errors) and afterwards try to find the real figure (accuracy). And depending on what part(s) of the image we are focusing on we will see another facet of the real entity. Looking at one type of error alone yields a detailed but only partial picture of accuracy. Focusing on all types of inaccuracy, on the other hand, will give an external contour without its internal cogs that are in unremitting interplay with each other.

Errors that occur during the learning process undergo continuous reorganisation due to interplay with the environment and the supply of resources (e.g. instruction in the classroom). Their complex nature automatically triggers both mutual interplay between several types of them as well as dynamic, chaotic behaviour in the development. Therefore, even if accuracy in general increases during the learning period we do not actually know if all types of error decrease to the same degree. Neither do we know if some errors are more resistant to change than others – in other words: the learner needs more time to understand the relationship between the form and meaning of words and structures.

We can better understand this relationship and its influence on overall accuracy and the learning process in general by gaining a deeper insight into the dynamics of several types of error. As was mentioned earlier in the chapter, for the needs of the present analysis errors have been divided into four categories: lexical-semantic errors, morphological errors, syntactic errors and spelling errors. Due to the adopted measure of accuracy, which was derived from the error ratio, an increase in accuracy involves a fall in error frequency. Of course, it would be more appropriate to investigate not lexical-semantic, morphologic, syntactic or spelling errors, but rather lexical-semantic, morphologic, syntactic and spelling accuracy. This point of view, unfortunately, can hardly be used for developmental, dynamically conducted studies due to the "no-dividing-by-zero" restriction. As has already been pointed out in earlier parts of this book, in the case of an error-free performance at one data collection point it would not be possible to calculate the dynamics of development in terms of growth rate or variability and therefore, in order to deliver reliable results, it is necessary to shift the focus in this case from accuracy to error.

As the figure below shows (Figure 6.13) the mean frequency of all error types clearly decreases. The most common errors are lexical-semantic and syntactic in character, while spelling and morphological errors make up the lowest percentage of all cases.

Lexical-semantic errors were the most common type of mistakes made by nearly all the students. However, in four learners (S1, S6, S11, S12) syntactic errors occurred most often – but only in the first experiment. These students made syntactic errors no more frequently than other learners, but in their own error constellation this type of error occurred most often

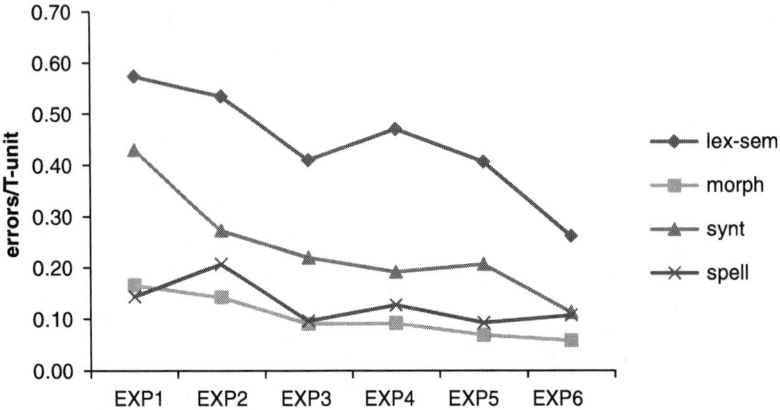

Figure 6.13. Development of mean error frequency

at the beginning of the study. What they have in common is that these are students with the highest accuracy levels in the entire group. One might ask if this high level of accuracy is possibly interconnected with a faster development of syntactic complexity in these students, which in the first phase of learning can cause such errors to occur. But this is not the case. Two of them actually had a higher ratio of syntactic complexity (DC/S), while the other two had a fairly average level of complexity after the first semester. A high level of complexity cannot thus be treated as the main reason for lower syntactic accuracy. The later development of syntactic correctness is rather a sign of a natural phenomenon in humans, especially at the beginning of the learning process, when they lack the cognitive ability to manage multiple operations simultaneously and with the same intensity. All four of these students begin very early to organize their new language system but they need more time to master syntactic connections between text units.

There is a great deal of inter-subject variation in all types of errors. None of the studied dimensions was characterized by such a divergence between students during the entire three-year period (see Figure 6.14). And these differences tended not to change at the end of the study, with growth rates between the first and the last experiment of $-10\% < R < +18\%$. Learners differ most not with regard to the complexity of their texts but rather in terms of accuracy. Variation in error frequency is not constant. Even if differences between the first and the last data collection point hardly exist, substantial changes are remarkable during the three-year period of the study. The developmental trajectory for morphological errors resembles a converted U-shape: students differed from each other mostly in the middle of the study. On the other hand, divergences in the occurrence of lexical and semantic errors remained almost at the same level.

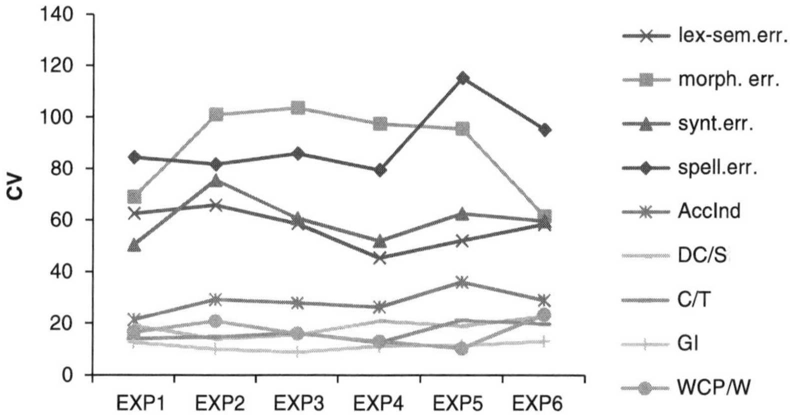

Figure 6.14. Inter-subject variation

The decline in the error ratio in all students during their three years of learning Swedish does not automatically mean that all learners will be at the same level at the end of the study. The homogeneity of the learning environment, the language background, the skill level in the new language, and the education level are not enough to even out individual differences interconnected with language aptitude, motivation, diligence, personality and many other factors. Even if the aim of many learners was to achieve a native-like competence in the second language, the ability to deliver an error-free text varied a great deal.

6.1.1. Development of lexical-semantic errors

As in the case of the other investigated phenomena the mean trajectory does not reflect the development of lexical-semantic errors in individuals. In only one student can we recognize any similarity with the mean route of the developmental path and an almost constant decline in inaccurate lexical items or semantic relations. Nor does the development of lexical-semantic errors correspond with the average trend for accuracy, where a substantial increase was already being observed in many participants in the second semester. In the case of lexical-semantic errors such progress could only be observed in three students. However, in the third experiment one semester later, about one half of the students had managed to considerably reduce the number of such errors they made (Figure 6.15). However, this decrease did not lead to stability in the development of the students' lexical and semantic systems. In the following periods growth rates between particular experiments were hardly ever lower than 20%. Hence, if we were only to analyse these particular systems we might not come to the conclusion that the third semester was a turning point for the development of these systems. However, when we compare this outcome with the development of complexity, which proceeds much less dynamically, we can state unreservedly that the greatest progress occurs in the beginning period of learning a new language.

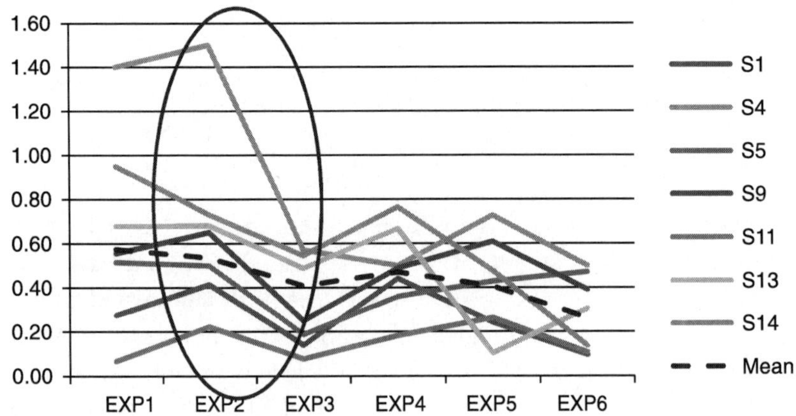

Figure 6.15. Students with a substantial decrease (≥ 25%) in lexical-semantic errors in the third semester

Due to high growth rates between experiments intra-individual variability is expected to be high. However, in the case of error frequency the mean absolute growth rate could not be used to estimate within-subject variability, because this variable could not be calculated for every student. When in one experiment the error ratio was zero and in the next it increased no growth rate could be calculated due to the mathematical condition that we cannot divide by zero. Therefore, instead of the mean absolute growth rate the mean absolute difference will be used in this part of the analysis. On the one hand, the absolute difference reflects a change in development. On the other hand, however, it is not a ratio value and thus it cannot give results that are as valid and comparable as the mean absolute growth rate.

As has been mentioned earlier, in macrodevelopmental studies intra-individual variability tends to reflect more the dynamics and the degree of change than the instability of systems. On the other hand it is the outcome of the interconnection and interplay between them. A striking, dynamic change at a given point in a learner's development is an indication of variability, but at the same time is also an indirect sign of the influence of other systems that have caused such variability. In the development of lexical and semantic systems intra-individual variability manifests itself above all periods in which there is a significant decrease or increase in errors. Such significant change at particular time points in the learning process was observed in the majority of students in the present study. Even if full accuracy is harder to achieve in a lexical-semantic system compared to morphology, syntax and spelling, we can observe periods in the development when error frequency declines considerably. Such a spurt in lexical-semantic accuracy triggers variability and predominantly occurs in students with a high error ratio. The calculated Spearman rho for the correlation between lexical-semantic errors and intra-individual variability, expressed as the mean absolute difference between experiments, is $\rho = .44$, which indicates a relatively high degree of interconnection between both features. Learners who make more errors vary more and develop more dynamically than those who are generally more accurate at the lexical-semantic level. However, we should not ignore the fact that variability in development occurs in almost every student. In only one learner did we observe a nearly constant level of errors throughout the entire learning period.

Inter-individual variation, on the other hand, which was presented in graphic form in the chapter above (Figure 6.14), did not change after three years of learning, which leads to three possible conclusions: (i) learners who made the most/least errors at the beginning of the study still have the highest/lowest ratio of inaccurate constructions at the end; (ii) those learners who were the best at the beginning became the worst at the end of the study, and vice versa, i.e. the "poorest" writer perhaps made the most progress and became the best; and (iii) changes in the development of learners with low or high error ratios are impossible to predict, i.e. some of the "poor" learners will become very good and some of the "quick starters" will not improve.

A deeper examination of the data reveals a clear polarising tendency among learners (Figure 6.16): they can be classified either as "good" or "poor" students, i.e. students with constantly low versus constantly high rates of error per T-unit. It should be stressed here that such a division is only valid with errors of this type. Furthermore, a drop-off in errors, followed by a further decline or by an attractor state is only characteristic of learners with the highest ratio of error in the first experiment (S4, S8, S10, S14 and S15). Such a developmental trend is again a sign of a strong relationship between the tempo and the dynamics of development – students who need more time to acquire a new language are more varied in their development, which resembles an S-curve.

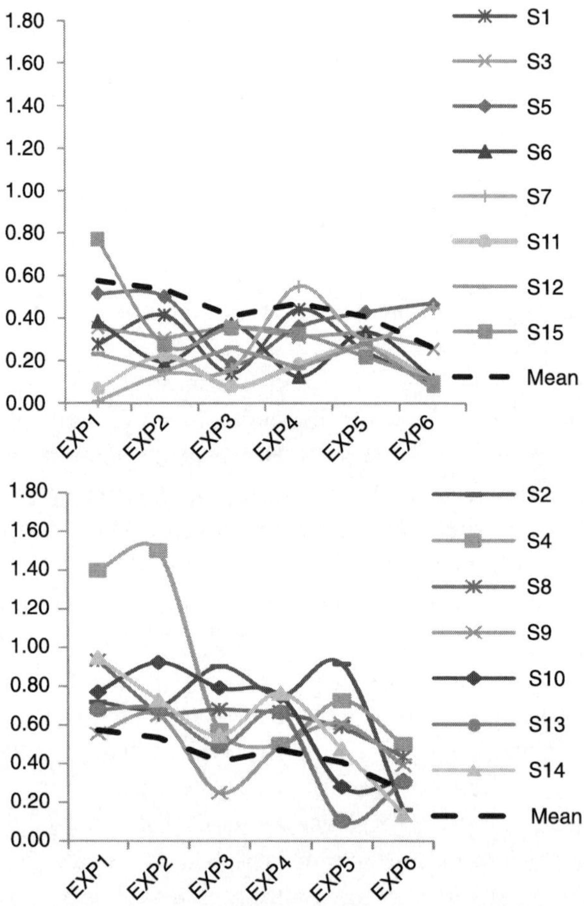

Figure 6.16. Development of lexical-semantic errors in individuals

While the development path of lexical-semantic errors in slower learning students is sigmoidal in shape (S-curve), the relevant trajectory in faster learners resembles a sinusoid, which in some ways may give the impression that the development path for these students is one of periodic motion, a kind of oscillation. Furthermore, as in the case of complexity, lexical-semantic errors exhibit another feature of chaotic motion – bifurcation (Figure 6.17). The necessary condition for this developmental shape – a change in the parameter value – is again a high growth rate and very rapid development in the beginning phases of language learning, in this case during the first five months. Learners who had a significantly lower ratio of lexical-semantic errors in the first experiment develop more unpredictably: they can stay at the same level (S3), reduce the occurrence of their errors (S1, S6, S12) or even make more and more errors as the learning period progresses (S7, S11). Unpredictability in development should not be understood in absolute terms. It does not mean that there will be learners who, e.g., will not improve their language skills at all. When we speak about unpredictability we do not equate it with an assumed cognitive inability to learn a language. Unpredictability is inextricably interlinked with the interconnectedness of systems. When we investigate the development of only one linguistic or cognitive feature the results can be unexpected and unpredictable due to the ongoing interplay of many systems. And these unpredictable results can occur at any time during the observation period – both at the end of the study period in the form of a decline and at several data collection points as an unchanged value of a variable.

Unpredictability in development can be confirmed in the interplay of lexical diversity, complexity and lexical-semantic errors.

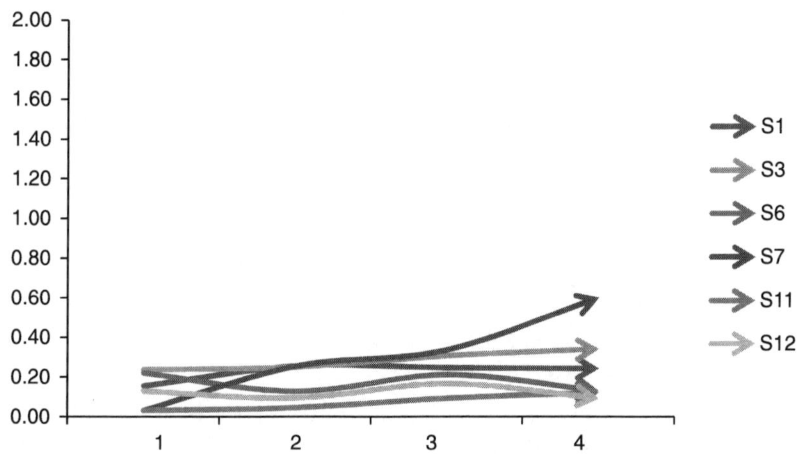

Figure 6.17. Bifurcation in the development of lexical-semantic errors (smoothed recalculated data)

Due to the interconnectedness of systems four assumptions are likely to occur. Firstly, learners with a lower lexical repertoire and lexical complexity will make fewer lexical and semantic errors because they are perhaps more watchful and use only those items they are sure that they have acquired and can use appropriately. On the other hand, students with a high level of lexical diversity and complexity will perhaps make more errors because they are more open to the idea of experimenting with language or will just focus on producing an interesting text that is not necessarily correct. The third possible expectation is that learners can handle the lexical and semantic systems very well and their development will not proceed at the cost of accuracy. The opposite assumption is that slower development in a learner's lexical and semantic repertoire and greater difficulty in using it actively will manifest itself in a higher error ratio. All these expectations can be reflected in the gap between lexical diversity/complexity on the one hand and the error ratio on the other. The bigger this discrepancy the higher the mutual relationship. Such divergence can be expressed as a ratio of errors made to lexical diversity/complexity. The higher the value the stronger the discrepancy between both phenomena. Figures 6.18a and 6.18b show a clear developmental trend at group level such that in the first period of learning second language learners differ most in their mental organisation of the lexical and semantic systems. Some students use limited vocabulary and make many errors while others are more cautious at the beginning, have a less diversified and complex vocabulary and are more accurate. During their three years of learning they develop the ability to manage the systems so that their progress in terms of lexical diversity and complexity does not proceed at the cost of accuracy.

Even if the general impression from the diagram above is that progress in lexical diversity and complexity during the three year period has an increasingly less negative impact on accuracy, clear learner profiles with their own developmental trajectories can be recognized in the peer group. The study confirms all four assumptions mentioned above, even if some modifications should be made so as to take into account the dynamic development of individuals.

The first expectation was that learners with a lower lexical repertoire would make fewer lexical and semantic errors. Student of this type can be called careful learners because the probability is high that such a profile is a sign that they are rather careful in their operation of the language, where the goal is presumably to avoid errors. However, this picture re-

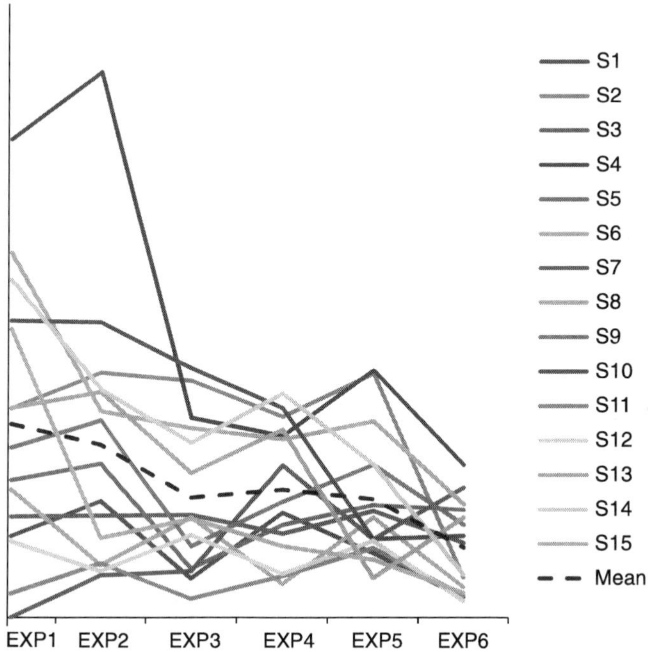

Figure 6.18a. Discrepancy between lex.-sem. errors and lexical diversity (GI)

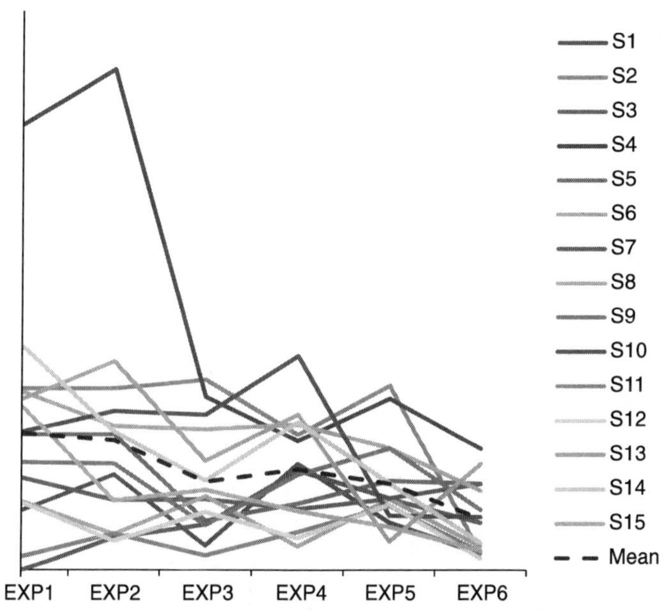

Figure 6.18b. Discrepancy between lex.-sem. errors and lexical complexity (WiCP/W)

quires some modification. In fact, there are learners who appear to pursue such a strategy, but not continuously. They also include those who were only careful at the beginning of the learning period, after which they then reached a high level of lexical diversity, which in turn did not lead to an increased error ratio. The term "careful" should also not be understood as a fixed feature in individuals. Some learners are cautious only in the beginning phases of learning, after which, when they feel more confident, they are capable of being more open and will try harder. On the other hand, other learners may need more time and may continue to be cautious in their use of the language for longer. In the present study four learners had such a profile (Figure 6.19). For the needs of clarity the data have been recalculated to 0–1 values so as to make them comparable.[8] Values under 0.50 have been interpreted as low, while those over 0.50 are deemed to be high.

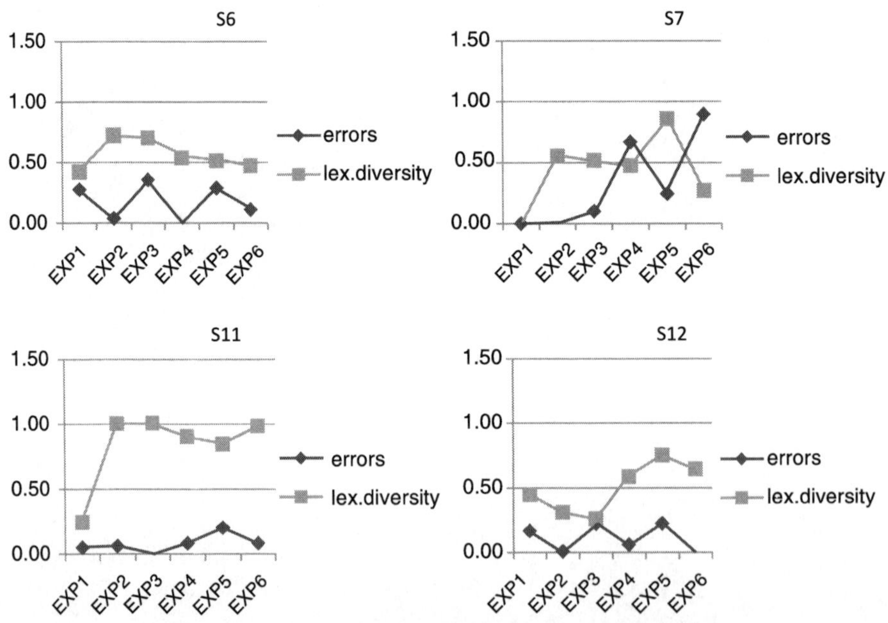

Figure 6.19. Development of lex.-sem. inaccuracy and lexical diversity in careful learners

[8] A description of how different kinds of values can be recalculated is found in: Versporr, Lowie, van Geert, van Dijk & Schmid (2011, pp. 161–162).

All these learners had a narrow lexical repertoire and a low error ratio at the beginning of the study and one of them (S12) continued to have low values in these areas until the third experiment. Afterwards, this discrepancy significantly increased. Their texts become more and more complex whilst the error ratio remained at a low level. The development of S7 is more complex and dynamic, especially in the second half of the study. In the case of the other three participants progress in lexical diversity did not lead to an increase in error frequency.

Another assumption was that students with a high level of lexical diversity and complexity will perhaps make more errors because they are more open to experimenting with language or just want to focus on producing an interesting text regardless of whether it will be correct or not. Learners of this type can be called risk-takers and S2, S9 and S13 fall within this category (Figure 6.20). Due to its dynamic developmental trajectory we cannot define this as a fixed characteristic, but for these learners the spread between (rather high) diversity and inaccuracy is low.

The third hypothesis was that learners would handle the lexical and semantic systems without a great deal of effort and their development

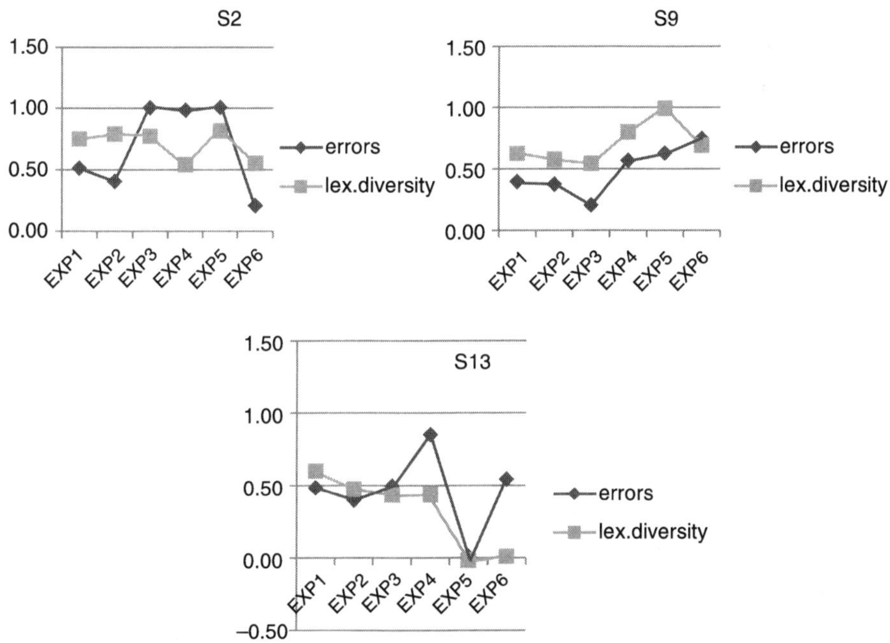

Figure 6.20. Development of lex.-sem. inaccuracy and lexical diversity in risk-takers

would not proceed at the cost of accuracy, which in turn would manifest itself in a high level of lexical diversity and a low error ratio. Also this assumption has been confirmed in the present study. In such "smart" students, as they may be called, some discrepancy between error frequency and lexical diversity is expected to occur. Three learners (Figure 6.21) fitted this profile during the majority of the three-year period. However, even S6, S11 and S12, who have tentatively been classified as careful learners, can also be included in this group, or represent a sub-group, because during the majority of their learning period they also demonstrated high levels of lexical diversity and low error frequency, even if they were more careful at the beginning.

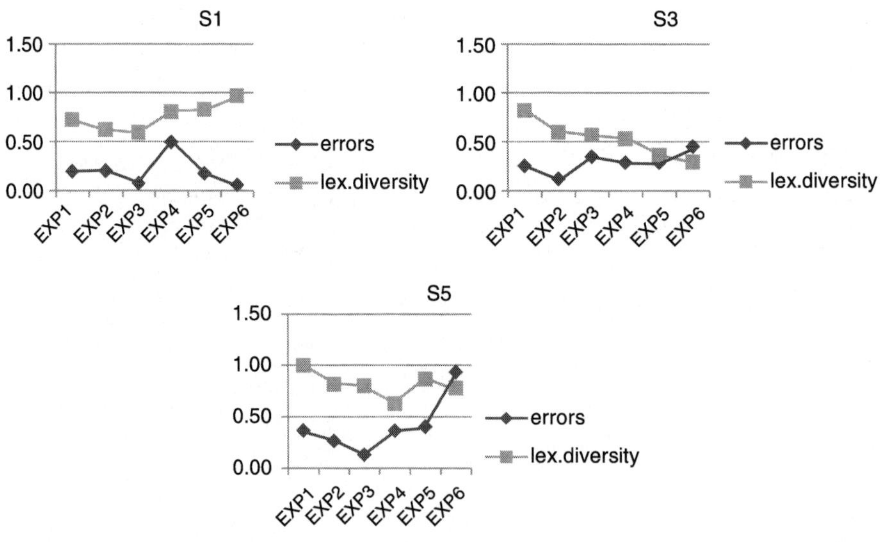

Figure 6.21. Development of lex.-sem. inaccuracy and lexical diversity in smart students

The last of these presumed patterns encompasses learners who develop more slowly and have greater difficulty in actively using lexical and the semantic systems, which will manifest itself in a high error ratio and low lexical diversity. Even students of this type could be found in the present study. As in the case of the other profiles, however, this group is not homogenous and cannot be treated as a closed set. As the figure below shows (Figure 6.22) such "wanderers," who find it difficult to accurately operate lexical items and semantic relations between words and therefore need more time and develop in different ways. In some learners (S8, S10) the increase in lexical diversity clearly proceeded at the cost of accuracy: even if their ability to build more diversified texts progressed, they still had major problems with accurately processing lexical and semantic relations. There were also two other learners (S4, S14) with constantly low levels of lexical diversity and high error ratios, who seemed to need more time than three years to develop an accurate lexical-semantic system in Swedish. The last of the "wanderers" (S15) actually belonged to this group for a very brief while. In the case of this learner considerable progress can already be observed after the second semester: there was a significant increase in lexical diversity, followed by a sharp decline in her error rate, such that she can undoubtedly already be reclassified as a "smart" learner by the end of the first year of learning.

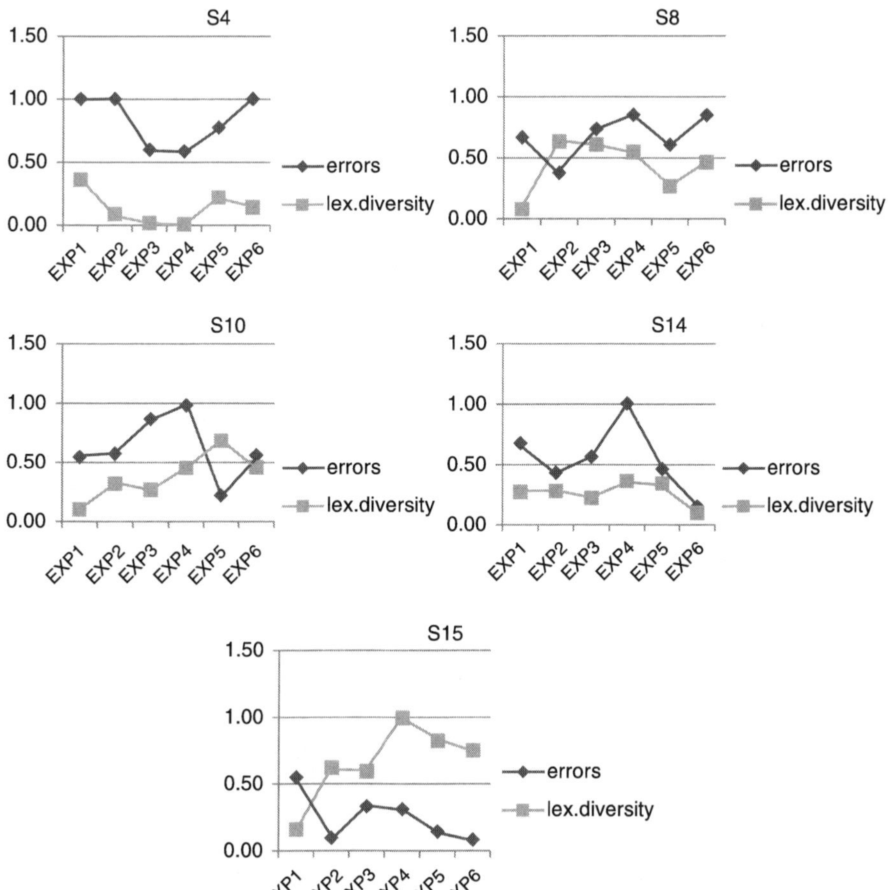

Figure 6.22. Development of lex.-sem. inaccuracy and lexical diversity in "Wanderers"

Labelling learners in this way is of course risky and may appear judgemental, especially in the case of such terms as "smart" or "wanderer." These students can be expected to achieve high or low grades, respectively, when the teacher has to evaluate their achievements in a classroom setting. On the other hand, when we find regularities in such development we need to find ways to define learners with similar characteristics and the above proposed expressions on no account aim to divide learners into good or bad categories or to judge them in any way. They are purely descriptive in character.

The chaotic, unpredictable behaviour of lexical-semantic errors is also a result of their complexity. These errors are not only the most common among all students. They also make up the most diversified category of errors and one that is most exposed to the influence of previously acquired/learned languages. As was mentioned earlier in the chapter, lexical-semantic errors include, e.g., incorrect word choice, which often involves items or structures transferred from other languages (L1 or L2s). And for this category of errors – even more than in the case of syntactic, morphological or spelling errors – crosslinguistic influence is an additional factor that should undoubtedly be taken into account. Lexical-semantic errors occur most often due to the fact that they concern linguistic systems that are least connected with the structure of language, are most ambiguous and thus hardest to learn. In order to understand the semantic system of a language the learner has to develop the ability to comprehend the way the world is perceived by a native user of the language, which in turn requires a set of factors, such as frequent exposure to the language, comprehension of the context of use and the ability to create a mental representation of the language.

6.1.2. Development of morphological errors

Errors in the inflection or morphological structure of words are in general the least common mistakes made by the majority of participants. The mean curve decreases steadily in an almost linear fashion. One of the reasons for the low frequency of such errors may be the language typology. Compared with Polish or German Swedish is less inflected, so students have to learn only a few inflectional paradigms. Nouns have two cases: nominative and genitive (German has four and Polish seven), verbs are inflected for tense and voice and not for person (German and Polish), number (German and Polish), aspect (Polish) or gender (Polish).

Swedish as one of a few languages that admittedly has a far more differentiated category of definiteness, a "double definiteness," where in some constellations both prenominal and enclitic articles occur. The question of double definiteness tends to be a syntactic and semantic phenomenon and from a structural point of view the opposition between an uninflected bare noun and an inflected noun with a definite suffix is not sophisticated.

Another reason for the low frequency of morphological errors lies in the fact that this particular group of students are accustomed to learning languages. They study Swedish philology and have prior knowledge of at least two other Germanic languages (German and English) that they had studied in classroom settings at primary and secondary school where grammar is one of the main topics. So we can assume that learning inflectional paradigms can proceed faster than in the case of e.g. untutored learners. The lower frequency of morphological errors can thus be interconnected both with language typology and learning habits – these students have mostly mastered the main inflectional patterns during the first months of learning Swedish. On the other hand, it does not automatically mean that they do not make any errors at all.

The following errors could be recognized in the analysed data:

1) errors in the morphological structure of words,
3) errors in the inflection of nouns,
2) errors in the inflection of verbs,
4) errors in the inflection of participles,
5) errors in the inflection of pronouns,
6) errors in the inflection of adjectives.

Errors in the morphological structure of words occurred when learners tried to build new words using assumed derivational or lexical morphemes, i.e. *sjukhusperso<u>nell</u>** – correct form: *sjukhusperso<u>nal</u>* (hospital staff), *vänt<u>ning</u>** – correct form: *vänt<u>an</u>* (anticipation), *fär<u>ig</u>** – correct form: *fär<u>jerik</u>* (colourful). Inaccurate inflection of nouns concerning above all plural forms: *dator** – correct form: *datum* (dates), *männ<u>er</u>** – correct form: *män* (mens), *handsk<u>or</u>** – correct form: *handsk<u>ar</u>* (gloves). In few cases incorrect building of the definite form of nouns occurred: *mor<u>en</u>** – correct form: *moder<u>n</u>* (the mother), *nyckel<u>en</u>** – correct form: *nyckel<u>n</u>* (the key), *part<u>en</u>** – correct form: *party<u>n</u>* (the party). In the inflection of verbs errors occurred in the building of the past tense, the present tense or the supine: *glömte**, *glömade** – correct form: *glömde*^{PAST} (forgot), *sittade** – correct form: *satt*^{PAST} (sat), *beto** – correct form: *betedde*^{PAST} (behaved), *minnas* – correct form: *minns*$^{\text{PRES.}}$ (remember), *tillbringer** – correct form: *tillbringar*$^{\text{PRES.}}$, *sagit** – correct form: *sagt*^{SUPINE} (from: say), *bett** – correct form: *betett*^{SUPINE} (from: behave). Samples for errors in the inflection of participle were: *fascineradde** – correct form: *fascinerande*$^{\text{PRES.PART.}}$ (fascinating), *överrasked** – correct form: *överraskad*$^{\text{PAST.PART.}}$ (surprized), *hyrde** – correct form: *hyrda*$^{\text{PAST.PART.PL.}}$ (hired). Errors in the inflection of pronouns concerned personal pronouns and their inflection: *de* – correct form: *dem*$^{\text{OBJECT FORM}}$ (them), *sig* – correct form: *mig*$^{\text{REFL.PRON.1.PERS}}$ (myself), *eras** – correct form: *oss*$^{\text{OBJECT FORM.1.PERS.PLUR}}$ (us). And errors in the inflection of adjectives were connected with comparison and/or congruence: *värste** – *värsta*$^{\text{SUPERL.DEF.PLUR.}}$ (worst), *svärsta** – correct form: *svåraste*$^{\text{SUPERL.DEF.}}$ (most difficult), *främmandet** – correct form: *främmande*$^{\text{NOT INFLECTABLE}}$ (foreign).

As Figure 6.23 shows, errors in the inflection of verbs are the most common category and are the only type of error that every learner made. Also very common were errors in the morphological structure of words. In this case, however, the problem is clearly interconnected with individual characteristics. Almost one half of all the errors of this type were made by one student (S9), who has been characterized as a "risk taker:" with a high level of lexical diversity and a high number of lexical-semantic errors. Errors in the morphological structure of words are without doubt a consequence of lexical creativity, where the learner tries to find expressions that help to build utterances in his/her next language, and this type of error is therefore connected with lexical-semantic errors.

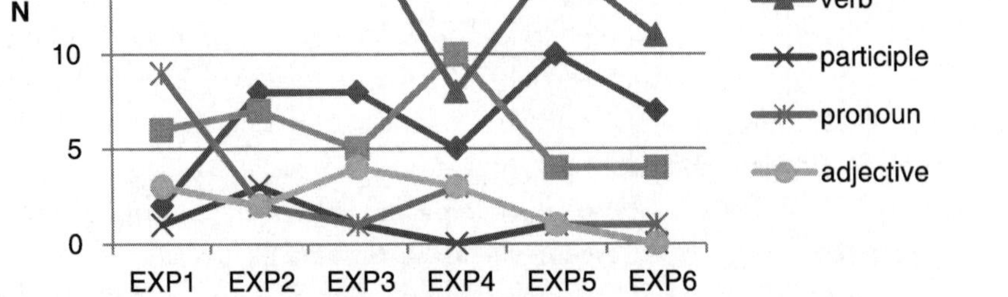

Figure 6.23. Development of morphological errors by type

The mean developmental trajectory for all morphological errors shows a steady decrease, with the first value being 0.17 morphological errors per T-unit. Compared with a value of 0.57 E/T, which was the corresponding result for lexical-semantic errors, we clearly see a huge difference. However, the almost linear drop-off in morphological errors could not be confirmed in individuals. No single participant in the present study could be labelled as "average." However, the ratio of this type of error decreased or remained at the same level in all the students. On the other hand, the frequency of morphological errors only remained unchanged in students who did not make any errors in the first experiment or made very few errors. In the distribution dynamics for this error we can recognize the pattern observed in the development of AccInd: the biggest decrease occurred at the beginning of the learning period (Figure 6.24). In 60% of the students the growth rate between the first and the second experiment was at least –38%. And this pattern was observed in both learners with low and high morphological error ratios in the first experiment. Two other learners (S6, S15) made very few morphological errors throughout the entire experimental period, so in their case they had already mastered the morphological systems of Swedish during the first semester. Four students needed more time to order in their minds the morphological pattern in Swedish. In their case such a substantial decrease in errors of this type occurred one or two semesters later.

The development of morphological errors corresponds to the development of general accuracy: the biggest improvement in Swedish morphology occurred early on in the study period. After 300 hours (two semesters) of foreign language instruction almost all the learners properly identified and used inflection patterns and morphological structures of words. This developmental path also corresponds with the assumptions of processability theory, where the processing of lexical morphemes lies at the next lowest level, which means that their acquisition occurred at a relatively early stage. In the context of Swedish at this level plural, definiteness on nouns, and past or present tense on verbs have been listed (Pienemann, 1998; Pienemann & Håkansson, 1999). And these errors were the most common mistakes made by the participants of the present study.

Even if the morphological level in general develops early, most students develop dynamically even in later periods. Their trajectories remain a sinusoid, which is a sign that the morphological system has still not been fully stabilized. On the other hand, there are some learners

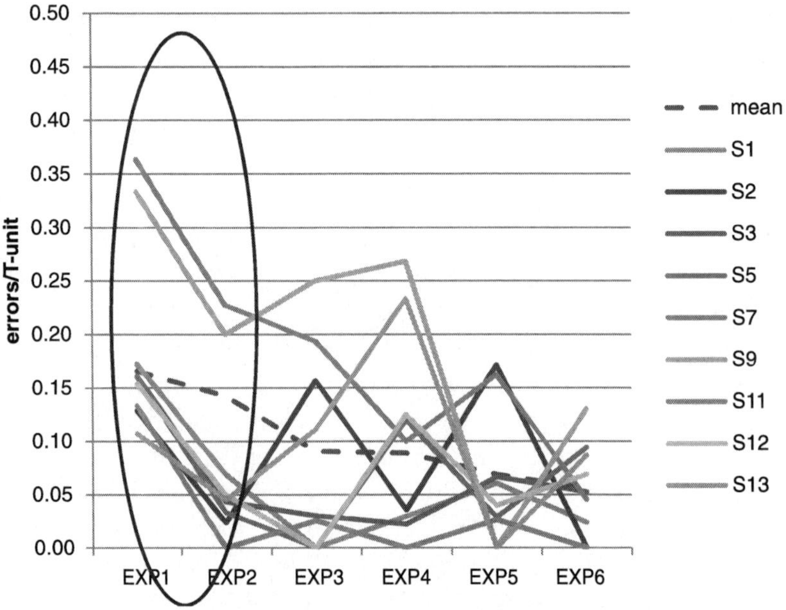

Figure 6.24. Learners achieving a considerable decrease in morphological errors during the second semester

(consisting exclusively of students with a low ratio of errors), whose mastering of Swedish morphology clearly resulted in their approaching an attractor state as early as the second semester (see Figure 6.25 – right diagram). Their intra-individual variability was considerably lower than it was for the other group of students. Variability in the development of the morphological systems is also clearly connected with the stability of the system: the process of internalisation is reflected in such variability.

But even this variability should be relativized. The highest error ratio in the group was 0.46, which means that the learner made a morphological error in every second T-unit. Such high values did not occur in other students and experiments, where the frequency of the inaccurate use of morphological features was no greater than one error in every third T-unit. Thus we can conclude without any doubt that morphological accuracy develops early.

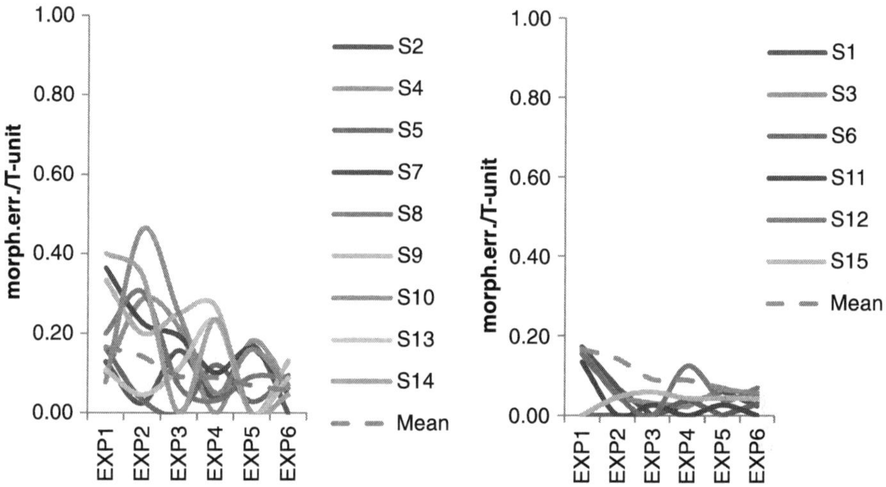

Figure 6.25. Students with high (left diagram) and low (right diagram) variability

6.1.3. Development of syntactic errors

Swedish syntax is much more difficult to learn than morphology, as is confirmed by the high ratio of syntactic errors. The mean value in the first experiment was 0.43 errors per T-unit and this makes these errors the next most common category of error after lexical-semantic errors. However, errors of this type develop most dynamically and during the three-year learning period their frequency decreased the most, with R = −74% (the corresponding values for other error categories were −54% for lexical-semantic errors, −66% for morphological errors and −25% for spelling errors). The general downward trend could be observed in almost all the participants, but as was the case with the other investigated features learners who developed earlier than their fellow students did not have such a high (negative) growth rate because they had approached the attractor earlier.

As in the case of the development of morphological errors the most significant decrease occurred in most students during the second semester (Figure 6.26) and this phenomenon is common in both learners with high and low error ratios. The first year of learning appears to be the period of greatest change in development and the most crucial phase in the learning of another language. Of course, not all learners can master Swedish syntax at the same level and no one student develops along a similar path to the average. As the illustration below shows the development of syntactic errors in individuals is much more variable than the mean curve suggests. The achievement is especially remarkable in students who at the beginning had most difficulty in building syntactically correct texts. The decline from about one error in every T-unit to one error in every fifth T-unit (S4) is an outcome that cannot pass unnoticed. This student was the "poorest" in terms of accuracy in almost all the experiments. And even though she made great progress she still had one of the highest error ratios compared with the other students in the group. And when we look exclusively at the results from every experiment we could overlook the fact that she made much harder work of learning than learners with "better" results, i.e. with lower error ratios.

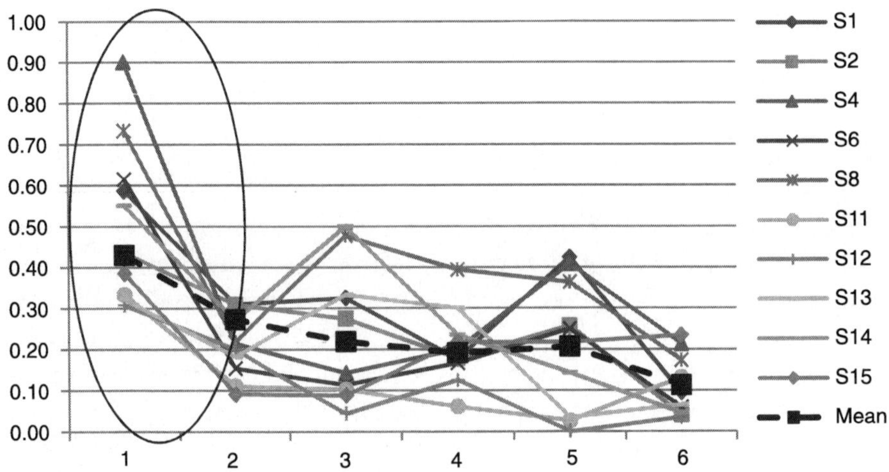

Figure 6.26. Learners with a considerable decrease in syntactic errors during the second semester

On the other hand, students with the lowest error ratios in the first experiment (S3, S5, S7, S9) developed in a completely different way: their trajectories tended to resemble sinusoids and no downward trend was visible (see Figure 6.27). With the exception of S9, whose accuracy in the beginning phases in particular varied a great deal, the other three learners seemed to have already approached an attractor state in the first months of their learning. The sinusoidal developmental trajectories should not confuse us: the within-subject variability in these students is among the lowest for the entire group. Their syntactic system in Swedish developed

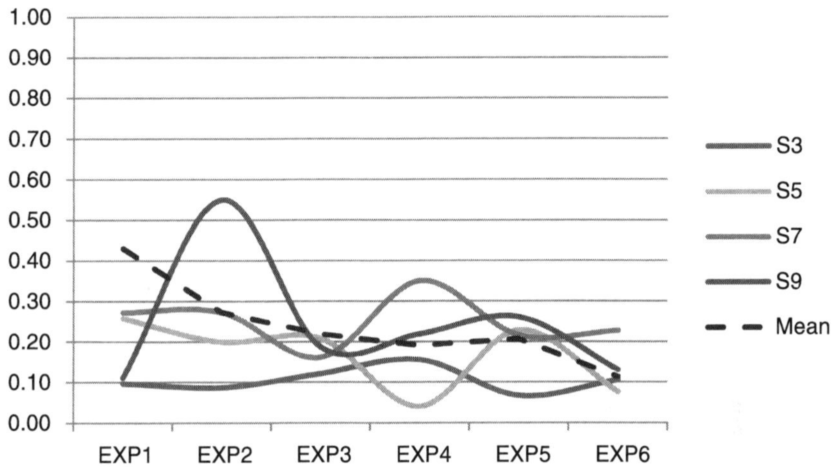

Figure 6.27. Development of syntactic errors in "quick starters"

and stabilised early in the learning process. They approached an attractor state, which, however, is not the same as equilibrium.

Due to the interconnectedness of the systems a correlation between syntactic complexity and syntactic accuracy may be expected. The development of correctness can either proceed at the cost of complexity or it can go hand in hand with complexity. One possible developmental tendency may therefore be for students who learn to comprehend and master syntactic relations in a new language to be more careful at the beginning and use simple constructions in order to avoid errors. As in the case of lexical and semantic accuracy, we can expect to see both careful learners and risk takers who in the earliest phases of learning a new language are already willing to use complex syntactic structures, which can lead to a higher error ratio. Also a parallel development is expected to occur when an increase in syntactic complexity does not result in an increase in error frequency.

The analysis has shown that the developmental patterns observed in the development of lexical-semantic systems were also noticeable in the case of syntax, although with no such clear splitting into groups. There were two careful and two smart students who could be distinguished and this characteristic concerned both the subordination ratio and syntactic diversity (see Figures 6.28 and 6.29). Only one of them (Figure 6.30) can be labelled a risk taker and one (Figure 6.31) a wanderer. No such distinct dependency between the level of syntactic complexity and inaccuracy was observed in the other students.

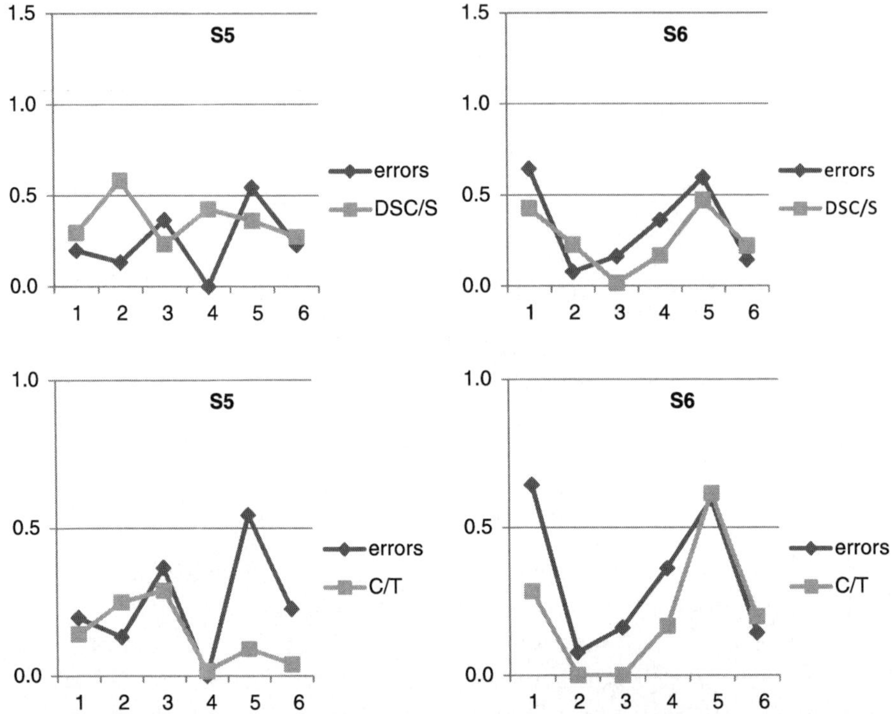

Figure 6.28. Development of syntactic inaccuracy and syntactic complexity (DSC/S, C/T) in careful learners

Individual developmental characteristics mostly overlap. Learner S6, for example, seemed to focus mostly on accuracy. She has been classified as careful with regard to both lexical-semantic and syntactic systems. In order to avoid errors she chose to build short (her narratives were among the shortest in the group) and simple texts. On the other hand, the "smart" learners S11 and S12 needed a little more time to manage the lexical and semantic systems in the new language than they did to manage its syntax, but in general they had no difficulties producing correct texts that were also diverse and complex. Student S5 exhibited another tendency: he tended to focus on building interesting utterances, using a complex and diversified vocabulary that was syntactically simple but correct. He has therefore been classified as a smart learner in terms of his mastering of the lexical-semantic system and as a careful learner in his development of Swedish syntax. Student S9 is very clearly a risk taker: she tried to use new words and structures that she had learned, with no focus on accuracy. Correctness in the new language seemed to

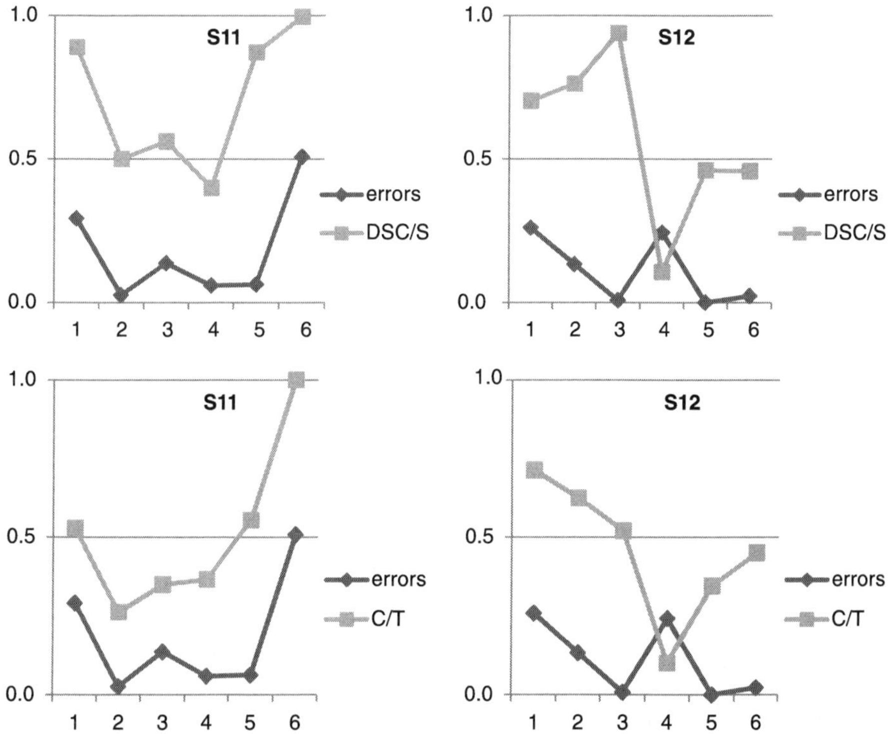

Figure 6.29. Development of syntactic inaccuracy and syntactic complexity (DSC/S, C/T) in smart learners

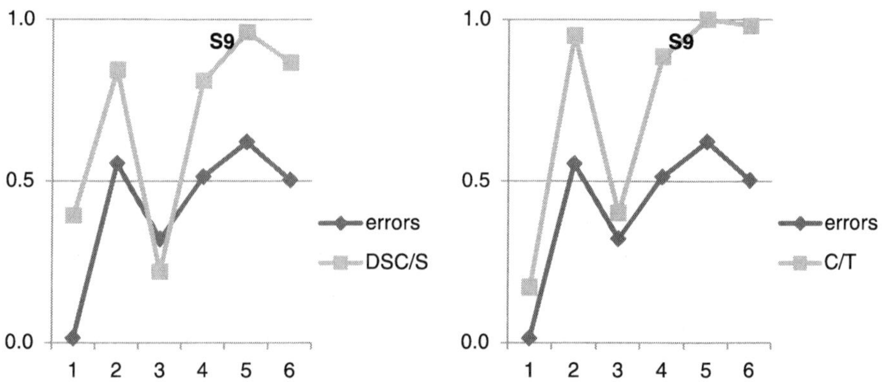

Figure 6.30. Development of syntactic inaccuracy and syntactic complexity (DSC/S, C/T) in the risk taker

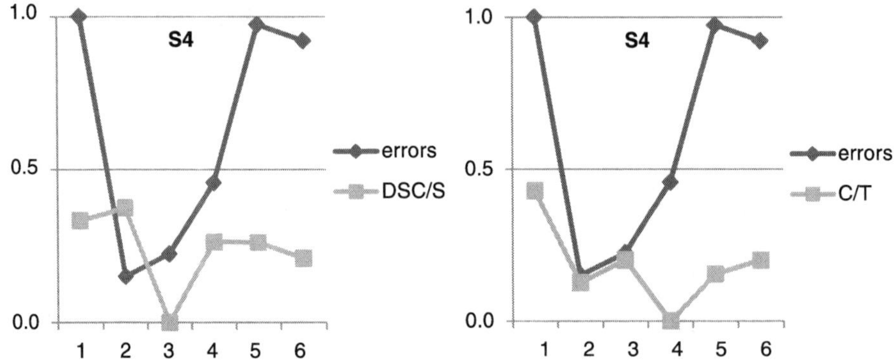

Figure 6.31. Development of syntactic inaccuracy and syntactic complexity (DSC/S, C/T) in the wanderer

be of secondary importance for her. Finally, learner S4, who was referred to as a "wanderer" due to the fact that her production in Swedish was characterized by a high error ratio and a low level of lexical diversity and complexity, behaved in the same way with regard to the syntactic system: she made many errors even though her sentences were not complex. The term "wanderer" reflects the dynamics of her development: as was described earlier in the chapter she made her greatest progress in syntactic accuracy during the second semester of learning, but she remained a learner with a highly variable development path and without any attractor state, while her lexical and syntactic diversity and complexity were simultaneously rather low.

As we can see from the individual learner characteristics above an unambiguous classification of language learners is not possible. Thus we cannot focus exclusively on one aspect when we find regularities in a learner's development. There are only a few individuals who represent a clear and identifiable profile. The continuous interplay of systems, the unpredictability of a learner's development and the constant reorganisation of these systems make it impossible to define a "typical" language learner or a "good"/ "bad" one. Moreover, they necessitate viewing second language development as a complex phenomenon.

6.1.4. Development of spelling errors

When a language is learned in a classroom setting the learner is often confronted with spelling rules that are binding, e.g. that nouns in German are capitalized, or that *h* never occurs at the end of Polish words (only *ch* is allowed). Sometimes they learn these rules explicitly, but in many cases they acquire them implicitly by reading texts in textbooks, doing grammar exercises or reading books in the language that they are actually learning. We can assume that learners will focus more on spelling in the second language when learning in the classroom than in natural settings. Furthermore, according to individual differences and the interconnectedness of systems it is likely that some learners focus more on spelling and that this focus will be reflected in other language systems. In other words, learners who do not pay attention to spelling perhaps concentrate more on fluency. Such interplay between systems can also be expressed in the correlation between spelling accuracy and lexical/semantic, morphologic or syntactic accuracy. Some learners may concentrate only on selected parts of the actually learned language, such as, for example, its external shape (spelling), which can have a negative effect on other features, such as word order or inflection.

It is not always clear what can be classified as a spelling error. Nauclér (1980) defines it as a violation of a spelling rule. One such spelling rule in Swedish is that names of nationalities are always written in small letters, while another is that the length of a consonant in a stressed syllable is marked by its doubling. Despite clearly defined rules spelling is in most cases not explicitly defined and reflects writing habits connected with the etymology, morphological structure or phonological aspects of a language. A common taxonomy of spelling errors is based on a division into four categories: substitutions, insertions, omissions (sometimes called deletions), and transpositions (Kay & Hanley, 1994; Okada, 2005; Cook, 1997). In her analysis of Swedish adults with writing and hearing dysfunctions Wengelin (1999) extends this basic taxonomy on the one hand by adding segmentation errors that are connected with compound writing, and on the other by establishing a separate language-specific category, called consonant doubling, to reflect the fact that a long consonant in a stressed syllable in Swedish is often marked by doubling. There is a difference in writing, depending on which part of the syllable is long. For example: both *dag* and *dagg* are correct words in Swedish, where the first has a long vowel /ɑ:/ and the second – a long consonant /ɠ:/. According to this approach, they have different meanings. *Dag* means 'day' and *dagg* – 'dew.' Luelsdorff (1990), who in turn analysed the spelling of German learners of English, distinguishes between two other types of spelling errors that characterize second language learners: overgeneralisation and transfer. As we can see from the taxonomies above, no single classification occurs. Besides the general and rather technical grouping of spelling errors into the four main categories of 'substitution,' 'inserting,' 'omission' and 'transposition,' spelling difficulties can vary, depending on the spellers and languages being investigated. The common tendency is, however, that typos are most often excluded from such taxonomies and analysed separately.

In the present study spelling errors have been divided into the following categories:

1. Substitution
2. Insertion
3. Omission
4. Transposition
5. Segmentation.

Substitution entails replacing a letter (or a letter combination) with another letter/letter combination, e.g. *oppnade* instead of *öppnade* (opened), or *semaster* instead of *semester* (holidays). Insertion is characterized by adding a letter: *familiji* instead of *familj* (family), *förskyld* instead of *förkyld* (has a cold), *kotelett* instead of *kotlett* (cutlet). A specific sub-category of insertion errors is dittography, which means repeating a letter. This group contains first of all consonant doubling: *gratullera* instead of *gratulera* (congratulate), *drömm* instead of *dröm* (dream), *kännde* instead of *kände* (felt). An omission occurs when (a) letter(s) is/are missing: *sifror* – the correct form *siffror* (digits), *busen* instead of *bussen* (bus), *överrasking* instead of *överraskning* (surprise). Transposition entails re-arranging a letter or a sequence of letters in a word: *skvarllade* instead of *skvallrade* (gossiped), *angråde* instead of *ångrade* (regretted). A specific sub-category in this group builds transpositions where consonant doubling has been re-arranged: *vännina* instead of *väninna* (friend), *hottelet* instead of *hotellet* (hotel), *vistte* instead of *visste* (knew). Segmentation errors occur when a compound is written as two separate words or when words that do not build a compound are written as one word: *favorit film* instead of *favoritfilm* (favourite movie), *jätte rädd* instead of *jätterädd* (very afraid), *stadensnamn* instead of *stadens namn* (name of the city). Spelling errors are only an external expression of language behaviour and the reason for their occurrence in a text lies in many factors, such as writing tempo, metalinguistic awareness or the influence of other languages. Therefore, such categories as transfer or overgeneralisation tend to be reasons for erroneous spelling rather than being spelling errors in themselves. They can take the form of, e.g., substitutions (*Sevärdheter* instead of *sevärdheter* 'monuments,' or *universität* instead of *universitet* 'university'), insertions (e.g. *theater* instead of *teater* 'theatre'), omissions (*hotel* instead of *hotell* 'hotel') or segmentation errors (*det samma* instead of *detsamma* 'he same,' or Polish 'to samo'). For this reason they have not been distinguished as separate categories in the current classification.

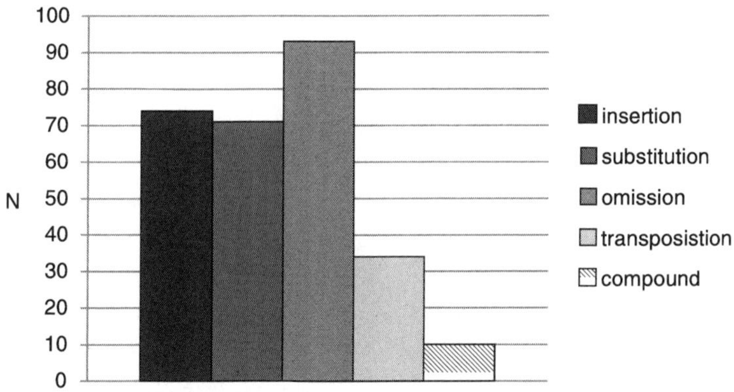

Figure 6.32. Distribution of spelling errors

While no one type of spelling error dominates, omissions, substitutions and insertions in general occur more frequently than transpositions and compound errors (see Figure 6.32). Due to the huge variation between subjects, these overall outcomes cannot be interpreted as a reflection of an individual writer's characteristics. While the majority of learners do not have a tendency to make more errors of a certain type, such a propensity could be observed in some of them. Two-thirds of the spelling errors made by one learner (S1) were due to inserting one additional letter, while substitutions predominated in another case (S10) and three learners (S4, S8 and S13) made omissions very often (50–85%). Regardless of the error category, nearly half of the errors were the result of difficulties in using double consonants properly. The learners either omitted the necessary repetition of a consonant (*dör** instead of *dörr* 'door'), inserted an additional consonant in situations where it should not been included (*skoggar** instead of *skogar* 'forests') or re-arranged the doubling (*raporrt** instead of *rapport* 'report'). Such errors occurred in every learner, even if three of them with the lowest error ratios in general made only one such mistake each. The use of a double consonant is closely connected with both phonological and metalinguistic awareness. When a learner knows which sound in a word is pronounced long they will write the word properly, i.e. with a double vs. a single consonant – as this will be a sign of high phonological awareness. On the other hand, a learner may have explicit knowledge of the relationship between short and long vowels and consonants in a word/a prosodic sequence, but they cannot differentiate which of the syllables is long and which sound (vowel or consonant) within this syllable is long, especially when their background languages do not have these oppositions. This can lead to overgeneralisations ('one of the syllables must have a long consonant and therefore I have to double it') or to omissions, when a learner cannot differentiate between long and short consonants within a word and every sound appears to be short and therefore not doubled.

As was mentioned earlier, spelling errors were, alongside morphological errors, a fairly rare occurrence among participants. These learners seemed to have had only one constant problem, namely the phonological system in Swedish and its visual representation in writing (e.g. the doubling of consonants). Otherwise, the infrequent occurrence of these inaccuracies might have been due to the task specifications. The participants had the chance to correct their texts during the experimental sessions and they often revised the spelling errors that they made by themselves so that only some of their faults were left uncorrected. In the case of writing, writers in general very frequently correct their own spelling errors, a fact which has been noted in, among others, studies on writing development in L1 (Strömqvist *et al.* 2002; Johansson, 2009). The same tendency has likewise been noticed in L2-writers. In her studies on online revisions and metalinguistic awareness in written texts produced by adult Polish learners of Swedish, Kowal showed that revisions of spelling errors were the most common category of error and they even increased during the learning period. Around 50% of self-corrections were due to the violation of a spelling rule, while only 10–16% occurred when students noticed a grammatical error and 5% were a consequence of trying to replace a lexical error. Other revisions were made at the conceptual rather than the normative level (Kowal, 2009; 2011). Students' explicit knowledge of spelling rules connected with their learning environment and learning habits was without doubt one of the reasons for the low frequency of their spelling errors in the final version of the texts.

Spelling errors were not only infrequent, but also the only error category in which a rather slight change was observed at the group level after three years of learning. The mean growth rate for these errors was R = –33%, while the corresponding value for lexical-semantic errors was R = –54%, for morphological errors it was R= –66% and for syntactic errors it was R= –74%. As with other errors also incorrect spelling was characterized by huge inter-subject variation, which means that individual differences were significant (see Figure 6.14). The slightly changing variation is even reflected in the developmental pattern: there were learners who only made single spelling errors and others who did so more frequently. On the other hand, regardless of whether we are speaking about students with high or low error ratios, about half of the participants made fewer and fewer spelling errors during the three-year period. In some students we did not observe any progressive/regressive trend in the development of spelling skills in Swedish. An upward tendency was even noted in some of the students. These divergent developmental patterns are presented in Figures 6.33–6.35.

The development of writing skills in a new language is an unpredictable process. Regardless of whether at the beginning of the learning period a writer is capable of managing the systems of writing rules very well or with greater difficulty, it is not at all clear whether he/she will get better, remain at the same level or even make more spelling errors. The adopted pre-requisite for bifurcation – a considerable improvement in language skills in the first period of learning, expressed in this case as a very low error ratio after the first semester – is also relevant for this feature. As

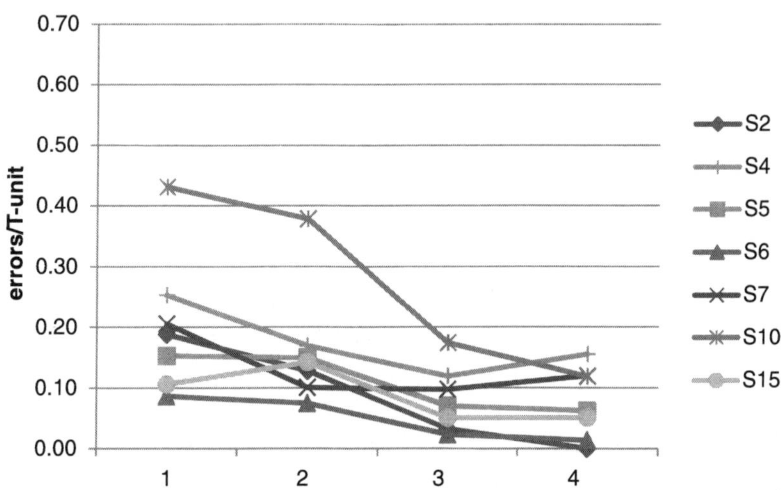

Figure 6.33. Decreasing frequency of spelling errors (smoothed data)

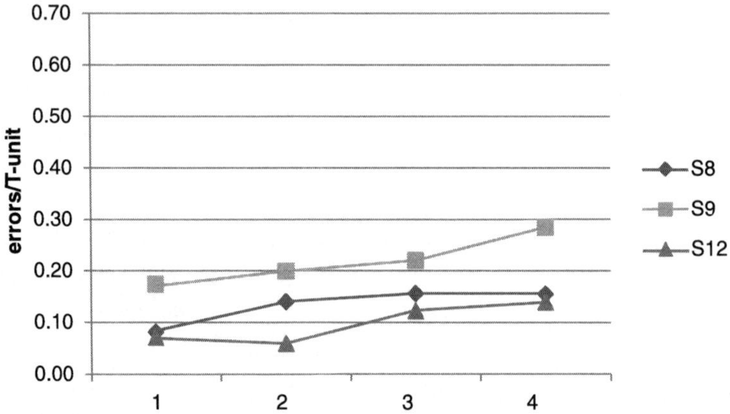

Figure 6.34. Increasing frequency of spelling errors (smoothed data)

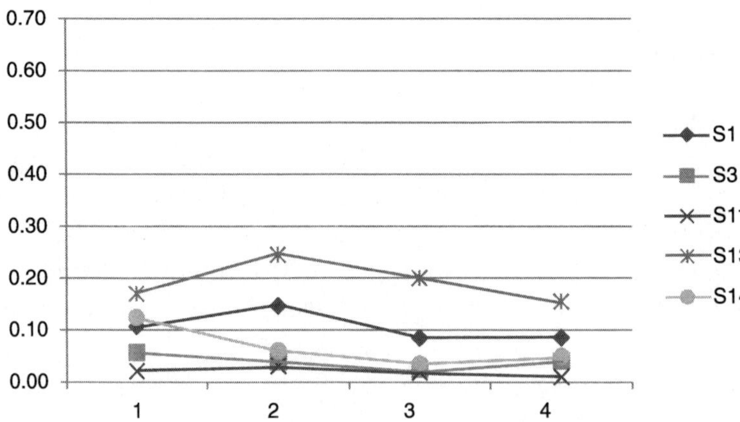

Figure 6.35. No progress/regression in spelling errors (smoothed data)

Figure 6.36 shows, in such spelling-focused students accuracy can most certainly develop in all directions, i.e. the error ratio remains constantly at the same low level, which is the most likely scenario, or inaccuracies in writing actually continue to decline in number or error frequency even increases. And in the latter case the change may not necessarily be insignificant. The low error frequency at the beginning of the learning period, i.e. at least 50% lower than the mean, may increase significantly as it did in students S8 and S12.

The occurrence of spelling errors is interconnected with writing tempo and automaticity in writing. The issue of fluency in writing will be discussed in the next chapter. However, at this point we will focus on the

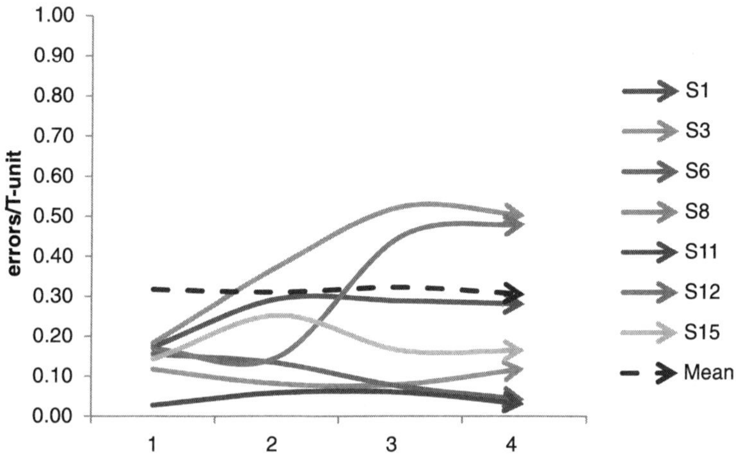

Figure 6.36. Bifurcation in the development of spelling errors (smoothed recalculated data)

specific interplay of writing tempo and spelling. Although all typos have been excluded from the analysis, due to Grabowski's (2008) assumption that fast typing can result in mistyping, typing speed is expected to have an impact on the occurrence of spelling errors. When the newly learned language has been automatized, the learner will write more quickly, because they will not spend much time on reflecting what word or what structure should be used. Also fluency will be expressed in writing speed: if a student can think and operate the new language in longer chunks, they will try to express it directly, maybe without any filter or deeper thoughts, which can lead to a high writing tempo. Furthermore, omissions in writing may be caused by such "fluency influence." The present study includes many examples of omissions that were a sign of fluent speech. For example, learners wrote the short, spoken-specific, version of the word *och* 'and' (*o*), or *mycket* 'much' (*mycke*), without making any pause after it, which undoubtedly not only shows that they are influenced by the spoken language, but even that this spoken language has been automatized due to the fact that these words were part of longer, undisrupted chunks.

Automaticity in another language will thus be reflected in typing speed, which in the present study could be evaluated in the form of transition time. As was described in the second chapter, the tool used in the present study (ScriptLog) provides insight into the time needed to move between keyboard keys. ScriptLog calculates how fast the writer moves between keystrokes within a word, i.e. how many seconds (fractions of a second) had passed before the next key was pressed. Slow writers will thus have a longer transition time than fast typists. This distinction was made by Strömqvist, who proposed it as the most reliable indicator of typing proficiency. He argues that within-word strokes are very common and rapid, and therefore less time is needed for planning or monitoring. The further assumption is that the execution is source demanding for less skilled writers while it is virtually automatic for fast writers (Strömqvist, 1999). In the context of second language writing it can be used as that aspect of fluency that is interconnected with automaticity in writing, with the focus on within-word automaticity. The assumption is that a writer with high automaticity in a second language can retrieve second language items faster than a writer whose cognitive processes have not been automatized and thus he/she will spend more time retrieving information from working memory, which in turn will lead to slower production of text chunks.

As Figures 6.37a and 6.37b show, the time needed to move between keys in a word decreases steadily, which shows that students write with ever greater automaticity. This general pattern concerns all participants – it is the only one of the features investigated in this study that allowed for such a homogenous developmental path. Another striking result is the homogenous attractor state, beginning from the fifth experiment. From this point no further automatisation in writing was observed in any of the learners. It should be stressed here that this improvement was not influenced by training to type in Swedish. As has already been mentioned, a Swedish keyboard was used in the experimental sessions, while during the time between the experiments (throughout the whole semester) the participants in the study wrote on computers with Polish keyboards, on which the keys are located differently. This might have confused them and even led to a slowdown in writing in subsequent experiments, which, however, was not observed. Their progress in typing speed was thus undeniably a result of increased automaticity in Swedish.

It is highly probable that increased writing speed will cause more frequent occurrences of spelling errors. On the one hand, this may reveal itself in the form of omissions, as the above described samples show, or on the other as transpositions, when the writer knows what word should be written but in his or her haste ends up writing the letters out of order. A Pearson correlation coefficient of $r = .63$ (p=0.179), calculated for the mean transition time (TT) and mean ratio of spelling errors (errors/T-

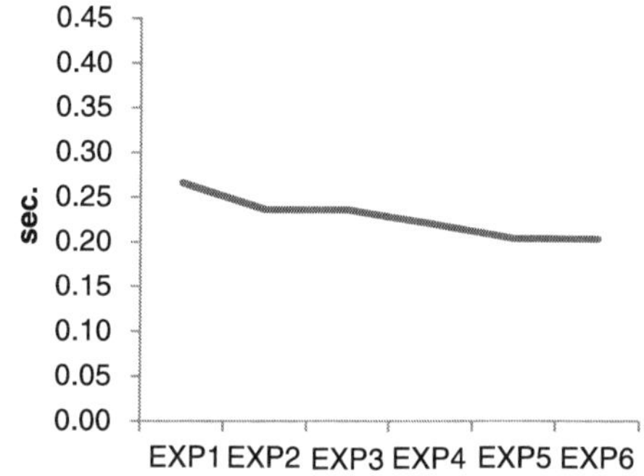

Figure 6.37a. Mean transition time

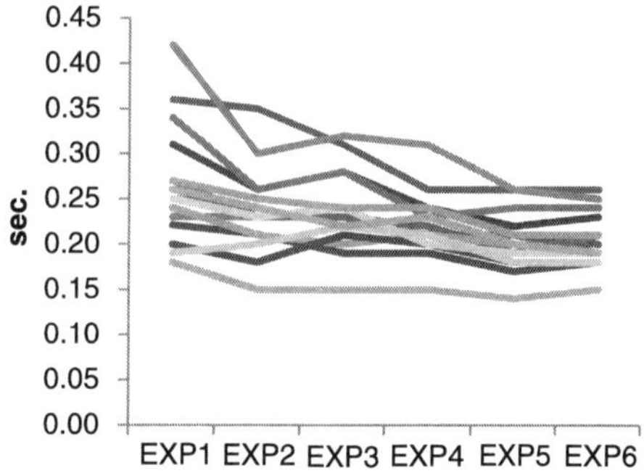

Figure 6.37b. Transition time in individuals

-unit), leads us to conclude that an acceleration in writing speed goes hand in hand with increasing competence in the observance of writing rules in Swedish. The above assumption has also not been confirmed. The development of automaticity in the new language does not appear to result in less vigilance in spelling. An analysis of individual data, however, leads to opposite conclusions. There is considerable variation in the learners, which prevents us from drawing such general conclusions. Only in six participants was the correlation at least moderately positive ($r \geq .30$), which may confirm the general trend observed on the basis of the mean values. In five of the learners, however, there is no direct interplay between writing tempo and the occurrence of spelling errors. However, the data reveals another interesting result worth pointing out, namely that only in three students was there a negative correlation between both features – those in whom spelling errors increased in frequency (see Figure 6.38). These learners behave in another way: for them an increase in automaticity in second language writing results in a more frequent occurrence of spelling errors. The unexpected outcome mentioned earlier, i.e. an increase in errors during the learning period, is in these learners directly connected with fluency (especially automaticity) development. As in many earlier described cases, every significant change and/or every unexpected developmental trajectory (in this case a decline in accuracy despite constant language instruction) is always a footprint indicating the interconnectedness of systems. In the case of spelling accuracy, an increase in automaticity clearly leads to less attention being paid to how words are written.

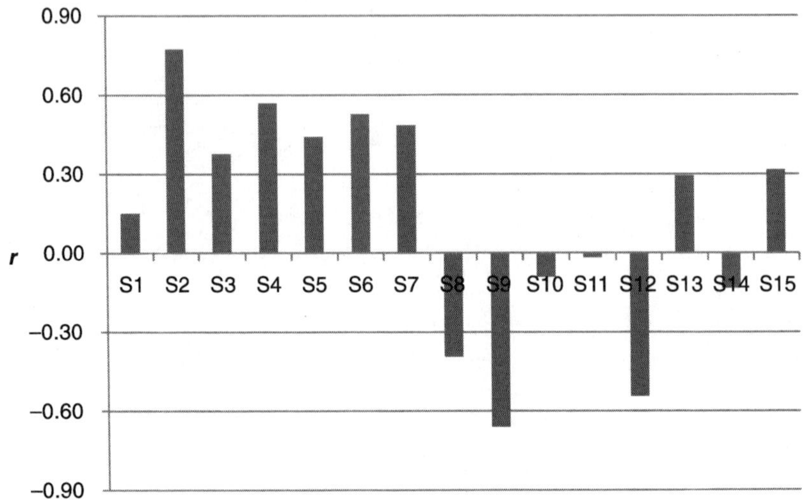

Figure 6.38. Correlation between the frequency of spelling errors (errors/T-unit) and writing speed (TT)

6.2. The interplay of error distribution in individuals

Due to the heterogeneity of language sub-systems we can assume that learners more or less focus on different aspects and thus can be more accurate in, for example, spelling than in morphology or syntax. On the other hand, discrepancies in accuracy between several systems may shed light on the order of their development in individuals and a learner's ability to reorganize and order mental representations of the new language.

The analysis shows that the majority of learners for the most part develop accuracy in several language systems in parallel, and this occurs regardless of the general level of correctness (see Figure 6.39). When students make many errors, the frequency tends to be high for all error types. When their accuracy is high, it is high at every language level. The illustration in the figure shows the occurrence of errors according to the mean value, expressed as 1 on the Y-axis. The bars below the reference value depict a lower error frequency, while those above that value represent an above-average error rate. The learners S3 and S11 used as examples here maintained uniformly high levels of accuracy in all error categories, while S4 and S10, on the other hand, achieved constantly lower levels of correctness in their respective language systems. This nonselective behavior is very noticeable in S13, who, when she made many errors, did so in all error categories, and when she built correct utterances – they were accurate at all levels: lexical-semantic, morphological, syntactic and spelling. This general pattern was evident in almost all the learners. Regardless of their developmental stage, the second language learners either managed all linguistic systems or none at all.

As could be expected, there are some learners whose error distribution was not as even as was is in their fellow students (see Figures 6.40

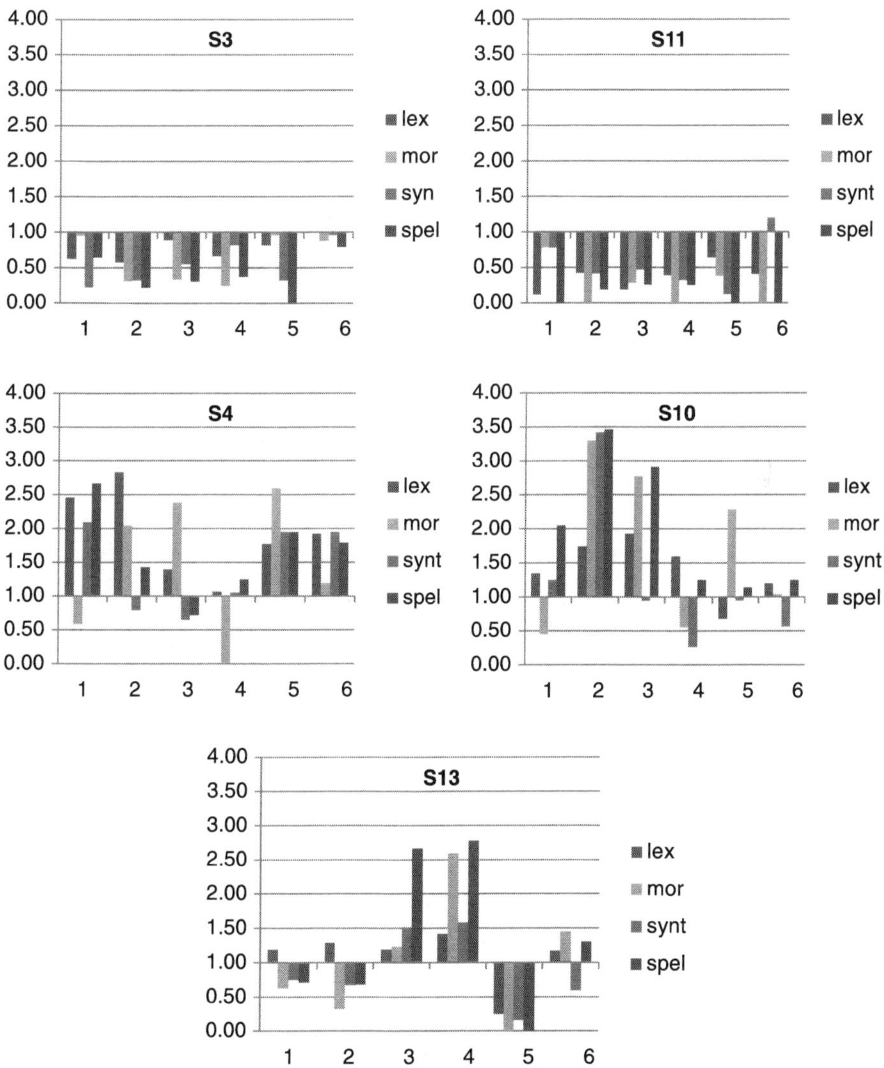

Figure 6.39. Learners with over- vs. under-average error frequency

and 6.41). Student S7 seems to have been better at handling the lexical-semantic system than morphology, which, however, changed in the last experiment. Learner S1, on the other hand, built texts with high levels of accuracy at the lexical-semantic, morphological and spelling levels, but was unable to pay much attention to Swedish syntax, which resulted either in an above-average error ratio or in a considerable discrepancy between the frequency of these errors, compared with other error categories.

Regardless of their actual level of accuracy during the next stage of their language development, individuals can vary in terms of the inter-

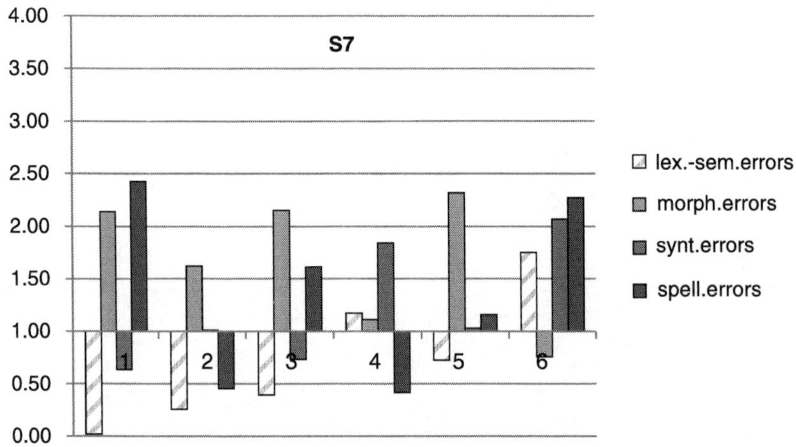

Figure 6.40. Learner with a greater focus on lexical-semantic accuracy

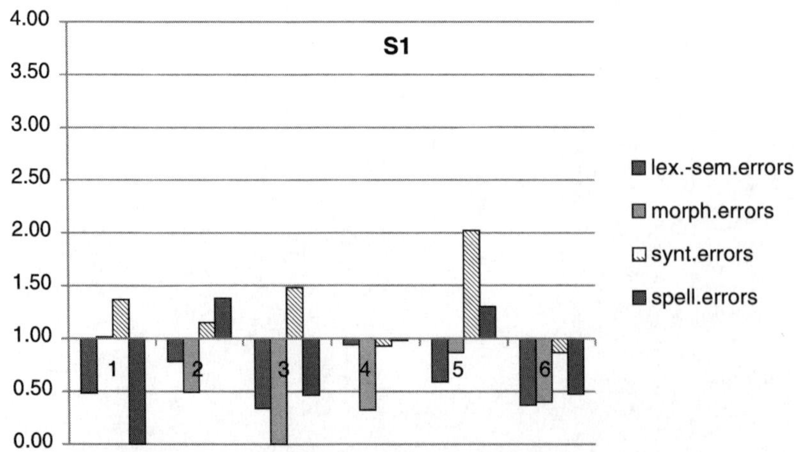

Figure 6.41. Learner with less focus on syntactic accuracy

nal distribution of their errors. A learner who, for example, is more inclined to error can at a given point make far more syntactic than lexical-semantic errors. Moreover, both types of inaccuracy occur more often than in other learners and they can have a different status in a learner's own error constellation. In some learners a few errors can be dispersed much more widely than is the case with other students in whom errors are spread quite evenly. Such intra-individual variability is a sign of the instability of learner's language sub-systems. The greater the dispersion between different error types the more likely it is that the learner can manage different language systems only selectively. A narrowing of this spread in a learner's development would indicate that he or she is managing the language's lexical, semantic, grammatical and spelling systems more effectively. Despite the fact that all learners find it most difficult to integrate lexical-semantic and syntactic systems in their minds, it would be interesting to gain some insight into the interplay of several language systems over time. As we have shown earlier, lexical-semantic and syntactic errors occurred most frequently. These errors as well morphological errors decreased most significantly. Spelling errors were not only the least represented but also the least resistant to change. The distribution and development of several error types in individuals was, however, very diversified. In some learners syntactic errors were only dominant at the beginning of the learning period, while in others spelling errors became more frequent and in yet others they decreased. There were also students who from the very beginning achieved a high level of accuracy in all systems. An analysis of the individual development of error distribution over time would also shed light on a learner's ability to integrate different language systems. For this purpose the development of error dispersion in individuals was analysed. Two general patterns emerged from this analysis. The first is a rather stable developmental path, without any outstanding systems that the learners focus on more than on others or that they fail to manage more often than others. These students, who achieved a balanced management of the language systems, are presented in Figure 6.42a below. Such a balance covers both cases when few errors occurred and those when there were many errors. In other words, here we have learners with relatively high (S7 and S9) and low (S3, S5, S11, S12) levels of error frequency.

The divergent pattern, presented in Figure 6.42b may indicate that learners who at the beginning of the learning period focused exclusively on selected parts of the language later shifted towards a more integrated

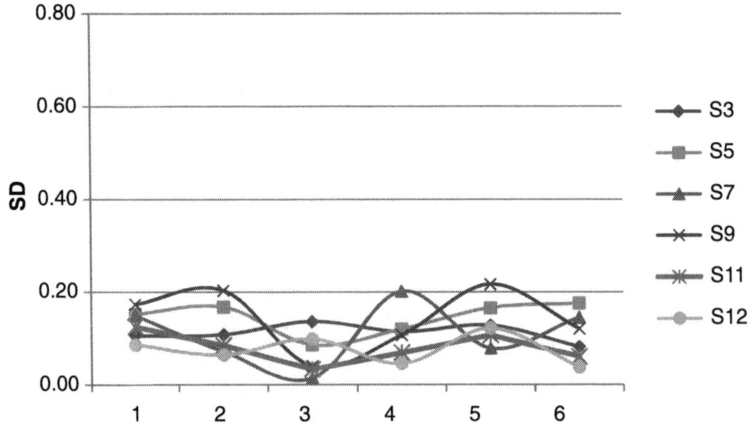

Figure 6.42a. Development of variation in error distribution

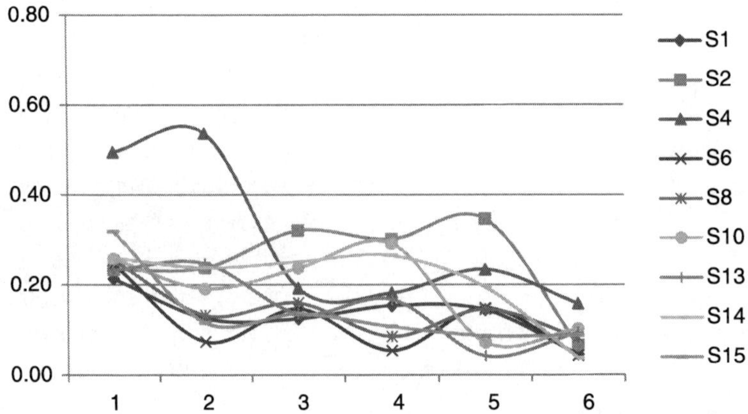

Figure 6.42b. Development of variation in error distribution

view of all language systems, which is reflected in the narrowing of the gap between different error types.

It should be stressed here that the illustrations presented above actually reflect intra-individual variability in learners with regard to their accuracy in the case of particular language systems. Within-subject variability as an inherent feature of dynamic systems can also behave unpredictably. The more systems involved the more complex become their mutual interconnections. On the one hand, we have variation in the accuracy of several language systems at a certain developmental point, while on the other, this variation changes in different ways depending on the learner: in some it develops more dynamically while in others it is a rather balanced feature.

An overall view of the development of accuracy reveals very dynamic growth over a three-year period of learning Swedish. The majority of the learners achieved the greatest improvement in correctness during the first three semesters. This pattern, however, is not homogenous for all sub-systems of accuracy. Morphological and syntactic accuracy increased earlier, i.e. during the first two semesters. However, the learners might have been expected to acquire their morphological systems even earlier, i.e. in the first five months, due to the fact that during the entire experimental period their morphological accuracy was at a much higher level than their syntactic and lexical-semantic correctness. It also changed less dynamically than other systems, which allows us to conclude that the trajectory had approached an attractor state in most students.

There was almost unchanging variation between subjects both with regard to their level of accuracy, the dynamics of their development and the interplay of their language systems. The differences between the learners are remarkable not only because of the divergent tempo in accuracy growth, but above all because of clearly recognizable learner profiles. Some of the students in the investigated group focused more on accuracy, which had an impact on the other systems. Four learner characteristics can be identified, depending on the interplay between systems. Risk Takers are more concerned with the content of the delivered texts than in their accuracy: they build lexically and/or syntactically complex texts that, however, often fail in accuracy. Careful learners, on the other hand, care deeply about correctness, but their texts are often very simple. They seem to champion the strategy of "less is more:" "I write briefly and simply but above all correctly." The third and fourth categories of second language learner are placed in two outstanding pools with regard to the convergence in the interplay of systems that occurs in their cases. Smart learners can build very accurate utterances in second languages, which at the same time are characterized by high levels of lexical diversity and syntactic complexity. The opposite tendency is evident in the wanderers, who need more time to integrate the complexity and accuracy of the new language. Even if their language competence is continuously growing, there is still a considerable discrepancy between the accuracy and complexity of their texts. These students by and large build texts that are unsophisticated and contain many errors.

Being a complex, dynamic system even accuracy behaves chaotically, i.e. its development can be described as unpredictable and characterized by bifurcation. This feature can be observed when the development of a certain parameter proceeds very quickly in the beginning phases. When the growth ratio in the first period of learning is very high, the developmental trajectory can go in all directions: the learner may have approached the attractor state and is unable to make any more improvement in a particular skill, some learners still progress while others became worse in a studied feature, because, for example, of a stronger focus on other sub-systems and dimensions. Such a developmental pattern is evident in the case of accuracy. In the case of lexical-semantic and spelling errors the development of learners who produced very accurate texts in the first experiment could also go in all directions, so that, e.g., the spelling accuracy of well above-average students worsened after three years, among other things, because of the continuous interplay of other systems.

The systems involved are interconnected with one another and they undergo uninterrupted reorganization due to the supply of new resources, such as language input, personal development, cooperation with fellow students and so forth. This reorganization is reflected in individual variability in managing systems. On the one hand, the learners exhibited a behavioural pattern that can be described as "all or nothing" in the sense that when the accuracy of their performance is at a low level, it concerns all language systems and vice versa: when they produce correct utterances they are accurate at all levels. On the other hand, we have observed some dispersion in the correctness of several language systems while two relevant developmental patterns were identified. In those learners who were able to integrate all language systems the dispersion between several errors was rather stable, while in other students, in whom considerable differences between particular error types were noted, these divergences decreased over time.

7

Development of Fluency

As a complex dimension, also fluency is expected to develop chaotically, unpredictably and dynamically. Due to the fact that differences between learners either remain at the same level (in the case of lexical complexity) or increase (in the case of syntactic complexity and accuracy), we cannot begin our deliberations on fluency with the assumption that between-learner variation will develop the same pattern because no such homogenous pattern has been observed for other proficiency dimensions. Nor can we begin any discussion on fluency with the commonly imagined developmental pattern for complexity or accuracy because also that pattern does not exist. So we have to analyse fluency independently of other skills and then try to find the interconnections between them. Three aspects of fluency will be investigated in this chapter, i.e. within-word automaticity, rapidity in text production and smoothness, which together should give us a differentiated picture of fluency and its development in second language writers.

7.1. Development of automaticity

In view of the above-mentioned complexity of fluency it seems reasonable to investigate particular aspects of this dimension both separately and in connection with one another. As was proposed above, automaticity in text production has been analyzed in the present study using transition time. The data presented earlier in Figures 6.37a and 6.37b (see p. 151) clearly show that an increase in this aspect of fluency is a homogenous feature of the language development of all learners. This development is for the most part not dynamic, with mean growth rates between experiments equal to $R \leq -10\%$ and the mean growth rate after three years of learning amounting to $R = -22\%$. However, the changes are more variable at the individual level. As Figures 7.1a and 7.2b show, in some learners the decrease in the time needed to move between keys is especially dynamic in the first period of learning Swedish, when their growth rates were at least 70% higher than the average. Such substantial progress in automaticity was observed in both slow (S4, S5, S9, S11) and fast (S8) writers. The dynamics of development is very strongly correlated with the level of automaticity at the beginning of the study. Spearman's rho for the relationship between the transition time level in the first experiment and the general growth rate after three years of learning is $\rho = -.93$ (p=0.000), which unambiguously shows that those students who were initially the slowest writers made the greatest progress in fluency. In the case of the faster students, on the other hand, automaticity in second language writing approached an attractor state early on, so that during the second and third year of learning no rapid changes were observed.

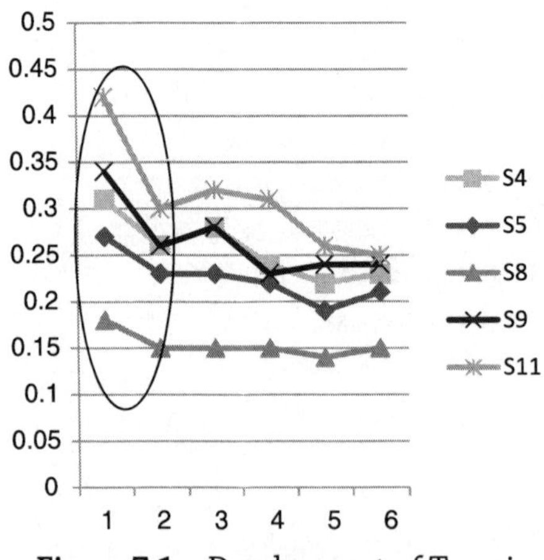

Figure 7.1a. Development of Transition Time in learners with substantial change at the beginning

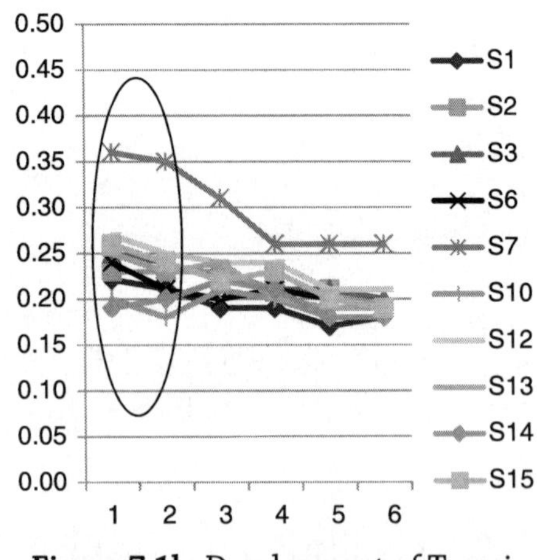

Figure 7.1b. Development of Transition Time in learners with no dynamic change at the beginning

Learners differed most in automaticity at the beginning of the study. Due to the fact that all of them began to learn Swedish at the same time and thus in the first experiment received the same amount of instruction, the discrepancy between them reflects the tempo of fluency development in the new language. Between-subject variation continuously falls during the investigated learning period (see Figure 7.2) and after three years of learning the discrepancy in fluency between learners is much lower than during the first months of language instruction.

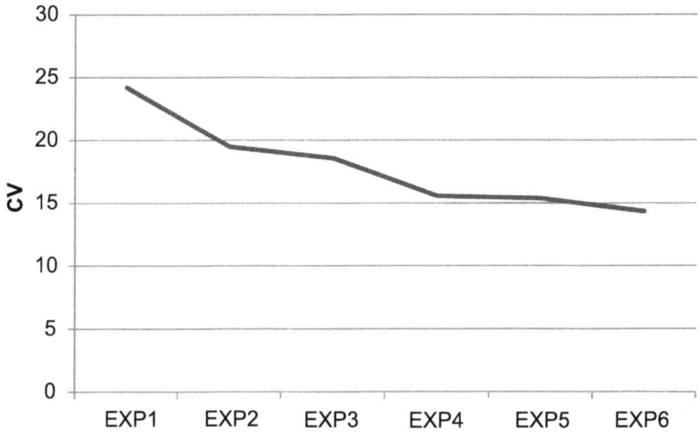

Figure 7.2. Inter-subject variation in the development of automaticity (TT)

This pattern is the opposite of that represented in the case of complexity and accuracy. In the case of syntactic complexity and accuracy differences between students became greater over the three-year period, while for lexical complexity they remained at the same level. In the developmental process within-word automaticity in second language became more homogenous. After three years of learning all learners are essentially fluent users of the new language, but they are not necessarily equal to one another in terms of diverse and accurate usage of the language.

It can be assumed that an improvement in automaticity is a consequence of stabilization in vocabulary. In other words, an increase in fluency can be interconnected with lexical development. Thus, the assumption is that such a developmental sequence will be reflected in an interconnectedness of lexical diversity and fluency. Both features may progress in parallel, but it is also possible that fluency will develop after the lexical system has been internalized in some way. However, it is difficult to determine unequivocally the order of such development. In almost all the learners a very strong interplay was observed between transition time and lexical diversity. The correlation between both characteristics, calculated for the mean group values, was $r \geq -.82$ (p = 0.045), which clearly indicates that an increase in vocabulary richness proceeds hand in hand with progress in within-word automatization. Such interconnectedness between the development of vocabulary and automaticity is also apparent when text length is considered. In this case the correlation between both features was $r = -.80$. Both results clearly confirm the thesis that vocabulary growth and the development of automaticity in second language learning are inseparable, interacting parts of an emerging system.

7.2. Development of rapidity in text production

Fluency as a complex system involves not only automaticity. Automaticity is a trigger, an enabling condition that leads to increased speed in producing utterances. Such rapidity can manifest itself in the time spent delivering a text. The more words a speaker can produce in a given time unit the higher his or her fluency is perceived to be. In our study the number of words written in one minute may serve as a relevant measure for this feature of fluency, a fact which corresponds with previous studies described above.

The overall writing speed generally increased during the three-year-period. This was a tendency that was observed at both the average and the individual levels, see Figures 7.3a and 7.3b. However, although the general trend was upward, looking solely at the mean developmental path would lead us to the misleading conclusion that fluency developed almost linearly (with growth rates not exceeding 20% in six-month intervals) and stabilized after two years of learning. A comparison of the average results with those noted for individuals leads us to reject this simplistic statement. In no student was such straightforward progress observed. Individual developmental trajectories in all study participants visibly diverge from the average line presented in Figure 7.3a. No one student becomes more fluent in a linear-like way. Their writing speed in most cases developed very dynamically, with growth rates between experimental sessions higher than 20%. What should be stressed here is that fluency did not decrease in any writer. Even those students who were already very fluent composing texts from the very beginning remained at least at the same level or even improved slightly. This leads us to the preliminary conclusion that the progression of complexity and accuracy does not automatically result in a less fluent performance. The interplay of all three dimensions will be discussed in the next chapter so no deeper analysis will be made at this point.

As in the case of automaticity, inter-subject variation decreases, with a growth rate of $R = -25\%$ between the first and the last experiment. However, both results show that fluency, compared with complexity and accuracy, is the only dimension of proficiency where differences between learners smoothed out. However, it is not only between-student varia-

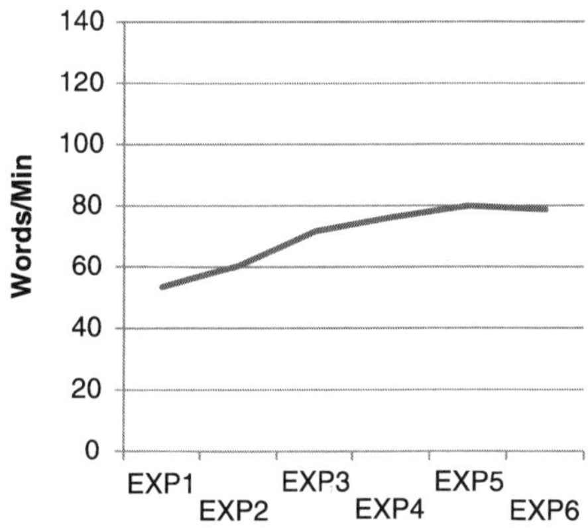

Figure 7.3a. Average development of writing speed

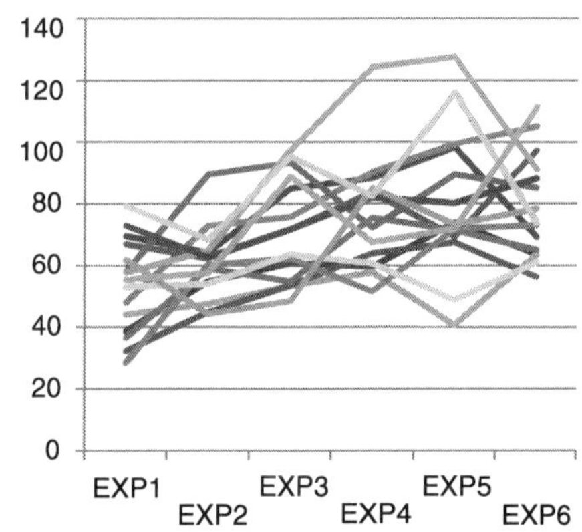

Figure 7.3b. Development of writing speed in individuals

tion that indicates how automaticity and speed in writing are two inherent features of the same dimension. We can even see this interconnection between the two in a correlation that was very strong in almost all the students (Table 7.1). In only three learners (S10, S12, S14) did the development of automaticity and speed not proceed hand in hand.

This should not come as a surprise. Even if the general tendency in the majority of second language learners is for automaticity to develop in parallel with rapidity in text production for some students these two aspects of fluency do not depend on each other in the same way as it does in the case in their fellow students. A likely scenario is that revisions and pauses may affect general fluency in these learners.

As has already been mentioned, the mean development does not correspond with the individual trajectories. The dynamics of fluency development are not only recognizable in the nonlinearity visible in the diagram. The individual growth rates provide a picture of the actual developmental path. It turns out that in the majority of learners fluency increased significantly during the first three semesters of learning Swedish (see Figures 7.4a and 7.4b) when the individual growth rates at six-month intervals were $32\% \leq R \leq 111\%$. As in the case of accuracy, fluency appears to be a property in second language that is often a kind of cornerstone for other language skills, such as, e.g., complexity. Due to the variation between students even this statement cannot be accepted without reservation. The majority does not mean all students and the remaining one third of the participants began to write much more fluently at the end of their second or not until their third year of learning Swedish.

Table 7.1. Correlation between automaticity[9] and speed

Subject	*R*
S1	.84
S2	.70
S3	.85
S4	.77
S5	.69
S6	.51
S7	.92
S8	.72
S9	.98
S10	.15
S11	.97
S12	.04
S13	.77
S14	.10
S15	.82

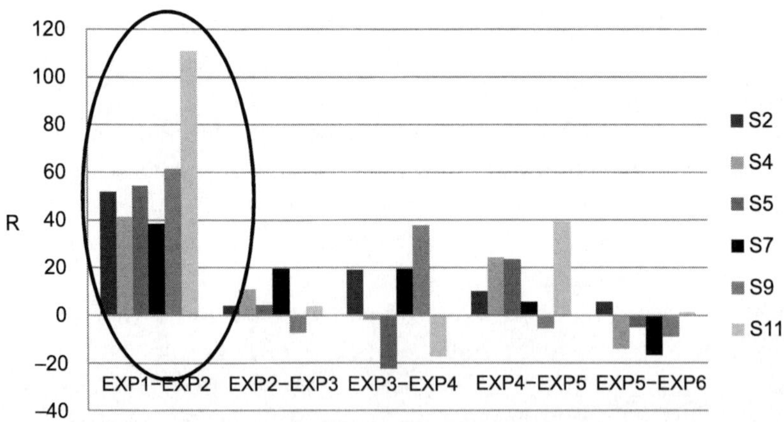

Figure 7.4a. Learners with highest growth rates for writing speed *during second semester*

[9] For a better visualization and in order to not confuse the reader by constantly reminding them that an increase in automaticity in this study means a decrease in transition time the value (TT) has been recalculated to $1//\sqrt{\text{TT}}$ so that we get an inversely proportional result, which allows us to interpret an increasing value as increasing automaticity.

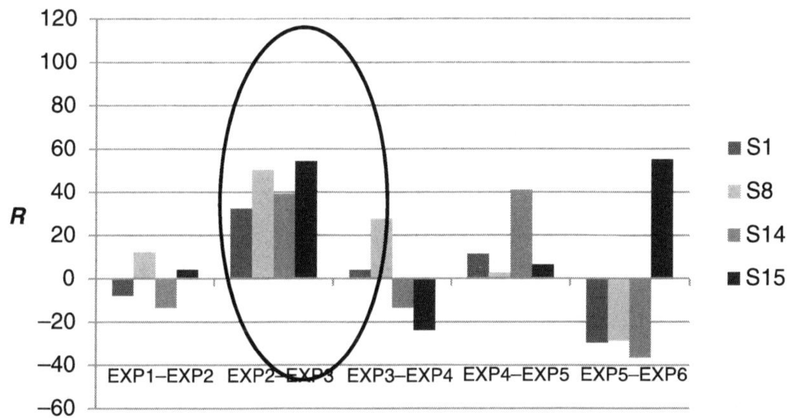

Figure 7.4b. Learners with highest growth rates for writing speedduring third semester

This divergence between learners once more illustrates another feature of dynamic systems, namely their chaotic and unpredictable character. The tempo of development is one of the most unpredictable variables in this area. When a learner differs quite significantly from their fellow students in the beginning phases of learning a new language, in other words, when the parameter of fluency has been set very high, further development can proceed unpredictably, such that a bifurcation may occur. This phenomenon has also been observed in the case of writing speed. The writing speed of the three learners with the highest level of fluency in the first experiment, exceeding the group average by at least 20%, had assumed two different development paths after three years: one of the students made further improvement, while two remained at the same level. From the perspective of the time of onset for the language, fluency in these writers obviously increased, as it did in other learners. However, in the case of such quick-starters unpredictability is much more likely than in other students. Their fluency had already approached an attractor state in the first months of learning the new language – even the student whose fluency increased had the lowest growth rate in the entire group, which shows us that stability, or less variability does not mean equilibrium when open and complex systems are in action.

Looking at the development of fluency from the other side, i.e. from the point of view of those students who were slowest in text production in the first experiment it turns out that these learners had made the greatest progress in fluency by the end the three-year study period.

Spearman's rho for the interplay of general growth and fluency levels after the first semester was ρ = –.75 (*p*=0.01), which clearly shows that the lower the fluency level at the beginning, i.e. the later fluency develops, the more long-term progress can be observed. And these two developmental patterns – quick starters who achieve fluency early on and then approach an attractor state, and slower learners, whose development is more dynamic in the long-term perspective – together build a picture of decreasing individual differences in fluency.

7.3. Development of smoothness

In order to be understood and not make too many disruptions in a text that could disturb the listener's comprehension and in extreme situations even reduce the cohesion of an utterance, the speaker is faced with the need to speak smoothly, i.e. not make too many pauses nor pauses that are too long as well as not make too many revisions of his or her text, nor revisions that are overly extensive. As was mentioned above, production of a written text takes place in different circumstances to those in which a spoken one is produced and a direct comparison is not possible. But even an analysis of how smoothly a text emerges can help us answer the question of how the third aspect of fluency, namely smoothness in text production, develops.

In the present study the way a smooth text is produced will be examined using the *Mean length of burst*. This value reflects the number of tokens between pauses or such editing activities as deletions or revisions and it can be seen as an indicator of smoothness in text production. Only online activities have been taken into account, i.e. pauses in reading a text after it had been produced or self-repairs that were the result of such a re-reading were excluded from the analysis. The time criterion for a pause was 2 seconds, which is in line with previous studies on L2-writing (1995; Severinsson-Eklundh & Kollberg, 1996; Strömqvist & Ahlsén, 1999; Wengelin, 1999a; 2002; Wengelin, 2007). Furthermore, as in the analysis of spelling errors, corrections of typos were excluded from the analysis. Gunnarsson (2012) also made such an exclusion in her study on the development of complexity, accuracy and fluency of L2-learners of French where the same tool (ScriptLog) was used.

As was illustrated in Figure 7.5 the average values indicate a steady increase in smooth text units during the first two years of learning Swedish, after which fluency stabilized at the level of 13 tokens (about two words) written in one course. The biggest increase occurred during the first year of learning, when the mean growth rate between the first and the second experiment was 28%, after which it steadily declined. This pattern corresponds with those observed for the other aspects of fluency, i.e. automaticity and rapidity, where the mean development was continuous during the first two years of learning before approaching an attractor state. Also the correlation between the mean values of automaticity ($1/\sqrt{TT}$), rapidity (Words written per minute) and smoothness (mlb) were very high ($.93 \leq r$ *1.0*)[10], which is an additional factor confirming how strongly all three aspects of fluency are interconnected with one other.

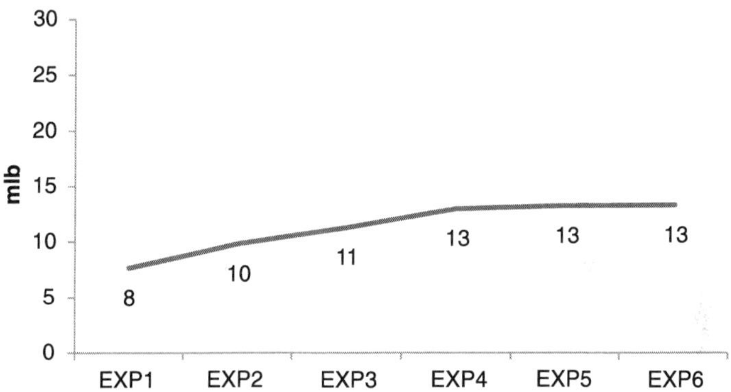

Figure 7.5. Mean development of fluency (smoothness)

The individual developmental paths are by no means as uniform as the mean curve would suggest. In many learners fluency changes very rapidly. In fact, the first three semesters of learning were characterized by a significant increase, with growth rates exceeding 20% (see Figures 7.6a and 7.6b). However, the system was far from stable and developed continuously in a visibly non-linear way. Even after this clear improvement in fluency had been achieved at the beginning of the learning period many students made continued progress with high growth rates. In no learner was the mean length of burst shorter after three years of second language instruction. Even those with very high levels of fluency at the beginning of the study continuously improved, although with much lower growth rates.

---

[10] $p = 0.007$ and $p = 0.000$, respectively.

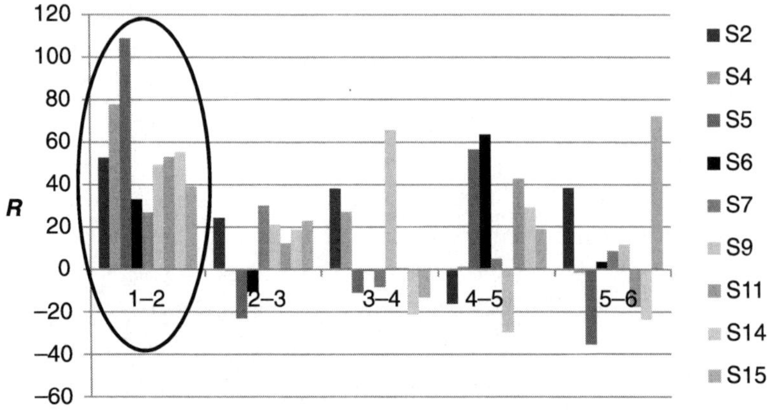

Figure 7.6a. Substantial growth in fluency during the first year

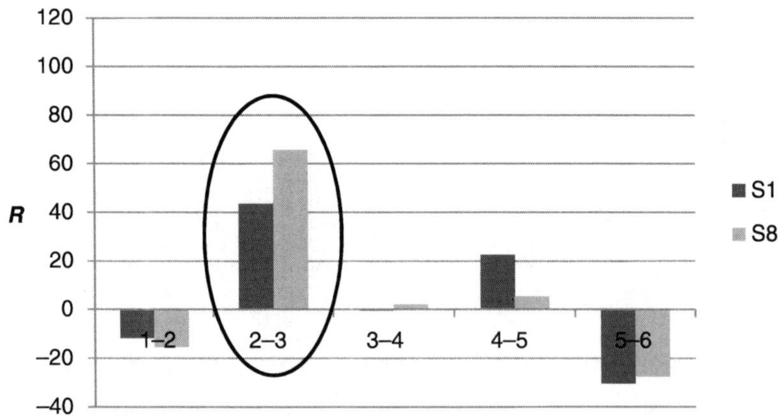

Figure 7.6b. Substantial growth in fluency during the third semester

Just as occurred with text production rapidity, so also in the case of smoothness those learners who were more careful and did not focus on fluency at the beginning of the study made the greatest progress in the long-term. The correlation between the level of fluency in the first experiment and the general growth rate after three years of learning was $\rho = .57$ ($p = 0.02$), which unequivocally shows that the lower the fluency level at the beginning of the learning period the more progress can be expected in the long-term. To learn fast does not automatically mean to learn best. Second language teachers often label students who develop more slowly as "poor" learners and in light of this and other previously described outcomes such stigmatization can lead to teachers disregarding the hard work and the great improvement that these learners actually make. The slower learning students did not develop as dynamically and variably as their faster learning fellow students. As Figure 7.7 shows their developmental paths resemble much more a line than a polygonal chain, which, on the other hand, is a characteristic feature of more fluent learners (Figure 7.87). There are two possible reasons for such discrepancies. The first results from the dichotomy between the functional and optimal levels. A chaotic developmental curve with many peaks may suggest that the learner oscillated between his or her optimal and functional levels at the data collection point. A more line-like pattern, on the other hand, may be interpreted as meaning that these learners' optimal and functional levels tend to lie close to each other. In other words – the development of lower achieving learners proceeds more smoothly. The second reason for such polarization in developmental patterns may lie in the general developmental behaviour of students. Regardless of the language structure, skill or proficiency dimension, some learners tend to learn more rapidly and may develop a "risk-taker" profile, while others develop in smaller steps without dramatic changes. Furthermore, such differences may be interconnected with personality, which, however, requires a separate study.

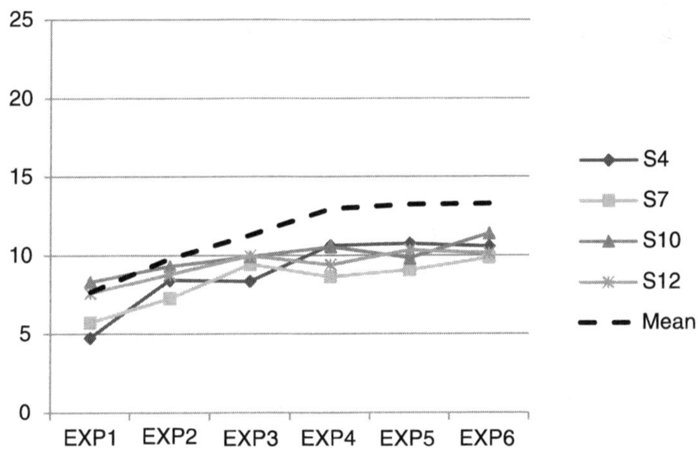

Figure 7.7. Mean length of burst in slower developing learners

As far as accuracy is concerned, the extreme spurts achieved by two learners ought to be mentioned here. These exceptional peaks in fluency were observed in students S3 and S15 (see Figure 7.8), whose growth rates in one experiment were 139% (S3) and 79% (S15). The very signifi-

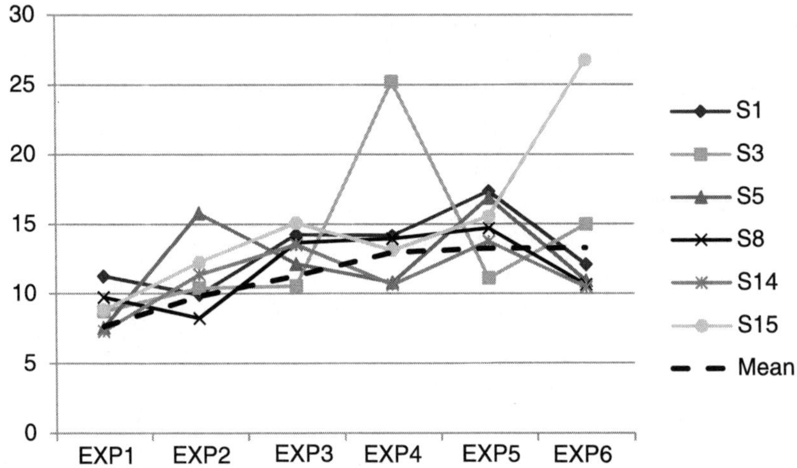

Figure 7.8. Mean length of burst in dynamically developing learners

cant increase in fluency achieved by writer S15 during the sixth semester was clearly a consequence of her learning environment. She was one of the students who spent one semester on a scholarship in Sweden, which surely contributed to substantial improvement in fluency. Again we can see how strongly systems are interconnected in the process of second language learning.

On the other hand, the explanation for student S3's fluency spurt is not so obvious. This learner was not in Sweden after the third experiment. Nor were her accuracy or complexity levels lower at the objective data collection point, which might have been expected in cases involving such a great improvement in fluency due to the Trade-Off Hypothesis. She clearly improved in all other dimensions of the language, but not as remarkably as in fluency. Her within-word automaticity or rapidity in text production increased, but not as dramatically as it did in the case of smoothness. In fact, she wrote a very long text (one of the longest) and the length seems to be the key factor here. The topic for the fourth experiment was "An adventure on my holidays" and presumably it was such an interesting subject for her that she wrote her text very fluently, without long pauses and without extensive revision – nevertheless her story was lexically and syntactically complex and accurate. There was one more learner (S9) who also peaked in the fourth experiment (with a growth rate of 66%) and whose text was as long as her (S3) text. In general, text length may be seen as a condition of fluency. When a learner toils over the drafting of a text he or she will not write at length nor fluently. A long text is an outcome of many factors, of which interest in the topic and sufficient language skills are the most crucial. Learner S3 presumably possessed both in the fourth experiment when she wrote down her holiday memories. A strong interconnection between length and fluency was also confirmed by measuring the correlation coefficient for length and fluency level in all learners. The Spearman rho ranged between $\rho = .45$ and $\rho = .72$, which indicates that the relationship between text length and fluency is strong. Only in the first experiment was this interconnection a little weaker ($\rho = .30$), which may be explained by a lower level of automatiziation and internalization of linguistic features in the second language. Due to the fact that participants in the present study had no time limit for writing their the narrative and thus could produce both long and short texts, the general conclusion to be drawn is that when we lack such tools as ScriptLog, which can provide insights into the entire writing process, the length of a written text can serve as an indirect indicator of fluency. This can of course be much more evident in cases where writers do not have so much time at their disposal. However, even in situations where no such limit is set a long text is the outcome or an indicator of high fluency.

The interplay of systems is evident not only in vocabulary growth or text length. All three aspects of fluency also strongly interact with one other. The interconnection between automaticity and rapidity in text production has already been discussed earlier in the chapter. However, also the smoothness of a text is clearly dependent on other aspects of fluency.

The table below (Table 7.2) presents the interplay of all three aspects of fluency, i.e. automaticity, rapidity and smoothness. The first column recalls Table 7.1, but for transparency reasons all subsystems have been presented together. This stems from the juxtaposition below, which shows there is a very strong interconnection between all aspects of fluency. The correlation coefficient (Pearson's r) is higher than ±.56, which demonstrates an at least moderately strong interplay during the developmental period of a second language. However, in the majority of learners this interplay between all the features is quite strong and oscillates around $r = \pm.80$. Also in those students in whom no correlation was observed between within-word automaticity and rapidity in text production (S10, S12 and S14), a strong interplay occurs between at least one of the other features. This result is further proof of the need to investigate more systems. To consider only one feature of second language development necessarily deprives the complexity of its fundamental characteristics. And as an evident consequence of it a simplification occurs which on the one hand can provide us with quick answers, and on the other hand, however, gives rise to the risk that the research results will be flattened out and interpreted only in a cursory manner.

Table 7.2. Correlation between subsystems of fluency

	Automaticity/rapidity ($1/\sqrt{TT}$ /Words per Minute)	Automaticity/ smoothness ($1/\sqrt{TT}$ /mlb)	Rapidity/smoothness (Words per minute/ mlb)
	R	*R*	*r*
S1	.84	.80	.98
S2	.70	.89	.95
S3	.85	.56	.62
S4	.77	.96	.87
S5	.69	.70	.74
S6	.51	.71	.11
S7	.92	.91	.84
S8	.72	.48	.90
S9	.98	.88	.91
S10	.15	.11	.72
S11	.97	.90	.89
S12	.04	.87	.29
S13	.77	.72	.82
S14	.10	–.20	.70
S15	.82	.88	.93

Dynamic systems are complex systems. As such system fluency, which involves automaticity, ease and rapidity in retrieving linguistic items from long-term memory, as well as smoothness, undoubtedly behaves like other complex systems. All the above discussed features of fluency develop chaotically, undergo unpredictable changes and are sensitive to initial conditions: a significant change in one parameter in the early phases of development triggers random behaviour in the entire system, such that predicting a learner's developmental pattern is not possible. All the subsystems are inherently interconnected with one other. The first of these – automaticity – enables the learner to produce utterances faster, and this developing rapidity in text production in turn results in fewer disruptions and pauses so that the learner speaks or writes smoothly, which in turn gives the listener the impression that the speaker/writer has utterance fluency. This scenario assumes that automaticity is an enabling condition for other fluency features and after achieving it the learner can produce texts faster and more smoothly. This hypothesis has in fact been confirmed in the present study. Automaticity was the only feature for which an attractor state was approached in all participants. It developed faster than rapidity and smoothness and was not exposed to such rapid changes as the two other indicators. The stability of this system enables other systems to reorganize and reach more mature stages. In the case of fluency these stages involve faster writing and thinking in a second language in longer and longer chunks.

8

The interplay of Complexity, Accuracy and Fluency

The dynamics of development and the complexity of systems involved in second language learning necessarily imply some form of interplay between the systems in action. As has been described earlier in this book this interconnection is supposed to proceed in accordance with the Trade-Off Hypothesis proposed by Skehan (2009), which suggests that all three proficiency dimensions, i.e. Complexity, Accuracy and Fluency, do not develop in parallel and focusing more on one of them at the expense of the other two will weaken the performance of the latter. In other words: second language learners are unable to handle all three simultaneously and when they pay more attention to, for example, fluency they will automatically concentrate less on accuracy and complexity, which may lead to a situation where they will speak quickly but at the same time their texts will be rather simple and contain many errors. When we base our observations on the averages for each dimension and look at the linear correlation between them (see Table 8.1) the interplay between all three cannot be ignored. In each case the correlation is at least moderately strong with the lowest interconnectedness between accuracy and syntactic complexity (subordination ratio) $r = .58$ and the highest between fluency (rapidity measured as the number of words written per minute) and syntactic diversity (number of different clauses per sentence) $r = .92$. When it comes to the interplay between complexity, accuracy and fluency for the group as a whole we could reject the Trade-Off Hypothesis. The outcomes presented below tend to confirm the continuing interplay of all systems and provide proof that the development of these proficiency dimensions generally occurs simultaneously. However, a more in-depth analysis of the data reveals an interesting regularity. Although in all three cases the correlation is strong or moderately strong a common pattern can be observed, namely that in general interconnection is weakest between accuracy and syntactic complexity (both in terms of the diversity of syntactic structures and the ratio of subordinated clauses), as well as between fluency and lexical complexity, i.e. the ability to connect words in more complex phrases. This observation could also lead to a re-formulation of the Trade-Off Hypothesis in the sense that learners can focus on two dimensions at the same time rather than only on one and, for example, improvements in fluency and accuracy go hand in hand with one another and only complexity is more neglected. This suggests the need to analyse developmental paths as a whole rather than focus on linear relationships.

Table 8.1. Correlation (Pearsons *r*) between Complexity, Accuracy and Fluency (for mean values)

		Accuracy	**Fluency**		
			Automaticity	Rapidity	Smoothness
Complexity	Lexical diversity	.85	.80	.86	.89
	Lexical complexity	.90	.70	.66	.68
	Syntactic diversity	.68	.84	.92	.88
	Syntactic complexity	.58	.78	.75	.70
Fluency	Automaticity	.87			
	Rapidity	.85			
	Smoothness	.84			

The most striking observation concerning the development of all facets of complexity, accuracy and fluency is the uniform direction they take at the beginning of the learning period – in the first three semesters (Figure 8.1). All the systems make steady progress, albeit at different rates. As was stated earlier in this book the most progress was achieved in fluency and accuracy, with complexity being the slowest developing dimension in this respect. From the end of the second year of learning the students' developmental paths diverge more and more from each other and here the most remarkable reorganization processes begin. The interplay of systems becomes increasingly dynamic.

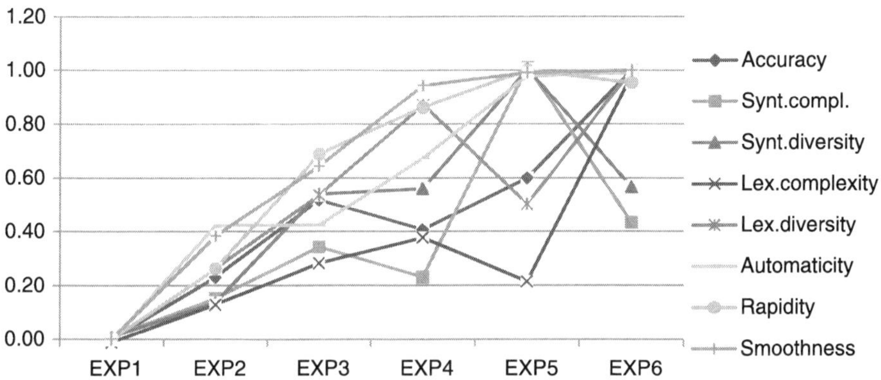

Figure 8.1. Development of mean Complexity, Accuracy and Fluency[11]

Due to one of the basic features of Dynamic Systems Theory, namely its analysis of complex systems, we cannot base our statements exclusively on data revealed by average values. As has been shown earlier in the book, mean values can be used only as a reference point for group-level development at a given point and not as an indicator of the general developmental path. The complexity of every component (in this case, for example, every learner) requires studying individual development and on the basis of such paths we can try to find regularities that, on the other hand, shed light on the unique development of individuals. This is especially important in light of the above discussion on the dynamic behaviour of systems demonstrated by mean values, which automatically leads to the assumption that the interplay of complexity, accuracy and fluency in individuals may reveal highly divergent patterns.

In order to refute or confirm the Trade-Off Hypothesis we should state what precisely such refutation or confirmation might indicate. A focus on one dimension that results in less attention being paid to the other two may mean that one aspect of proficiency will increase during the learning period while the other two will decrease. Due to the nonlinear character of dynamic system behaviour another assumption may be that all dimensions will develop in the same direction, i.e. they will increase or decrease simultaneously, but with different dynamics. A greater focus on one may mean that this particular aspect will develop faster or more dynamically than the other two, which can be observed in higher growth

[11] Due to the spread of numeric values for the respective dimensions the values have been recalculated to 0–1 in order to present them in one diagram.

rates during the learning period. However, as the outcomes for mean values have shown, it may happen that learners pay attention not simply to one dimension at a time, but actually manage two dimensions in tandem, only one of which can be treated as less important at a given point.

The justification for the Trade-Off Hypothesis will thus include confirmation of the following assumptions:

1) An increase in one dimension leads to a decrease in the other two and/or
2) An increase in one dimension is greater than the increase in the other two and/or
3) An increase in two dimensions leads to a decrease in the third and/or
4) An increase in two dimensions is greater than the increase in the third.

These postulates can thus appear in a stronger version, i.e. the dimensions compete with each other, which will result in a dichotomy, i.e. an increase in one or two of the dimensions is accompanied by a decrease in the other dimension(s), or they can appear in a softer version, where the growth rate in one or two of the dimensions is higher than the growth rate in the other dimension(s).

The analysis of complexity, accuracy and fluency has shown that in general fluency and accuracy develop more dynamically than complexity and that this strong development continues for the first three semesters. For complexity to develop, on the other hand, a longer period is needed. An analysis of growth rates in individuals for all the investigated dimensions (lexical diversity and complexity, syntactic diversity and complexity, accuracy, automaticity, rapidity and smoothness) revealed that in no single student did all the dimensions develop in parallel. In Figures 8.27 and 8.3 below sample growth rates are given for individual students. The diagrams should be interpreted as follows: those parts of the bars that lie above the X-axis represent a positive growth rate, i.e. an increase in one particular proficiency aspect, and the parts below the X-axis – a negative growth rate, i.e. a decrease. When a bar comprises both positive and negative values it indicates a strong version of the Trade-Off Hypothesis and thus progress has been achieved in certain dimensions at the expense of a decline in others. The more equally the dimensions are spread at both parts of the X-axis the greater the interplay of the systems and the more all the dimensions compete with one another. The development of all three dimensions in student S4 is presented in Figure 8.2. Here we have an example of a learner in whom these dimensions strongly compete with one other almost all the time, except for the time between the second and the third experiments, when we have observed an increase in all aspects of language: complexity, accuracy and fluency. However, this progress proceeded very unevenly. There was a huge increase in accuracy (51%), a rather moderate increase in fluency (8–11%) as well as lexical and syntactic complexity (8–10%) and a very slight increase in lexical and syntactic diversity (3–4%). At every other stage in the student's development, the increase in certain dimensions led to a reduced performance in others. In the final experiment, for example, the learner wrote a text that was more accurate and had a more diversified vocabulary but was at the same time syntactically simpler and written less fluently. Even if no values are displayed on the bars we can clearly see that at no point in the learner's development did the dimensions change to the same degree, which is evident in the unequal size of the fields. Every time one or two dimensions progressed more dynamically, it led to a decrease in (an)other dimension(s). For example, a great improvement in fluency was observed between the first and the second experiments, but this led to a (slight) decline in syntactic complexity. In the fourth experiment, on the other hand, fluency and lexical complexity increased, which in turn was paralleled by a decrease in syntactic complexity. In the next experiment the student was more fluent and her text showed a higher level of syntactic complexity and a more diversified vocabulary, as a consequence of which, however, her story contained more errors. And finally, in the last experiment, accuracy and lexical diversity increased, but at the cost of fluency and syntactic complexity and diversity.

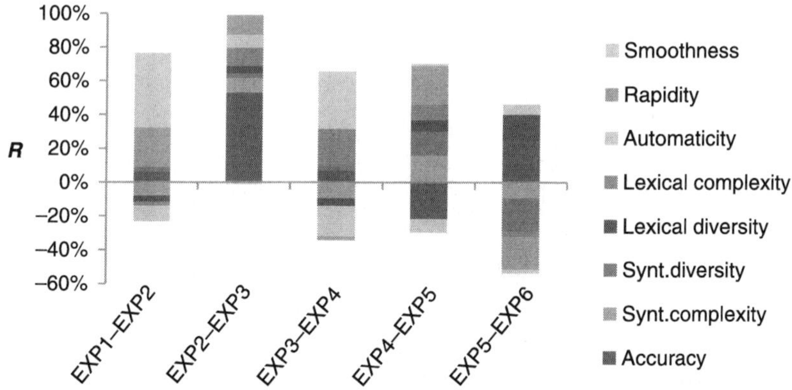

Figure 8.2. Individual growth rates for Complexity, Accuracy and Fluency in student S4

Figure 8.3 illustrates the development of all dimensions of proficiency in a student in whom a rather softer version of the Trade-Off Hypothesis can be observed. Except for the student's performance in the fifth experimental session, where an increase in fluency and syntactic complexity led to a decline in accuracy and lexical diversity, at all other time points an increase in the majority of the dimensions resulted in a poorer performance in only one other dimension, or slightly less progress in another: in the second experiment a significant increase in fluency was followed by a decline in syntactic diversity and a barely noticeable increase in accuracy. Half a year later the student made the most improvement in lexical and syntactic complexity, while fluency and accuracy did not progress hand in hand, but rather remained at the same level. Afterwards fluency and accuracy were the preferred dimensions, while both lexical and syntactic complexity either did not change or decreased a little. In the last experiment the learner improved in all dimensions, although to varying degrees. Her main area of improvement was accuracy, while her lexical complexity and fluency increased to a lesser degree.

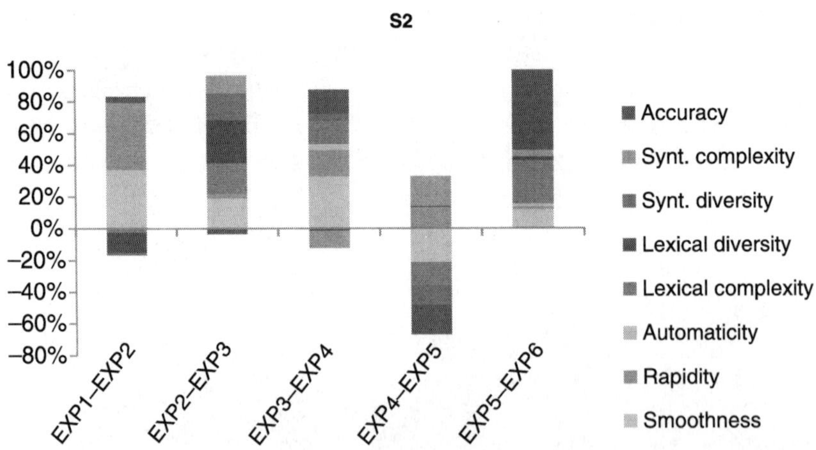

Figure 8.3. Individual growth rates for Complexity, Accuracy and Fluency in student S2

The above described students are typical of the entire group in the sense that they represent two versions of the Trade-Off Hypothesis. However, the stronger version (illustrated by the example of student S4) is much more frequent and was observed in thirteen students. In no learner did an improvement in one dimension lead to a decrease in all the others. The interplay of systems reminds us of a driver's behaviour at traffic lights. A green light means that the driver can continue driving and does not have to stop or be more careful. They can pay full attention to driving. When the amber light appears briefly, the driver either slows down or speeds up in order to avoid stopping in the middle of an intersection. No further driving is allowed when the light turns red. When we compare these signals with the interplay of complexity, accuracy and fluency the most focused dimension is equivalent to the driver's behaviour at a green light. The learner pays the greatest attention to it and this is the area in which he or she improves the most. The less focused dimension(s), i.e. this(those) in which we also can see progress not as remarkable as in the strongest dimension, can be compared with the amber light – the driver is allowed to drive but not as freely as with the green light. Finally, the competing dimension(s), which by necessity is(are) neglected when the learner improves in others, can then be symbolized by the red light.

It should be stressed here that we cannot deprive these dimensions of their complexity. Therefore, it would be a simplification to state that, e.g., an improvement in accuracy leads to a poorer performance in complexity overall, due to the fact that complexity by itself can have many facets and reveal itself at the lexical and syntactic levels. Hence, in the examples set out above learner S2 improved in syntactic complexity in the fifth experiment, which weakened her performance at the lexical level and thus led to a lower growth rate in lexical diversity and complexity. Furthermore, complexity and the chaotic behaviour of systems ensure that the learner does not prioritize one dimension all the time. As has been demonstrated earlier, some students, called risk takers, focused more on lexical diversity and less on accuracy, while careful learners, on the other hand, paid more attention to accuracy than vocabulary richness. However, even in their case the interplay between all dimensions leads to this privileged performance becoming of secondary importance when greater progress is achieved in another dimension. This can be demonstrated using the example of student S6 who, because of her lower ratio of lexical-semantic errors and low level of lexical diversity, has been described as a careful learner who preferred to build texts that lack sophisticated vocabulary but are at the same time correct. As Figure 8.4 below shows, accuracy (marked as the dotted field) was not always the dimension that increased the most while lexical diversity (marked as a white field) was not the most neglected aspect of proficiency. Hence, an individual preference or individual profiles do not necessarily mean that the learner will develop most dynamically in that particular dimension, while another, corresponding dimension will be treated as less important.

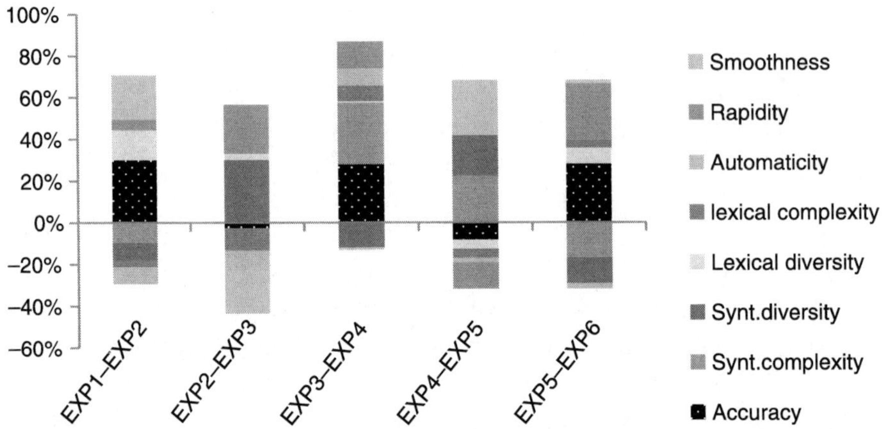

Figure 8.4. Individual growth rates for Complexity, Accuracy and Fluency in student S6

Although all systems develop chaotically and no predictions can be made about the character of these interconnections, some dimensions compete with each other more often. This wrestling between them is very common due to the fact that the Trade-Off Hypothesis occurs in the majority of learners. Competition between dimensions was observed in some learners throughout the entire learning period, while in others these particular aspects of proficiency squeezed each other out only at singular points during the learner's development. The dimensions that competed most with each other turned out to be accuracy and syntactic complexity. Both clearly alternated with one another in terms of priority in five learners throughout their entire development (Figure 8.5). In other students an increase in accuracy did not automatically mean that a text got simpler at the syntactic level. However, a competing interplay between accuracy and lexical complexity was observed in three learners (S3, S7, S13). These facts taken together indicate that in almost half of all learners the dimensions that competed most with one another were accuracy and complexity: either lexical or syntactic (in the case of S13, even both). In the interplay between accuracy and fluency competition was constant between both dimensions in three learners (S3, S9, S13).

Competition between fluency and complexity was likewise only observed in three students (S6, S7, S10). Student S13 was the only learner in the entire group who can be described as a representative of the strong version of the Trade-Off Hypothesis. During the three years of S13's second language learning a clear correlation could be seen between accuracy on the one hand and lower levels of complexity and fluency on the other.

Based on the discussion above the Trade-Off Hypothesis can be confirmed to exist. All assumptions involving the interplay of dimensions

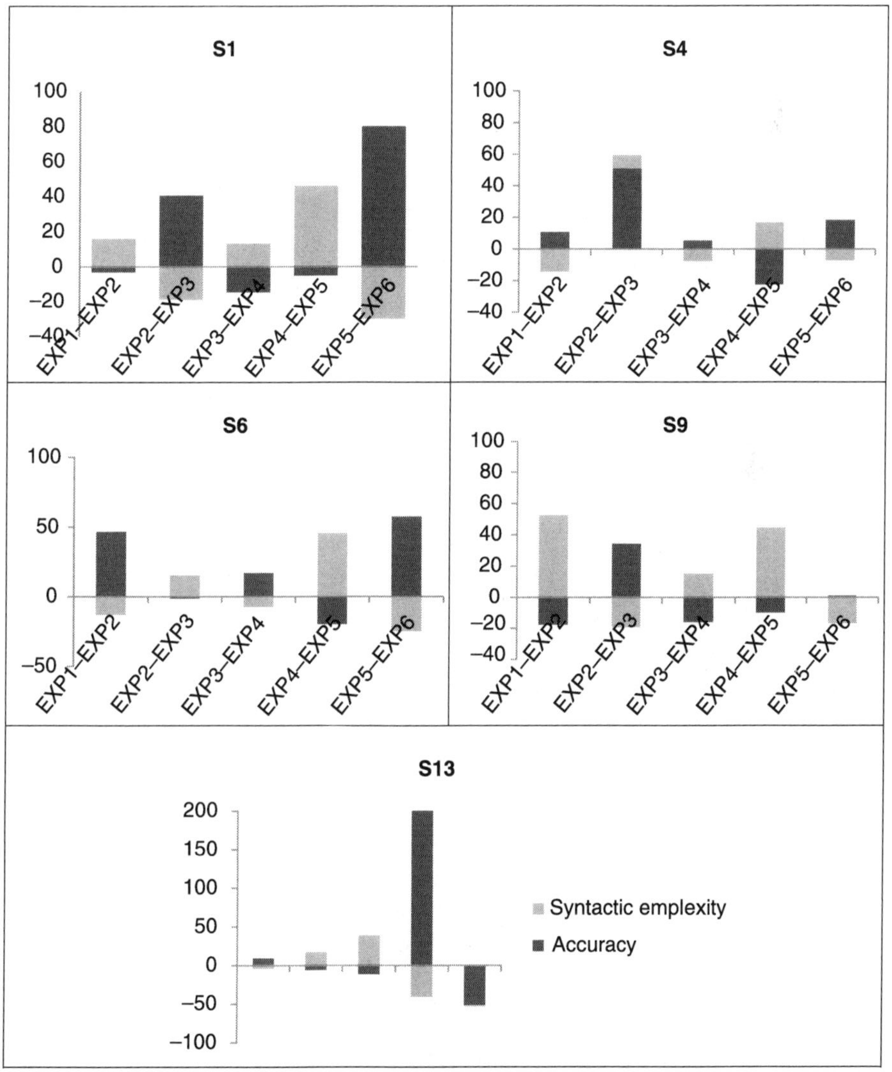

Figure 8.5. Competing interplay of accuracy and syntactic complexity

in both the Hypothesis' softer and stronger versions are reflected in the analyzed data. The second language learners did not focus on all dimensions of proficiency to the same degree, as a consequence of which an increase in one or more aspects led either to less growth in other dimensions or to a decrease in them. On the other hand, nonlinear development necessarily resulted in the uneven development of all features of second language proficiency. Therefore, to describe the interplay between all aspects of complexity, accuracy and fluency we have sought analogies with the behaviour of drivers at traffic lights. One or two dimensions are always in the foreground (green light) in a learner's mind, while others are of secondary importance and therefore do not increase at the same rate (amber light) while a clear check is placed on the others in a learner's mind (red light), so that these neglected aspects are fairly weak in performance terms. Although every student develops in his or her own way and no generalizations can be made with regard to the interplay between all three dimensions one slight tendency observed is for the development of accuracy, which was the most dynamic dimension in development terms, to lead to a dip in complexity and vice versa: when complexity increases, a learner's performance becomes more error prone. The interplay between accuracy and fluency on the one hand, and fluency and complexity on the other, does not show such a strong propensity for competition.

The most important characteristic of development is that it is a process in which change leads to a more mature state. This state can be achieved not only as a consequence of growth, but also through a re-organisation of systems that, in turn, become more differentiated and integrated. Such differentiation can be recognized in the changing interplay between systems, while integration, on the other hand, involves learners' ability to handle them appropriately so that they not only compete with each other but also complement one other. Such integration of complexity, accuracy and fluency can be studied in individuals by looking at the development of all these dimensions in every individual and see how the process of reorganization proceeds. In the present study the integration of all dimensions was analyzed using the Gini coefficient. This index is broadly applied in econometrics to measure inequality between values. It shows how widely, for example, incomes are spread in the world. The higher the calculated value the more differences exist between analysed elements. A low ratio, on the other hand, indicates a high concentration of elements at the same level. The Gini coefficient does not indicate how high or low the levels are. It only tells us to what degree the analysed values are cumulative. The ratio can have values ranging between zero and one, where zero means that all the variables are the same and thus we have full equality. When the ratio is one, a maximum distance between values exists, but in the sense that one variable represents full possession of a certain feature while all others are located at the opposite pole. In econometrics such a pattern symbolises a situation where one person possesses maximum income and the rest of the population (in a given country) does not earn anything at all. When we apply this to our own study we can assume that a high Gini ratio will occur when complexity, accuracy and fluency are not integrated in the learner's mind. This will be reflected in a competitive interplay between dimensions; i.e. when, for example, accuracy is high, fluency is lower and complexity very low. Or when one dimension is very high and the others are very low. Such a situation would result in a Gini coefficient of close to one. On the other hand, if all aspects of accuracy, complexity and fluency were at a similar level (high or low) the coefficient would be around zero and it would mean that the learner has integrated the proficiency dimensions in his or her mind and they are not competing with one another. However, according to the results presented above, which indicate that the Trade-Off Hypothesis works, we will not achieve a zero value because one dimension is always more privileged in the learner's mind so we will rarely encounter a situation in which all dimensions are at the same level. Software developed by Wessa (2015) was used for calculation purposes. As Table 8.2 shows the interplay between complexity, accuracy and fluency developed from "parts separated" to "parts joined," which unambiguously confirms the assumption that during the learning period these systems become more and more integrated in the learners' minds. This development path was visible in all students with one exception (S13), who will be discussed separately.

At the beginning of the learning period the Gini ratio was very high. In 80% of the students it was above 0.6, which must be interpreted as reflecting a very high dispersion between all features of the studied dimensions. In the remaining three students it is slightly lower ($0.44 \leq G \leq 0.53$), but the outcomes should definitely be interpreted as showing a low level of integration between accuracy, complexity and fluency. Overall, we can state that after first six months of second language development learners cannot focus on more than one aspect of the new language and the tendency is for them to pay more attention to one performance dimension, while leaving all the others in the background. That is why the Gini ratio is so close to1 in so many learners. The developmental path is unique for all learners and after three years of learning all learners had integrated all dimensions so that they tended to complement one other in the production of utterances in the second language. The Gini coefficient decreased dramatically and after three years it did not exceed 0.3 in the majority of learners. This increase in system integration is particularly strong in the first phases of the learning period, when the growth rates in all learners were highest in the first three semesters. This result once more emphasizes the fact that development was most dynamic and most progress made in language skills in the first period of second language learning.

Table 8.2. Dispersion of Complexity, Accuracy and Fluency in individuals (Gini index)

Subject	EXP1	EXP2	EXP3	EXP4	EXP5	EXP6
S1	0.53	0.52	0.38	0.31	0.23	0.30
S2	0.82	0.67	0.42	0.31	0.29	0.04
S3	0.84	0.53	0.30	0.10	0.32	0.17
S4	0.78	0.54	0.26	0.36	0.13	0.14
S5	0.75	0.45	0.27	0.21	0.16	0.29
S6	0.70	0.40	0.36	0.29	0.40	0.23
S7	0.87	0.21	0.26	0.11	0.13	0.14
S8	0.81	0.48	0.17	0.29	0.19	0.22
S9	0.84	0.37	0.28	0.27	0.31	0.19
S10	0.46	0.42	0.27	0.31	0.25	0.25
S11	0.67	0.39	0.23	0.29	0.25	0.04
S12	0.71	0.24	0.23	0.33	0.33	0.08
S13	0.44	0.48	0.44	0.18	0.36	0.52
S14	0.61	0.50	0.31	0.37	0.26	0.41
S15	0.87	0.41	0.19	0.32	0.20	0.10
Mean	**0.71**	**0.44**	**0.29**	**0.27**	**0.25**	**0.21**

As was mentioned above, one learner (S13) does not fit into this developmental pattern. In this student's case the dispersion between complexity, accuracy and fluency increased continuously throughout the learning period. This result should be analyzed together with the interplay of systems discussed above, which is expressed in their mutual interaction. This student was the only one in the entire group to be described as a perfect representative of the strong version of the Trade-Off Hypothesis: in her case there was clear competition between all systems throughout the entire three-year learning period. Her improvement in accuracy was achieved at the cost of complexity and/or fluency. All performance areas had definitely not yet stabilized in this learner. The process of integration, i.e. the development of several proficiency aspects in the second language, clearly took longer in this learner than in others.

8.1. Individual learner profiles

The interconnectedness of systems in language learning is evident not only in the more or less conscious juggling of several performance areas in a learner's mind, resulting in the uneven quality of particular utterance aspects, but also in the interplay apparent in general learner profiles. On the one hand, from the point of view of Dynamic Systems Theory, it may be impossible to distinguish between such common developmental tendencies in second language learners, due to the fact that dynamic systems behave chaotically and unpredictably. Furthermore, they develop nonlinearly and are greatly dependent on external resources that lead to their continuous reorganization, thanks to which it may be difficult to pick up the development attractor point, from which we would be able to look backwards and describe the process. The next obstacle may be the specificity of the target group. As was described earlier, development in adults is characterized by much greater variability than in children. Adult learners continue to move between optimal and functional levels, depending on the support they receive from the environment. This, in turn, makes their development more complex and more unpredictable.

On the other hand, however, the present study has repeatedly shown that despite the unicity and singularity of developmental paths and directions, a number of general tendencies were identified and some common learner characteristics emerged. We observed, for example, that some learners develop more dynamically than others, that students, who have been called "quick starters," i.e. those who develop faster than others, in later periods behave more unpredictably, on the one hand, but less dynamically, on the other. Furthermore, learners who need more time to internalize second language systems improve more in the long term. Finally, based on the interplay between selected systems four learner characteristics have been distinguished: risk-takers, careful learners, smart students and wanderers. At the same time, we stressed that due to variability these characteristics can change during the learning period, i.e. students may be careful at the beginning but later develop into smart learners. To sum up, we can also identify complexity and system interconnectedness within the same learner. Quick starters can become smart students or appear to be risk takers; careful learners can develop into smart students or turn into wanderers. However, in order to make more general statements or to determine if such common profiles in general exist, all proficiency dimensions should be analyzed in the context of their interaction within individuals and also with reference to other students. In order words: a retrodiction of development at both individual and group level is necessary.

As we have already shown, the interplay of systems in a learner's mind can be described using the traffic light metaphor. One dimension will be privileged more than the others and thus get the green light in second language production, while a second dimension will be less active but still present in the learner's mind (amber light) and the third will remain more neglected and not keep up with the development of the others (red light). Such behaviour has been observed when changes in development have been analyzed. However, one interesting task would be to discover if learners in general tend to prefer one performance aspect over another, not only in transition, i.e. when some of these increase and others decrease, but also whether such a focus is an inherent characteristic in individuals. Previous findings have suggested that these profiles in fact may exist: we have identified learners who for the most part produce more complex texts, learners who build correct but simple utterances (careful learners), and learners who produce lexically diverse but erroneous stories. From this point of view the development of all three dimensions needs to be studied in every learner.

Learner S1

This learner belongs undeniably to long-text writers. In all experiments the length of her texts far exceeded the average value. Figure 8.6 shows the values for all of the dimensions in every experiment. The diagram illustrates all aspects of complexity, accuracy and fluency in relation to the mean values for the entire group. The value "1" on the Y-axis represents the mean. Hence the fields above the X-axis represent a high (higher than the average) value for a given dimension, while the fields below the X-axis, on the other hand, represent a low (lower than the average) value. As the diagram illustrates, those long stories produced by learner S1 are characterized by highly diverse vocabulary. Moreover, this learner often achieved high levels in other aspects of complexity. At the same time, she wrote fluently – the high values for the mean length of burst suggest that she can write longer passages without a break. This student has the capacity to think complexly and does not focus on single words but tends instead to think in phrases or longer text units. The high level of both her complexity and fluency necessarily resulted in reduced accuracy. In general, however, the gap between complexity and fluency on the one hand, and accuracy on the other, is not so great. Accuracy tends to complement the development of other dimensions rather than compete with them. We can therefore describe this learner as a smart student, or a good learner, who has the capacity to integrate all proficiency dimensions in a second language. This corresponds with the concentration ratio for complexity, accuracy and fluency presented above, which in this student was already low at the very beginning of the learning period. This provides further support for the statement that she is able to manage all proficiency dimensions very well and can be described as a smart learner.

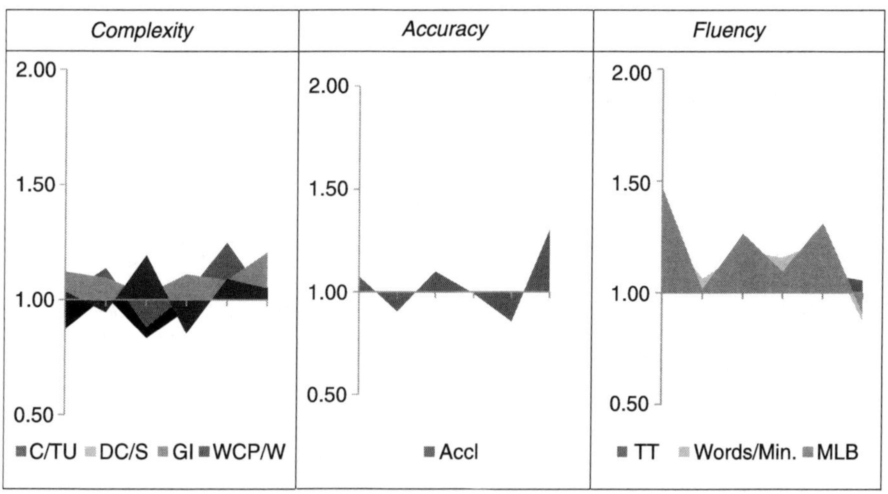

Figure 8.6. Levels of Complexity, Accuracy and Fluency in S1

Learner S2

Learner S2 undoubtedly focused on fluency (see Figure 8.7). Apart from the first experiment, when she wrote more slowly and less smoothly she constantly achieved a high level of fluency. At the same time, her stories are complex, especially in syntactical terms. However, fluency is this learner's most privileged dimension. However, thanks to a green light for fluency and amber for complexity, red is set for accuracy. Her fluently written and quite elaborate stories contain many errors. The integration of complexity, accuracy and fluency occurred no earlier than in the final experiment when all performance aspects were at a very high level. As has been mentioned earlier, this student spent a semester on a scholarship in Sweden and this occurred precisely during the sixth semester, such that her immersion in a new, Swedish speaking environment very clearly resulted in the integration of all performance dimensions. The specific interplay of systems in this student's case shows that she tended to be a risk taker with a focus on fluency.

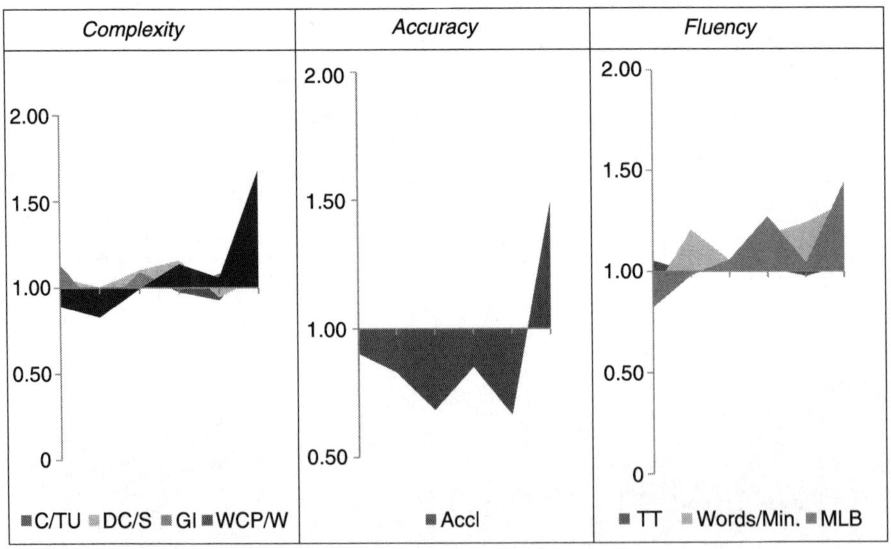

Figure 8.7. Levels of Complexity, Accuracy and Fluency in S2

Learner S3

As Figure 8.8 below shows, this student for the most part produced correct texts. Only at the final data collection point was her story not very accurate. Nevertheless, her most desired aim in second language learning was to avoid making errors. Her focus on accuracy did not negatively impact on her fluency. She can retrieve items in second language very quickly and has no problems processing them in her memory. On the other hand, she did not entirely neglect complexity, although it was undoubtedly the case that she focused less on this dimension than the other two. However, one dimension she can manage very well is syntactic complexity. The only underrepresented dimension appears to be lexical complexity. Also, even if her texts did not contain diverse and elaborate vocabulary she very often expressed her thoughts in the form of complex, diverse constructions. All these characteristics allow us to classify her as a smart student.

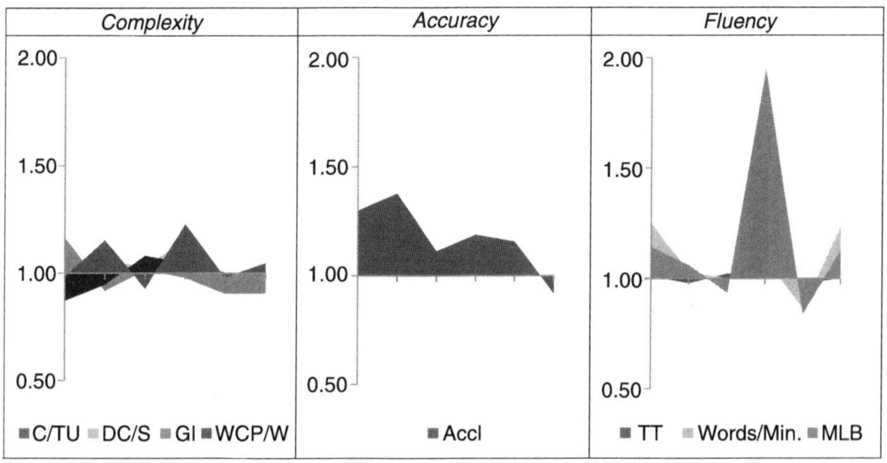

Figure 8.8. Levels of Complexity, Accuracy and Fluency in S3

Learner S4

This student had constant difficulties managing all proficiency dimensions in her mind (see Figure 8.9). Her complexity and accuracy levels were among the lowest. The results below show her to be the weakest learner in relation in her fellow students. Compared with the others she made the most errors and wrote the simplest texts. However, her fluency was good. From the discrepancy observed between the mean length of burst and general rapidity (the number of words produced in a minute) we can conclude that she was unable to process longer text units but tended to prefer to retrieve single words from her long-term memory, as a consequence of which for the most part she wrote quickly but with frequent pauses and corrections. However, this fluency clearly developed at the cost of accuracy and complexity. The strong polarization between several aspects of proficiency in her case is remarkable. As a result, she displayed the features of a wanderer, a slower developing learner. If we begin with the hypothesis that the weakest link reflects the behaviour of the entire system we could risk the conclusion that fluency is the first dimension that second language learners develop. They base themselves on simple linguistic entities, such as words or simple structures, and it is against this background that they develop other linguistic skills. This claim has, however, already been made in this study, in the sense that this dimension developed in the majority of the learners at the very beginning of the study, during the first year of second language learning.

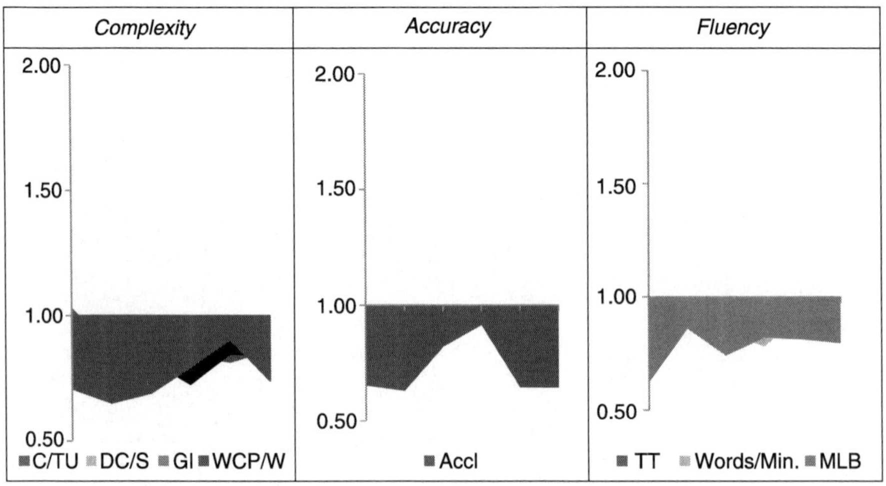

Figure 8.9. Levels of Complexity, Accuracy and Fluency in S4

Learner S5

Learner S5 definitely does not provide a homogenous picture as the students presented above (see Figure 8.10). As we can see from the diagrams below there is a wide spread between several aspects of proficiency in this learner. Some areas of complexity are still underrepresented while others are privileged. Accuracy is sometimes high, sometimes low, and even fluency varies greatly. However, what we did observe is that this student focused on using a wide variety of different words. He demonstrated a high level of lexical diversity in all the experiments. This was combined with high and even very high levels of fluency. The texts produced by the student were rather simple and varied in their accuracy. His language behaviour remained in some way similar to that of learner S2, in the sense that both are fluent writers with one aspect of complexity in the foreground. In the case of S5, however, it is not the interconnectedness of items that is of importance. Rather, he tends to prefer to deliver an interesting story by using a wide range of words. However, contrary to S2, he did not exhibit the features of a risk taker due to the fact that his accuracy levels were much higher than those of his fellow students. He resembles far more a smart learner, but with a tendency to write simple and interesting texts that do not necessary involve complex structures.

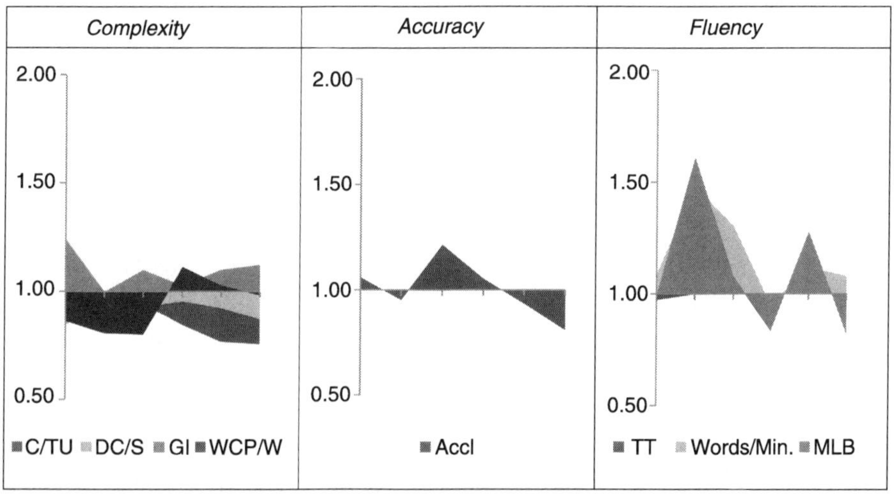

Figure 8.10. Levels of Complexity, Accuracy and Fluency in S5

Learner S6

This student paid most attention to accuracy (see Figure 8.11). Therefore, this dimension of proficiency got green light in her mind. At the same time her texts are not simple. They were characterized by a high degree of lexical complexity. In the narratives produced by this learner the sentences are very often composed of complex phrases rather than single words put together to form a clause. However, this complexity cannot be observed at a syntactic level. She used few subordinated clauses and even the clauses and structures she built are not diverse. Hence, we cannot argue that her texts were complex overall – they were complex only at a lexical level. Furthermore, she was not fluent. It also took her a great deal of time to form her correct and lexically complex utterances and during her text production in her second language she often stopped in order to think about the next sequence or correct herself – probably in order to produce as correct a text as possible. Low fluency and syntactic complexity also resulted from her focus on accuracy. She should therefore be classified as a careful learner.

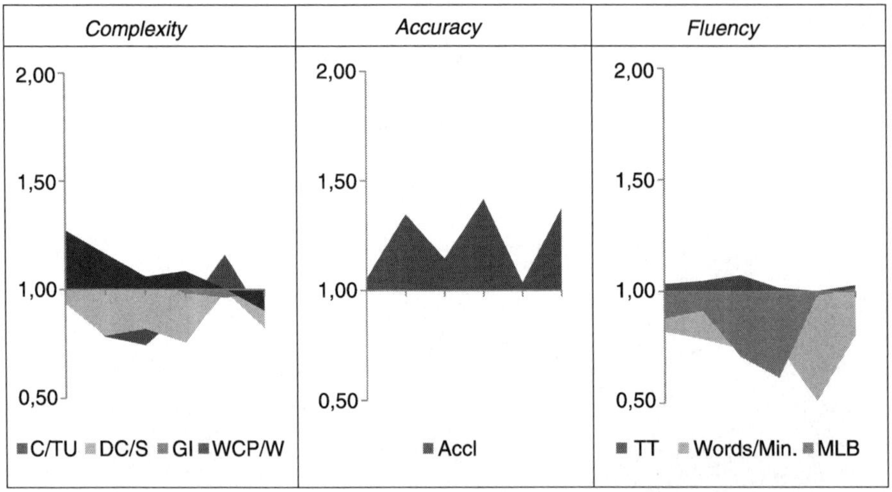

Figure 8.11. Levels of Complexity, Accuracy and Fluency in S6

Learner S7

Learner S7 represents a very interesting profile (see Figure 8.12). When we look at her levels of complexity, accuracy and fluency the first impression is that she is a student with a tendency to write simple and incorrect texts, but who is quite fluent. However, the development of this learner is much more complex than this description would suggest. She is the kind of learner who makes many errors when they produce texts in a second language, and when she did so she often stopped and wrote in shorter units. This characteristic was observed throughout the entire study. Beginning from the second half her second year of learning Swedish, however, she improved significantly in terms of complexity. From being very simple her stories became more complex and, above all else, more diversified: both lexically and syntactically. Her way of thinking in short chunks shows her to be a fluent writer. However, she is fluent in terms of her rapidity in text production. Neither the increase in her complexity nor the fairly high level of her fluency led to any progress in accuracy, which in turn appears to be the dimension she had the greatest difficulties in processing. As was the case with learner S4 she was one of the slower developing participants in the study, focusing on the stylistic side of her utterances (which manifested itself in a high level of lexical and syntactic diversity) and to some degree also on fluency.

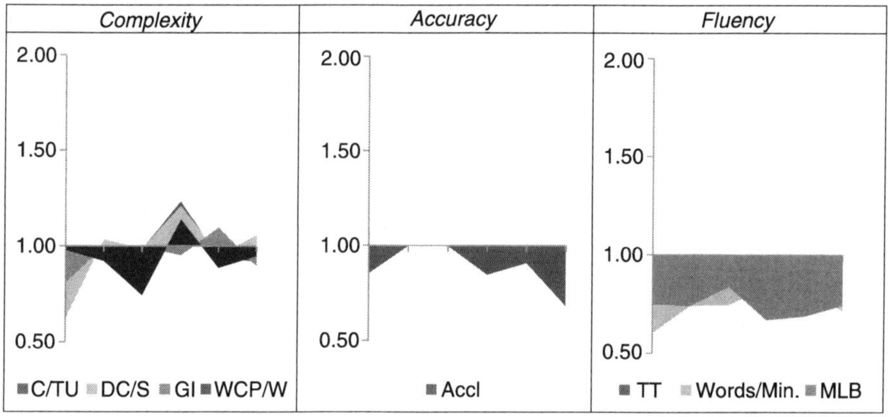

Figure 8.12. Levels of Complexity, Accuracy and Fluency in S7

Learner S8

Learner S8 (see Figure 8.13) has the profile of a risk taker. She writes very complex texts and does so with a high level of fluency, which, however, greatly affected her accuracy as she had one of the lowest levels in the group throughout the entire three-year learning period. The main feature of this student's texts was that they include a wide range of different clauses and clause-like constructions, which makes them highly diversified. At the lexical level, however, her texts tended not to be so elaborate. Based on an analysis of this learner's lexical-semantic errors she can be classified as a wanderer due to a low level of accuracy and low lexical diversity. However, a deeper examination of all dimensions leads us to the conclusion that this student was actually taking risks, using very complex sentences, without slowing down the tempo of her writing and without reflecting upon the correctness of her texts.

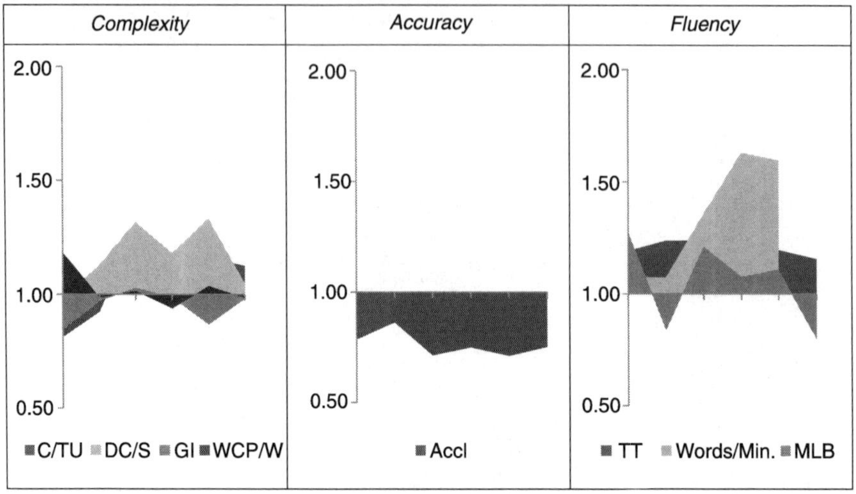

Figure 8.13. Levels of Complexity, Accuracy and Fluency in S8

Learner S9

As the figure below (Figure 8.14) illustrates, learner S9 was characterised by constantly low levels of accuracy and very high levels of complexity and fluency. In this sense her profile remains the same as that of learner S8 described above. She expressed her thoughts in very complex forms in her second language and did so with a very high level of fluency. The difference between her and student S8 is, however, that she not only produced many diversified sentences but also had the tendency to use a lot of subordinated clauses, which made her texts even more complex than those written by S8. This learner should also be classified as a risk-taker.

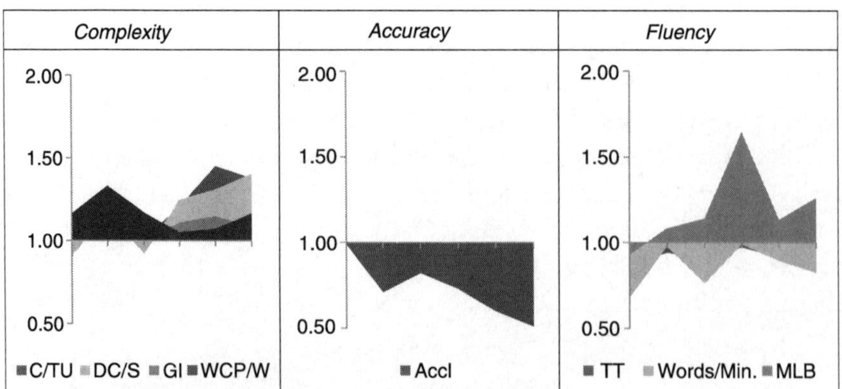

Figure 8.14. Levels of Complexity, Accuracy and Fluency in S9

Learner S10

As presented in Figure 8.15 below, the accuracy of this student was low throughout the entire period of study, but remarkable progress can be observed in the second part of the three-year period, when the normative level of her texts did not diverge as much from the average as it did during the first three semesters. She is a fluent writer but one who prefers to write quickly, although in short units. Therefore, both her automaticity and rapidity in text production were at a high level, while her mean length of burst was low. In this student we observed an interconnection between a decline in smoothness on the one hand and accuracy on the other. As soon as she began to make more frequent pauses her accuracy increased. This learner only achieved a high score in one aspect of complexity: lexical interconnection between words. She tended to use simple vocabulary, although she managed to weave it into a variety of structures. Based on this characteristic this learner could be classified as a risk taker. However, this feature is not as clearly evident in learner S10 as it is, for example, in S8 or S9, where more facets of complexity were in the foreground. This profile is more applicable in the first half of the study when she very clearly wrote complex sentences, had a high level of fluency and a very low level of accuracy. Afterwards she became a more careful learner, focusing more on accuracy than she did at the beginning of the learning period.

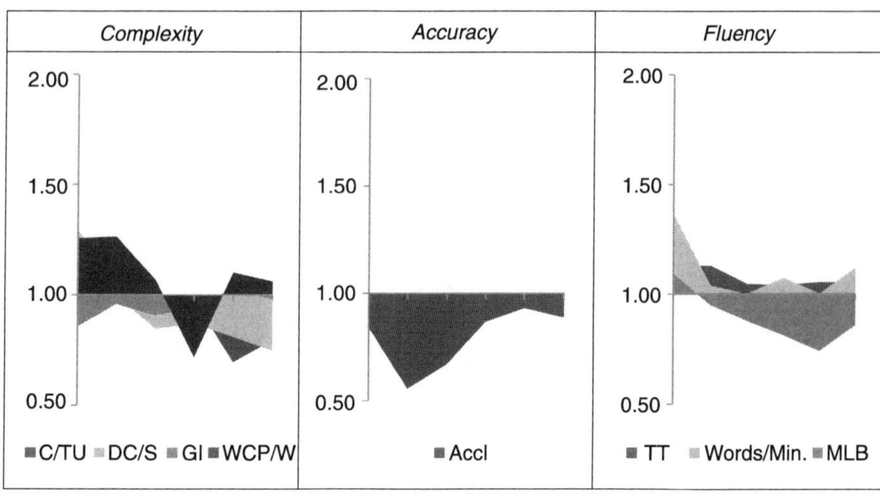

Figure 8.15. Levels of Complexity, Accuracy and Fluency in S10

Learner S11

The most striking observation from the figure below (Figure 8.16) is that this learner continuously achieved a very high level of accuracy. In fact, he outperformed all students in this dimension. Also, his complexity remained high during the entire learning period. This focus on correctness had no impact on the interconnectedness between lexical and syntactic items. However, as the Trade-Off Hypothesis predicts, this dimension did not have the same priority in his mind as accuracy and therefore only received "amber light" treatment. However, the exceptionally high values achieved for accuracy and complexity translated into very low fluency. This learner appears to have checked himself all the time and his desire to build elaborate and correct texts necessarily resulted in a low tempo and many disruptions during the writing process. An analysis of the learner's lexical and syntactic accuracy reveals him to be either a smart learner or a learner who was careful only at the beginning before becoming a smart learner. When we take fluency into consideration we must without doubt classify him as a careful learner who achieved good results for the most part after a long process of thinking, re-formulating and self-correction.

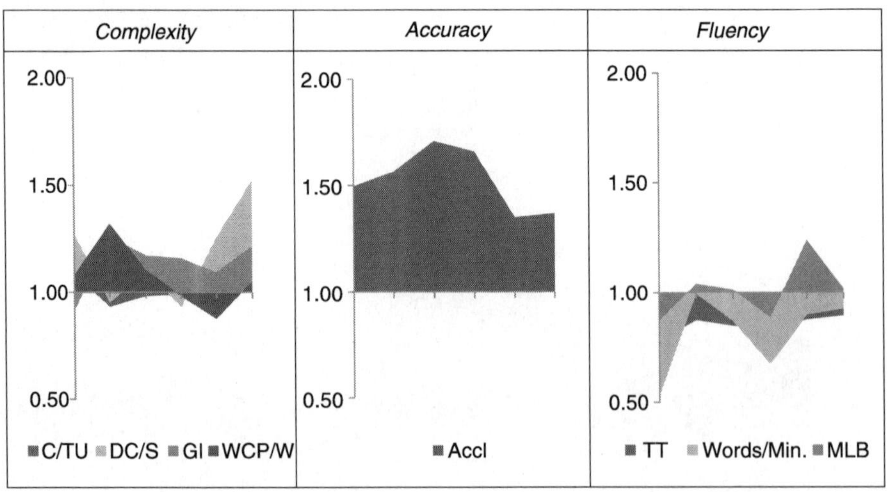

Figure 8.16. Levels of Complexity, Accuracy and Fluency in S11

Learner S12

The profile of this learner is in many aspects the same as that of S11 described above. In addition, this student wrote very correct stories, although at the cost of poor fluency. Not only did this learner have a slower tempo in general, but most importantly her smoothness was at a low level: she seemed to think about every word she wrote, which is reflected in her short mean length of burst. As with student S11 she was able to build complex utterances, which was particularly remarkable at the beginning of the study. According to these characteristics, she should be described as a careful learner.

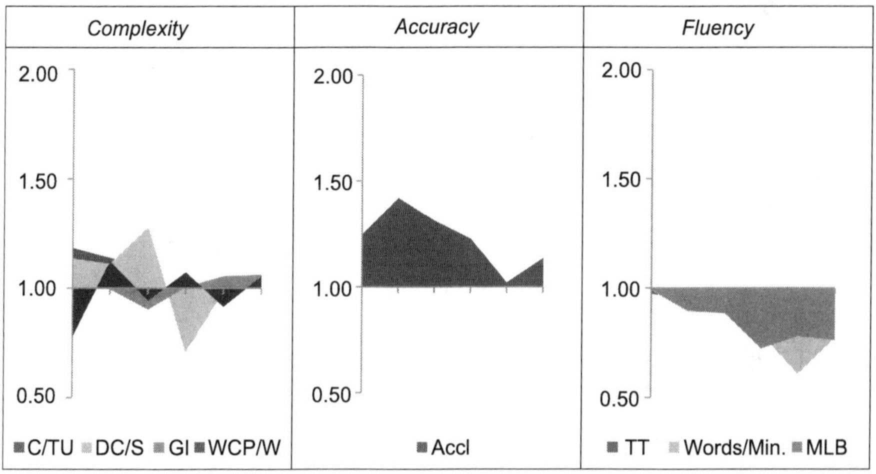

Figure 8.17. Levels of Complexity, Accuracy and Fluency in S12

Learner S13

We stated earlier that this learner represents a strong version of the Trade--Off Hypothesis. She was the only student in the entire group in whom the dispersion between all proficiency dimensions did not decrease during the three-year study period and who probably needs more time to operate these aspects in her mind. The singularity of this student is also noticeable in the interplay of complexity, accuracy and fluency in her case, when seen from a group perspective. As the figure below shows (Figure 8.18) she is the only learner whose profile is very unambiguous, compared with the student above discussed. Her development corresponds to that of a quick-starter profile. In her first experiment she produced a complex and fluent text that was fairly correct. Beginning from the second experiment, however, she clearly started to write very slowly with many breaks, used simple constructions and made numerous errors. She is also a learner who developed very dynamically. We can observe single peaks in her complexity and accuracy, which have already been discussed in previous chapters. Despite these accidental spurts in various dimensions, indicating a high degree of splitting in this learner's dimensions, she can be described as a wanderer, i.e. a student whose development was slower than that of others.

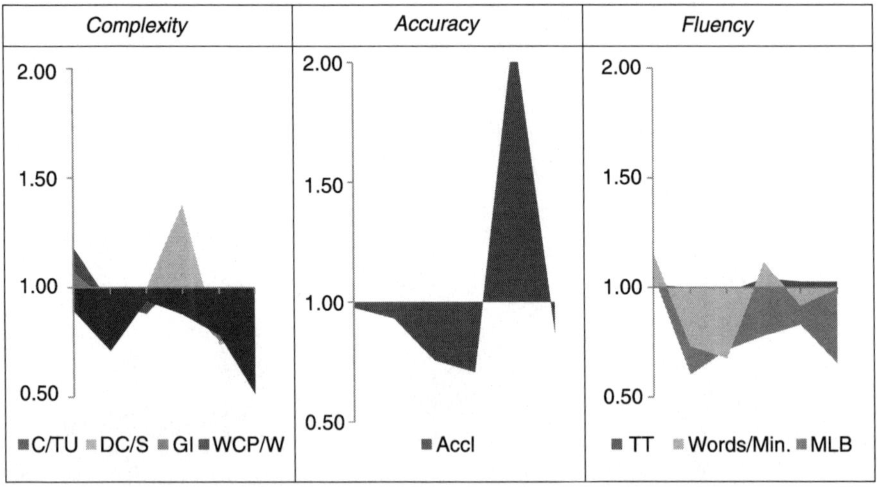

Figure 8.18. Levels of Complexity, Accuracy and Fluency in S13

Learner S14

As we can see from the figure below (Figure 8.19) student S14 is clearly a learner whose accuracy is low and fluency high. In his case these two dimensions were clearly competing with one another. On the other hand, his complexity is not as unique in form as his other two proficiency areas are. He is definitely a learner who is highly capable of connecting words in complex phrases such that he could be described as a learner of high complexity. In the first experiment, learner S14 also had the highest level of syntactic complexity. On the other hand, all other aspects of complexity were low, which gives us the impression that he tried to write complex texts but needed more time to internalize new words and new structures in his second language, which would have enabled him to make use of all aspects of complexity in his texts. Learner S14's high levels of fluency and complexity, combined with his poor accuracy indicates that he tends to be a risk taker who additionally exhibits quick-starter-properties.

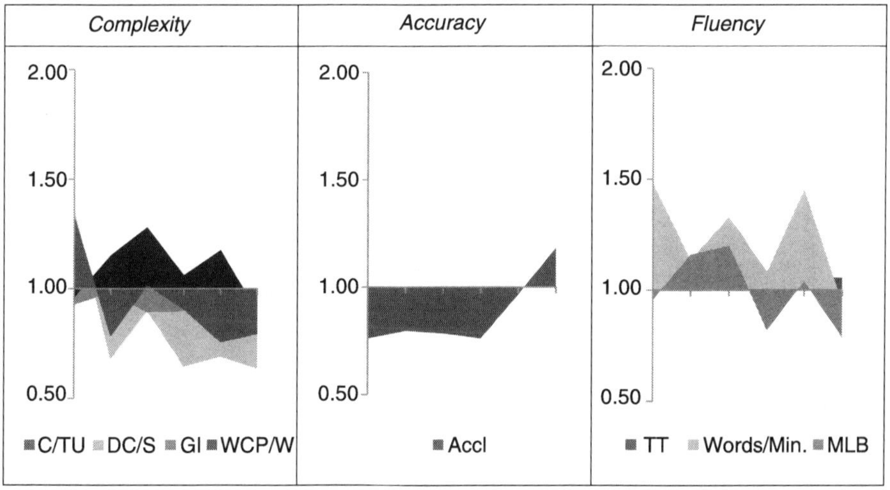

Figure 8.19. Levels of Complexity, Accuracy and Fluency in S14

Learner S15

The last of the fifteen students in the study stands out due to her very high level of fluency (see Figure 8.20), not only in terms of the rapidity of her text production but above all due to her smoothness. She has the ability to think and operate the new language in longer passes, which was especially remarkable in the last experiment when she demonstrated the highest level of fluency in the entire group. However, this learner also achieved high scores in other dimensions. She wrote lexically and syntactically complex texts and did so with above average accuracy. Although she clearly focused more on fluency and complexity than accuracy, she is undoubtedly a smart learner in whom the interplay between systems tended to be more complementary than competitive in character. When we compare her with other smart learners in this group we can argue that she was able to internalize all dimensions better than any of the other students.

As the analysis above shows, no two learners exhibited the same second language behaviour. We admittedly identified four profiles, depending on what dimension(s) were most prioritised during the entire study period. However, due to the diversity and complexity of several aspects of all three dimensions, even within these categories obvious differences existed within individuals. The general characteristics of the "risk taker" profile encompassed learners who demonstrated high levels of fluency and complexity, but whose accuracy was poor. Students in this group are

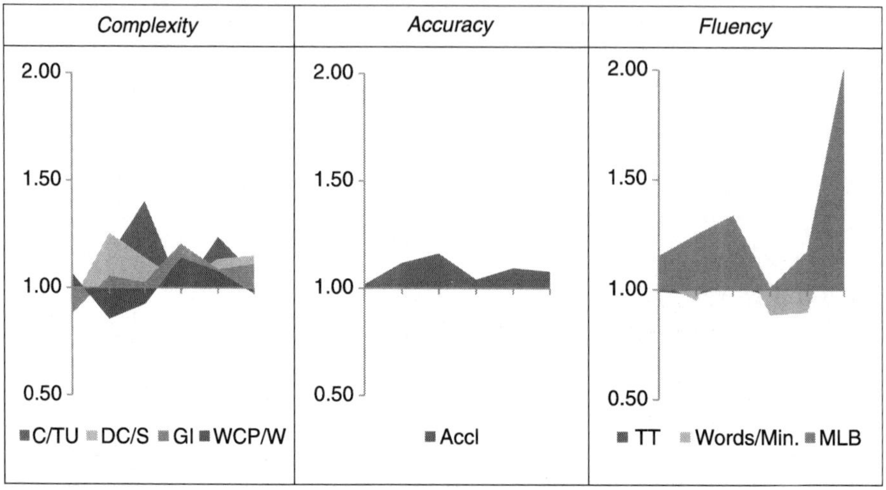

Figure 8.20. Levels of Complexity, Accuracy and Fluency in S15

assumed to take risks in the sense that they try to use elaborate vocabulary and complex structures but fail in their ability to process it correctly. Their high level of fluency indicates that they do not even think very long about what they wish to communicate in text form in their new language. Five of the learners in the investigated group (S2, S8, S9, S10 and S14) were identified as risk-takers. The opposite profile is composed of careful learners. This group is characterized by high levels of accuracy and complexity with simultaneously low levels of fluency. These students will for the most part produce utterances that are correct. They also possess a rich vocabulary and a wide range of different syntactic structures. Setting such high demands for themselves necessarily leads to a low tempo of writing due to the fact that they often check themselves, make corrections, reorganize their texts in order to make them as correct as possible from both a normative and a stylistic point of view. Such learners often receive very high grades from second language teachers and appear to be good students whose aim is to take advantage of newly learned words and structures. Three learners in the present study (S6, S11, S12) belong to this profile. The next characteristic concerns learners who may in some way resemble careful learners. They definitely do not experiment with their newly learned language but tend to still be in the process of finding the key to it. Such students have been called "wanderers" due to the fact that they seem to be in search of ways to integrate the new systems in themselves. Wanderers perform poorly in all three dimensions, which is an indicator that, perhaps due to the slower tempo of their development, they do not feel stable in the world of their new language and therefore have not yet chosen which aspect they will focus on. Three of the learners (S4, S7, S13) in this study were classified as wanderers. This picture leads to the assumption, however, that the key may lie in fluency, because this dimension was best developed in all these students: it was also the only dimension where some continuity at a higher level was observed. In the case of learner S13 it did not occur until the second part of the study, although fluency undoubtedly appears to have been the first dimension to develop. The final group of learners was referred to as "smart learners" due to the fact that they scored highly in all three dimensions. This outcome, of course, does not rule out the Trade-Off Hypothesis, because, as we have shown, with each individual one dimension is always given more focus than others. On the other hand, differences have been observed even between these higher levels of complexity, accuracy and fluency. Four learners (S1, S3, S5, S15) in this group have this profile and each one paid more attention to another dimension.

When discussing individual learner profiles we need to be aware of their limitations. Firstly, their purpose should not be to appraise character but rather should be treated solely as a means of describing characteristics. Therefore, the "wanderer" profile should be understood exclusively to mean a learner who develops more slowly rather than being seen as a "poor learner." A "careful learner" should in no way be associated with individuals who are worse than "risk takers," because they avoid experimenting with new linguistic features etc. These profiles have been distinguished because of certain differentiating features shared by individual learners. This rather stable tendency to behave like a risk taker, a careful learner, a wanderer or a smart student matches very well with one feature of chaotic behaviour that has not been emphasized until now but which is one of its three basic features. As was described earlier in the book, chaotic behaviour is characterized by a sensitivity to initial conditions, unpredictability and boundedness. The first two have been discussed at length in this book. For example, when a learner's development is very rapid at the beginning, bifurcation may occur. Unpredictability, on the other hand, was observed at many points when we discussed nonlinearity in the development of certain dimensions and it shows that we never can predict what direction a developmental trajectory can take in individuals. Boundedness, however, has not been discussed. As a feature that describes situations where the elements of systems do not leave their state space, even when behaving unpredictably, it cannot be precisely detected in the case of learner profiles. Even if learners develop dynamically and sometimes peak in one dimension, or begin at a very high level, they cannot exceed their own capacity, or, in other words, completely change their learner profile – so they do not leave their own state space. Of course, this does not rule out the possibility of further development, but we could risk arguing that a careful learner will never be a risk taker or a smart learner – wanderer. In this sense the boundedness of systems should be understood in the context of second language development.

8.2. The developmental sequence of Complexity, Accuracy and Fluency

A description of all the proficiency dimensions would have been expected to reveal a developmental sequence, based on the assumptions of Housen, Kuiken & Vadder (2012) and Skehan and Foster (2012). In this sequence, complexity is the dimension that should develop earliest in learners, followed by accuracy and, finally, fluency. However, in light of the present study, another order emerges that can be presented as follows:

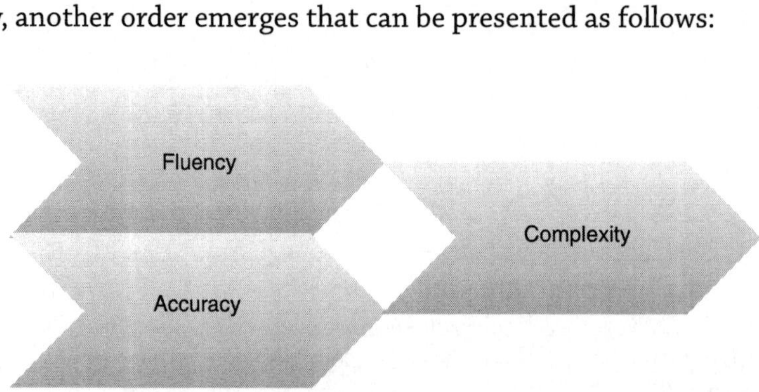

Figure 8.21. Developmental sequence of Complexity, Accuracy and Fluency

In many places we observed a huge increase in both fluency and accuracy in the first three semesters of learning Swedish, which corresponds to approximately 500 hours of learning. Complexity, however, began to develop later and higher growth rates were observed in individuals in the second year of the study. Almost all the learners achieved rapid development in fluency and accuracy during this period. Due to the variation between individuals we cannot state unequivocally which dimension develops first. In some students both fluency and accuracy were already developing in their first year of learning, while in others either the former or the latter had priority of development. Apart from this, we additionally observed that the strongest dimension of subjects who had been characterized as wanderers was fluency. The third argument suggesting that learners prefer to begin with fluency and/or accuracy concerns the developmental patterns of complexity. Students who tried to use complex constructions at the beginning of the study tended to abandon this way of writing, which in some ways may resemble being "short of breath" through overtraining. When we set the bar too high our body/mind cannot keep up with this tempo of development. These observations lead us to assume that second language learners tend to build their new language on the basis of simple constructions, internalizing and automatizing these unelaborate units, so that they can be prepared for the next step, i.e. reorganizing these simple elements, and putting them together in larger networks. When they begin with fluency and accuracy, they create a kind of framework, a skeleton that they afterwards fill with muscles, i.e. complexity.

9

Conclusions

Dynamic Systems Theory investigates complex systems and describes how these systems change over time. The transformation of complex, dynamic systems is never linear in fashion. They behave chaotically and their development is thus unpredictable. A minor change in the initial phases can have major consequences in the future. Therefore, such chaotic behaviour makes it impossible to predict how a transition from one state to another will proceed. Furthermore, when considering complex systems we cannot treat them separately from one another because all their parts are interconnected. A change in behaviour in one system by necessity leads to the reorganization of others. There is also considerable variation both within several systems and between them. In developmental studies intra-individual variability indicates that a system is undergoing dynamic change and is far from being in a state of equilibrium. Variation between systems, on the other hand, suggests that they are in different phases of development.

Because Dynamic Systems Theory focus on the behaviour of complex systems and describes how they change over time it has also proven useful in second language studies. In this area it investigates how a new language emerges in second language learners. Hitherto studies, conducted from the point of view of DST, have investigated second language development in a few learners and with a dense data collection point. What was missing, however, were longitudinal studies analyzing a larger set of individuals, where the focus is not on investigating different groups at different levels, but rather on tracing the development of the individuals forming a single group. The present study was conceived with a view to filling this gap. Its aim was to follow the development of fifteen young adults with Polish as their L1 who were beginning to learn a new language (Swedish) in a classroom environment. Their development was followed in all stages, starting from the first semester and ending with the end of the third year of learning Swedish. The study was not microdevelopmental but rather macrodevelopmental in character due to the fact that experimental sessions took place at the end of every semester, i.e. after about every 120–150 hours of second language classes.

The overriding aim of the project was to follow the dynamics of the development of Complexity, Accuracy and Fluency during a three-year period of second language learning and trace the interplay of several dimensions both in individuals and at group level. In this study a wide range of aspects of every dimension was investigated and a number of new measures proposed. In the case of complexity, both lexical and syntactic complexity were discussed. More specifically, within both these aspects the diversity of systems and their interconnection was studied both separately and in the mutual interplay between them. When it came to accuracy, on the other hand, not only was the general correctness studied but so too was the distribution of particular errors, such as morphological, syntactic, lexical-semantic and spelling mistakes. Fluency, in turn, was examined from the point of view of automaticity, rapidity in text production, and smoothness. According to the necessary interplay of dynamic systems the mutual impact of every dimension on particular aspects was also traced, as a consequence of which four learner profiles could be identified. Finally, the conducted analysis provided the basis for a proposed developmental sequence for complexity, accuracy and fluency.

The most important feature of complexity is that it does not develop dynamically, either on the basis of the average values for the group as a whole or in individuals. It should be stressed that in general the mean values very seldom correspond with individual developmental trajectories and therefore they should serve more as a reference point for the analysis of the developmental stage in individuals than as a universal indicator of change. Another drawback of mean values in developmental studies is that they smooth out the real growth rates and can distort the development dynamics.

Lexical diversity tended to increase slowly, with low growth rates between experiments and only in five learners was any dynamic development observed in the first year of learning Swedish. The majority of the students did not achieve dynamic progress in lexical diversity. Their six-month growth rates were slow. This sluggish development was also reflected in intra-indiviudal variability, where only three students showed any significant fluctuation during the three-year study while all the others reorganized their vocabulary diversity without any such dramatic change. Differences between individuals turned out to be slight, with the coefficient of variation remaining stable at 10% during the entire period, which indicates that the students had comparable levels of vocabulary diversity. Furthermore, lexical interconnectedness developed differently from the mean. In the majority of students the path to connecting words in complex phrases proceeds more dynamically than did the development of lexical diversity. In a few learners it had already developed by the end of the first year of learning Swedish, but others needed at least half a year more to create networks of words they had learned in the new language.

Syntactic complexity also appeared to develop on a highly individual basis rather than proceed harmoniously with the mean. Contrary to lexical complexity, however, the learners were clearly polarised in this case, which was also reflected in greater inter-subject variation. Some students were characterised by ongoing, high syntactic complexity, expressed both in their subordination ratio and in the diversity of the syntactic constructions they used. Others, on the other hand, were second language users with consistently low levels of complexity and even though both groups developed, these differences between learners even increased during the study. For subjects with low levels of syntactic complexity there is a tendency to develop during the first two years and to achieve an attractor point, after which complexity hardly changes at all. For those writers who achieved an extremely high level of complexity after just six months of learning Swedish, a bifurcation was observed and the developmental trajectories clearly diverged from each other. Very rapid development at the beginning of second language learning can thus lead to unpredictable results in long-term achievement. Learners may have a greater capacity to improve in particular dimensions, but they can also remain at the same level or their ability to operate a given feature can even decrease. Regardless of whether we look at the development of high achievers or students with lower levels of complexity, their intra-individual variability remains at a low level, just as it does in the case of lexical complexity, which indicates that complexity in the second language is not developing dynamically.

Accuracy has the ability to develop very dynamically and considerable progress was observed in almost all the learners. The new proposed measure made it possible to trace the development of correctness by focusing on error frequency. As in the case of complexity, the mean developmental path tended to suggest a smooth, almost linear increase in accuracy, with half-year growth rates not exceeding 20%. Individual trajectories, however, reveal an altogether different picture. In almost all the students a spurt in accuracy occurred during their first three semesters of learning Swedish when individual growth rates can reach up to 50%. After this period accuracy tended to stabilize and only in a few students was any additional dynamic increase observed at the end of the study. Students differed considerably from each other in terms of their accuracy levels during the entire three-year period. Inter-subject variation was twice as high as it was for complexity and did not fall, which again is a sign of significant polarization between learners, and despite the considerable progress made by individuals these differences remain unchanged. Unchanging variation in development is not only proof of individual differences that exist permanently and are not smoothed out in the same learning environment, initial conditions, amount of input, age etc., but is also an indirect indicator of different tempos of development in individuals.

An analysis of the different types of errors made by the students revealed that the most common mistakes were lexical-semantic in character. Such inaccuracies declined very sharply over the course of the entire study. To process lexical-semantic systems in a second language appears to be the most difficult part of second language achievement. In half of the students progress in lexical-semantic accuracy began no earlier than in the second year of learning and it continued throughout the entire period without reaching an attractor point. The polarization of the learners revealed two developmental patterns: in learners with a higher error ratio language development remained an S-curve, where following a prolonged phase of high error frequency a sharp decline was observed, after which the system stabilized. On the other hand, in the case of students who operated more effectively in the lexical-semantic system, development resembled a sinusoid with low variability, which indicates that an attractor had been approached. However, in learners with extremely high accuracy levels the developmental trajectories had once more already diverged from each other in the first semester of learning Swedish, which resulted in bifurcation.

When it comes to morphologic accuracy development another picture emerges. Most students mastered this language sub-system very early on and the greatest progress in this aspect of accuracy was primarily noted during the first year of learning, which was a common characteristic in both learners with low and high error ratios. As in the case of lexical-semantic accuracy discrepancies were observed in the developmental trajectories of individuals, such that an attractor state was approached in students with high accuracy levels much earlier. Moreover, their development was characterized by much lower within-subject variability than is the case with learners who need more time to internalize morphologic structures in second language learning and therefore make more errors.

The development of syntactic accuracy proceeded similarly to morphologic accuracy and the most significant progress in almost all students occurred in the first year of learning. The extent of this change is, however, even greater than it is for morphologic accuracy, which may be interconnected with the developmental sequence of these systems. Second language morphology probably developed earlier, perhaps already in the first few months, while syntax needs a little more time to be internalized in a learners' mind so that the most significant spurt in morphologic accuracy would have occurred before the experimental sessions began. Also, the same patterns were observed in the case of syntactic accuracy, namely that learners who develop earlier, behave less dynamically in later phases, while slower developing students are characterized by greater intra-individual variability.

In the classroom context, and especially in second language learning at university level, spelling has an important function in the development of a new language. Unlike in the informal, natural environment, mastering spelling rules constitutes an inherent part of second language internalization. In the present study spelling errors constituted the least frequent error category with the doubling of consonants being the most frequent error type. However, it turned out to be the only category with such diversified developmental trajectories. In some learners spelling accuracy increased, while in others it remained at the same level and in others accuracy declined. Moreover, this unpredictable developmental direction was primarily evident in learners with the highest level of spelling accuracy at the beginning of the study, which necessarily led to a bifurcation in development. Although typos were excluded from the analysis, the assumption exists that the frequency of spelling errors may be interconnected with typing speed. This hypothesis was not confirmed in the present study. In the interplay between the time needed to move between the keyboard keys and the ratio of spelling errors speed only had a negative impact on spelling accuracy in 20% of the students. In the majority of learners the development of typing speed and spelling accuracy even went hand in hand.

Differences between learners in overall accuracy are more evident in the distribution of errors in individuals. The analysis shows that regardless of the error ratio many learners develop accuracy in several language systems in parallel. When they make many errors, the frequency is high in all types of them. When their accuracy is high, it is high at every language level. And this occurred not only throughout the entire study but also at single points in language development, which should be interpreted as a normal situation due to the fact that adult learners in particular often shift from the optimal to the functional level and therefore sometimes perform better, and sometimes worse, depending on the resources supplied. On the other hand, some learners constantly focus more on selected aspects of the language and thus perform better at the syntactic or the lexical level. Finally, learners' attention can shift between particular aspects of the second language during their development and they may change their focus from, e.g. syntax towards vocabulary in later phases. In light of these characteristics we can never predict how systems will interact and how this will take shape in an individual's development. Even if the general assumption and expectation that second language learners will improve in accuracy after three years of learning has been confirmed, the complexity and chaotic behaviour of all systems deprives us of the ability to predict the tempo and trajectory of second language development.

The third dimension analysed in this study – fluency – must, just like the other two, be treated as a complex and dynamic system. In the present study this complexity was mirrored by an analysis of three aspects of fluency: automaticity, rapidity in text production and smoothness. Overall, fluency turned out to be the only investigated feature in which a unique developmental pattern was observed. It increased steadily in all learners throughout the entire learning period, although at a different tempo and with different growth rates. Students, whose language use became automatic during the first 300 hours of their second language instruction, approached an attractor state earlier and their later development was characterized by much lower dynamics than those observed in learners who needed more time to automatize new words and structures in their new language. This divergence, however, evened out after three years, as was observed in the decreasing inter-learner variation, so that the learners achieved a similar level of fluency after ca 800 hours of second language instruction. Such decreasing variation between learners only concerned this dimension. In the case of both accuracy and complexity divergences between students oscillated around the same level.

Rapidity and smoothness develop much more dynamically than automaticity, but both are characterized by the same feature: they increase most sharply at the beginning of the learning period, i.e. in the first three semesters, with half-year growth rates reaching 100%, which parallels the development of accuracy, where the first phases of learning were most crucial. Individual developmental trajectories do not reflect the pattern that emerged from the mean values, which, again, reveals a smoothed, almost linear and therefore distorted picture of a student's development. All three aspects of fluency were closely interconnected with each other and they developed in parallel with each other in every learner. This interconnectedness occurred not only between automaticity, rapidity and smoothness, but also extended to other systems, such as, e.g., lexical diversity. Automaticity, as an effect of an increased vocabulary richness, develops earlier than rapidity and smoothness achieves an attractor state and triggers the reorganization and further development of other aspects of fluency – faster text production and thinking in longer text units.

The dynamics in development and the complexity of systems involved in second language learning necessarily implies some interplay between the systems in action. The previous hypothesis implied that second language learners cannot focus on all proficiency dimensions simultaneously and with the same attention. This so-called Trade-Off Hypothesis was confirmed in the present study, although manifested in two versions: a stronger and a softer one. In the strong version progress in one or two dimensions necessary causes a decrease in two others (or in one other). In the softer version, on the other hand, the learner prioritises one (or two) dimension(s) as privileged, while the other (two) remain in the background and develop with lower growth rates than those placed in the foreground. This second language behaviour has been compared in this book with driving at a road junction with traffic lights. The dimension given the most focus is compared to the green light. The learner pays the greatest attention to it and this is the dimension in which he or she makes the most improvement. The less focused dimension(s), i.e. that(those) in which we can also see progress but not as remarkable as in the case of the strongest dimension, can be described as representing the amber light – you are allowed to drive but not as freely as with the green light. Finally, the competing dimension(s), which is (are) by necessity neglected when the learner improves in others, can then be symbolized with a red light. Inter-subject variation and the ongoing reorganization of systems ensured that no single dimension was prioritised by all the learners during the entire three-year period. In some cases accuracy was the feature given most focus, while in others it was complexity and in yet others it was fluency. And even if some students placed one or two dimensions in the foreground for the majority of the learning period, there were points in their development where another dimension came first. The discrepancy between the "green" dimension and the other two developed in line with another characteristic of dynamic systems, namely the principle of system reorganization. With the exception of one learner, who during the entire learning period represented the strong version of the Trade-Off Hypothesis, all other learners exhibited a unique developmental tendency. At the beginning of the second language learning process accuracy, complexity and fluency are not integrated in a learner's mind and they tend to act in an arbitrary fashion. This manifests itself in situations where one dimension clearly gains more attention than the other two. During second language development integration of all dimensions proceeds steadily and after three years of learning the discrepancy between different aspects of proficiency is very low.

The interplay between accuracy, complexity and fluency in second language learners undergoes constant change and the chaotic behaviour of the systems involved makes it impossible to predict how development in individuals will proceed and how the dimensions will interact with each other. However, the present study has shown again and again that despite the unicity and singularity of developmental paths and directions, some general tendencies were observed and some common learner characteristics emerged. We noted, for example, that some learners develop more dynamically than others, that students who have been called "quick starters," i.e. those who develop more quickly than others, behave more unpredictably in later periods, although less dynamically. Furthermore, learners who need more time to internalize second language systems make more improvement in the long term. Moreover, an analysis of the interplay between lexical-semantic accuracy and lexical diversity showed that four types of learners can be recognized. The first group is called risk-takers. These are students who achieved high levels of complexity and fluency, but who do not pay much attention to correctness. Learners who belong to this group are assumed to be risk takers in the sense that they try to use elaborate vocabulary and complex structures but fail in their ability to process these structures accurately. Their high level of fluency indicates that they do not even think very long about what they deliver in the form of a text in their new language. The next group, i.e. careful learners, builds the opposite profile. This group is characterized by high levels of accuracy and complexity while simultaneously achieving low levels of fluency. These students will for the most part produce utterances that are correct, involve a rich vocabulary and a wide range of different syntactic structures. By setting such high standards for themselves they inevitably write at a slow tempo due to the fact that they often check themselves, make corrections, and reorganize their texts in order to make them as correct as possible from both a normative and a stylistic point of view. Such learners often receive very high grades from their second language teachers and appear to be good students whose goal is to take advantage of their newly learned words and structures. The next learner profile is the "wanderer," due to the fact that this type of learner appears to be looking for ways to integrate new systems in themselves. Wanderers are characterized by low levels of all three dimensions, which is an indicator that, maybe due to their slower tempo of development, they do not feel stable in the world of the new language and therefore have not yet chosen which aspect they will focus on. The final group of students are called "smart learners," due to the fact that they are strong in all three dimensions and even if their focus is never spread equally between all of them, they can manage complexity, accuracy and fluency very well. On the other hand, this does not automatically mean that they learn faster than other students. In this profile we can find students who at the beginning are more careful and have, for example, lower levels of fluency. It should be stressed here that these four learner profiles should be treated solely as describing characteristics. Therefore, the "wanderer" profile is to be understood as a learner who develops more slowly and not as a "poor learner." A "carful learner," on the other hand, should in no way be associated with persons who are worse than "risk takers" because they avoid experimenting with new linguistic features etc.

The interconnectedness between systems and their reorganization during the developmental process result in unpredictable outcomes. On the other hand, however, the Trade-Off Hypothesis in some way forces a developmental sequence of systems in action. Development in general involves a process of unfolding into a mature state. And this transformation does not proceed linearly and often with substantial dynamics. The dynamics are characterized by a high degree of variability and high growth rates. The greater the variability and the higher the (both positive and negative) growth rates, the more active is the process of development. Weaker dynamics, in other words changes that are less dynamic in character combined with greater stability, mean that the system is oscillating around its attractor point. This behaviour suggests a need to revise our assumptions regarding the developmental sequence of complexity, accuracy and fluency. Until now the hypothesis was that complexity was the dimension that should develop earliest in learners. After that accuracy was assumed to appear, while fluency is achieved at the end. However, in light of the present study, another order emerges, namely that fluency and/or accuracy are the first dimensions to develop while complexity requires more time. This statement is based on observations of the development dynamics of second language learners. Fluency and accuracy were the dimensions that developed with the highest growth rates at the beginning, i.e. during the first two-three semesters of learning Swedish, after which the systems stabilised in the majority of the learners, while complexity developed at a slower pace, with more progress being achieved in the second and third years. Second language learners appear to build the basis of a new language by using simple constructions and internalizing and automating these unelaborate units, so that they can be prepared for the next step, i.e. reorganizing these simple elements and putting them together in larger networks. When they begin with fluency and accuracy they create a kind of framework, a skeleton that they later fill with muscles, i.e. complexity.

Dynamic systems theory has undoubtedly been a reliable tool in Second Language Development and its applicability in this research area has been further confirmed in the present study. Second language develops in nonlinear fashion and is sensitive to initial conditions: very significant progress at the beginning of the learning process triggers bifurcation. Development proceeds chaotically and therefore we cannot predict how much time will be needed for the learner to internalize new linguistic features and which system they will pay most attention to and in which they will thus perform best. There is considerable variability both at the individual level and between learners and only in the case of fluency does this variation decrease during the learning period. All systems are interconnected with each other and a change in one necessarily leads to reorganization in others. The interplay and transformation of systems during second language development entails a process where unintegrated and rather independently acting systems shift towards ever greater integration in the learners' mind. Therefore, the only way to look at such complex, dynamic systems is to observe them in their mutual interplay rather than separately from one another. Only such an approach can be treated as a dynamic understanding of Second Language Development.

References

Adamson, H.D., Fonseca-Greber, B., Kataoka, K., Scardino, V., & Takano, S. (1996). Tense marking in the English of Spanish-speaking adolescents. In R. Bayley & D.R. Preston (Eds.), *Second Language Acquisition and Linguistic Variation* (pp. 121–134). Amsterdam/Philadeplhia: John Benjamins B.V.

Alligood, K., Sauer, T. & Yorke, J. (1996). *Chaos. An Introduction to Dynamical Systems.* New York: Springer.

Arnaud, P. (1992). Objective lexical and grammatical characteristics of L2 written compositions and the validity of separate-component tests. In P. Arnaud & H. Bejoint (Eds.), *Vocabulary and Applied Linguistics* (pp. 133–145). London: Macmillan.

Aronin, L. & Singleton, D. (2008). Multilingualism as a new linguistic dispensation. *International Journal of Multilingualism*, *5*(1), pp. 1–16.

Arthur, B. (1979). Short-term changes in EFL compositions skills. In C.A. Yorio, K. Perkins & J. Schachter (Eds.), *On TESOL '79: The Learner in Focus* (pp. 330–342). Washington, D.C.: TESOL.

Ashby, W. (1962). Principles of the self-organizing system. In J.H. Von Foerster & G.W. Zopf (Ed.), *Principles of Self-Organization: Transactions of the University of Illinois Symposium* (pp. 255–278). London: Pergamon Press.

Ashwell, T. (2000). Patterns of Teatcher responce to student writing in a multiple-draft composition classroom: Is content feedback followed by form feedback the best method? *Journal of Second Language Writing, 9*(3), pp. 227–257.

Bachman, L. (1990). *Fundamental Considerations in Language Testing.* Oxford: Oxford University Press.

Balibrea, F. (2006). Chaos, periodicity and complexity on dynamical systems. In A. Sengupta (Ed.), *Chaos, Nonlinearity, Complexity. The Dynamical Paradigm of Nature* (pp. 1–52). Berlin Heidelberg: Springer-Verlag.

Bardovi-Harlig, K. & Bofman, T. (1989). Attainment of syntactic and morphological accuracy by advanced language learners. *Studies in Second Language Acquisition, 11*, pp. 17–34.

Bergé, P., Pomeau, Y. & Vidal, C. (1986). *Order within Chaos: Toward a Deterministic Approach to Turbulence.* New York: Wiley.

Bickerton, D. (1975). *Dynamics of a Creole System.* Cambridge: Cambridge University Press.

Briggs, J. & Peat, F. (1989). *Turbulent Mirror: An Illustrated Guide to Chaos Theory and the Science of Wholeness.* New York: Harper & Row.

Broer, H. & Takens, F. (2011). *Dynamical Systems and Chaos.* New York: Springer.

Brown, R. (1973). *A First Language.* London: George Allen & Unwin Ltd.

Bulté, B. & Housen, A. (2012). Defining and operationalising L2 complexity. In A. Housen , F. Kuiken & I. Vedder (Eds.), *Dimensions of L2 Performance and Proficiency* (pp. 21–46). Amsterdam/Philadelphia: John Benjamins Publishing Company.

Byrne, D. (1998). *Complexity Theory and the Social Sciences: An Introduction.* Florence, KY: Routledge.

Byrne, D. (2002). *Interpreting Quantitative Data.* London: Sage.

Canale, M. & Swain, M. (1980). Theoretical bases of communicative approaches to second language teaching and testing. *Applied Linguistics, 1*(1), pp. 1–47.

Carroll, J.B. (1968). The psychology of language testing. In A. Davies (Ed.), *Language Testing Symposium: A Psycholinguistic Approach* (pp. 46–69). London: Oxford University Press.

Cartwright, M. & Littlewood, J. (1945). On non-linear differential equations of the second order: I. the equation formula – k(1–y2)formula + y = bλk cos(λl + α), k large. *Journal of the London Mathematical Society, 20*(3), 180–189.

Casanave, C. P. (1994). Language development in students' journal. *Journal of Second Language Writing, 3*, pp. 179–201.

Caspi, T. (2010). *A Dynamic Perspective on Second Language Development (Doctoral dissertaion).* Retrieved from http://irs.ub.rug.nl/ppn/329338412 [accessed 21.07.2013].

Common European Framework of reference for Languages: Learnig, Teaching, Assessment (2001). Cambridge: Cambridge University Press. Retrieved from http://www.coe.int/t/dg4/linguistic/Source/Framework_EN.pdf [accessed 16.07.2015].

Chenoweth, N.A. & Hayes, J.R. (2001). Fluency in writing: Generating text in L1 and L2. *Written Communication, 18*, pp. 80–98.

Cook, V. (1992). Evidence for multicompetence. *Language Learning, 42*(4), pp. 557–591.

Cook, V. (1997). L2 users and English spelling. *Journal of Multilingual and Multicultural Development, 18*(6), pp. 474–488.

Corder, S.P. (1967). The significance of learner's errors. *International Review of Applied Linguistics in Language Teaching, 4*, pp. 161–170.

Dahl, Ö. (2004). *The Growth and Maintenance of Linguistic Complexity.* Philadelphia: John Benjamins Publishing Company.

de Angelis, J. (2007). *Third or Additional Language Acquisition.* Clevedon: Multilingual Matters.

de Bot, K. (2008). Introduction: Second language development as a dynamic process. *The Modern Language Journal, 92*, pp. 166–178.

de Bot, K. & Larsen-Freeman, D. (2011). Researching second language development from a Dynamic Systems Theory perspective. In M. Verspoor, K. de Bot, & W. Lowie (Eds.), *A Dynamic Approach to Second Language Development* (pp. 5–23). Amsterdam/Philadelphia: John Benjamins Publishing Company.
de Bot K., Lowie, W., & Verspoor, M. (2005). *Second Language Acquisition. An Advanced Resource Book.* London and New York: Routledge.
de Bot, K., Lowie, W. & Verspoor, M. (2007). A dynamic systems approach to second language acquisition. *Bilingualism: Language and Cognition, 10*, pp. 7–21 and 51–55.
de Jong, N. & Perfetti, C.A. (2011). Fluency training in the ESL classroom: An experimental study of fluency development and proceduralization. *Language Learning, 61*, pp. 533–568.
DeKeyser, R.M. (1998). Beyond focus on form: Cognitive perspectives on learning and practicing second language grammar. In C. Doughty & J. Williams (Eds.). Cambridge: Cambridge University Press.
Dörney, Z. & Murphey, T. (2009). *Group Dynamics in the Language Classroom.* Cambridge: Cambridge University Press.
Ellis, D.P. (2010). An introduction to signal processing for speech. In W.J. Hardcastle, L. John & F.E. Gibbon (Eds.), *The Handbook of Phonetic Sciences* (2 ed., pp. 757–780). Hoboken, NJ: Wiley-Blackwell.
Ellis, D.P. (2012). An introduction to signal processing for speech. In W.J. Hardcastle, L. John & F.E. Gibbon (Eds.), *The Handbook of Phonetic Sciences* (2 ed., pp. 757–780). Hoboken, NJ: Wiley-Blackwell.
Ellis, R. (1994). *The Study of Second Language Acquisition.* Oxford: Oxford University Press.
Ellis, R. (1997). *Second Language Acquisition.* Oxford: Oxford University Press.
Ellis, R. (2008). *The Study of Second Language Acquisition* (2 ed.). Oxford: Oxford University Press.
Ellis, R. & Barkhuizen, G. (2005). *Analysing Learner Language.* Oxford: Oxford University Press.
Ellis, R. & Yuan, F. (2004). The effects of planning on fluency, complexity and accuracy in second language narrative writing. *Studies in Second Language Acquisition, 29*, pp. 59–84.
Engber, S. (1995). The relationship of lexical proficiency to the quality of ESL compositions. *Journal of Second Language Writing*, Vol. 4(2), pp. 139–156.
Evans, N.W., Hartshorn, K.J., McCollum, R.M. & Wolfersberger, M. (2010). Contextualizing corrective feedback in second language writing pedagogy. *Language Teaching Research, 14*(4), pp. 445–463.
Evola, J., Mamer, E. & Lentz, B. (1980). Discrete points versus global scoring for cohesive devices. In J. Oller, & K. Perkins (Eds.), *Research in language testing* (pp. 177–181). Rowley, MA: Newbury House.
Favre, A., Guitton, H., Lichnerowicz, A. & Wolff, E. (1988). *Chaos and Determinism.* Baltimore/London: The John Hopkins University Press.

Ferrari, S. (2012). A lingitudinal study of complexity, accuracy and fluency variation in second language development. In A. Housen, F. Kuiken & I. Vedder (Eds.), *Dimensions of L2 Performance and Proficiency. Complexity, Accuracy and Fluency in SLA* (pp. 277–297). Amsterdam/Philadelphia: John Benjamins Publishing Company.

Fillmore, C.J. (1979). On Fluency. In C. Fillmore, D. Kempler & W. Wang (Eds.), *Individual Differences in Language Ability and Language Behaviour* (pp. 85–101). New York: Academic Press.

Fischer, K., Yan, Z. & Stewart, J. (2003). Adult cognitive development: Dynamics in the developmental web. In J. Valsiner & K. Connolly (Eds.), *Psychology, Handbook of Developmental Psychology* (pp. 491–516). London/Thousand Oaks/New Delhi: SAGE Publications.

Fischer, R.A. (1984). Testing written communicative competence in French. *Modern Language Journal, 68*(1), pp. 13–20.

Foster, P. & Skehan, P. (1996). The influence of planning on performance in task-based learning. *Studies in Second Language Acquisition, 18*(3), pp. 299–324.

Foster, P., Tonkyn, A. & Wigglesworth, G. (2000). Measuring spoken language: A unit for all reasons. *Applied Linguistics, 21*(3), pp. 354–375.

Fouser, R. (2001). Too close for comfort? Sociolinguistic transfer from Japanese into Korean as an L≥3. In J. Cenoz, B. Hufeisen & U. Jessner (Eds.), *Cross-linguistic influence in third language acquisition: Psycholinguistic perspectives* (pp. 149–169). Clevedon: Multilingual Matters.

Freed, B.F. (1995). What makes us think that students who study abroad become fluent? In B.F. Freed (Ed.), *Second Language Acquisition in a study abroad context* (pp. 123–148). Philadelphia: John Benjamins.

Gilabert, R. (2007). The simultaneous manipulation of task complexity along planning time and (+/– Here-and-Now): Effects on L2 oral production. In M. Garcia Mayo (Ed.), *Investigating Tasks in Formal Language Learning* (pp. 44–68). Clevedon: Multilingual Matters.

Goldin-Meadow, S. & Alibali, M. (2002). Looking at the hands through time: A microgenetic perspective on learning and instruction. In N. Granott & J. Parziale (Eds.), *Microdevelopment. Transition Processes in Development and Learning* (pp. 80–105). New York: Cambridge University Press.

Grabowski, J. (2008). The internal structure of university students' keyboard skills. *Journal of Writing Research, 1*(1), pp. 27–52.

Granott, N. & Parziale, J. (2002). Microdevelopment: A process-oriented perspective for studying development and learning. In N. Granott & J. Parziale (Eds.), *Microdevelopment. Transition Processes in Development and Learning* (pp. 1–28). New York: Cambridge University Press.

Grosjean, F. (1982). *Life with Two Languages: An Introduction to Bilingualism.* Cambridge, MA: Harvard University Press.

Guiraud, P. (1954). *Les caractères statisticues du vocabulaire.* Paris: Presses universitaires de France.

Gunnarsson, C. (2012). The development of complexity, accuracy and fluency in the written production of L2 French. In A. Housen, F. Kuiken & I. Vedder (Eds.), *Dimensions of L2 Performance and Proficiency. Complexity, Accuracy and Fluency in SLA* (pp. 247–276). Amsterdam/Philadelphia: John Benjamins Publishing Company.

Hakuta, K. (1975). Learning to speak a second language: What exactly does the child learn? In D.P. Dato (Ed.). Washington, D.C.: Georgetown University Press.

Halliday, M. & Matthiessen, C. (1999). *Construing Experience through Meaning: A Language-based Approach to Cognition.* London: Cassell.

Hammarberg, B. (2010). The languages of the multilingual: Some conceptual and terminological issues. *International Review of Applied Linguistics in Language Teaching (IRAL)*, *48*(2–3), pp. 91–104.

Herdina, P. & Jessner, U. (2002). *A Dynamic Model of Multilingualism. Perspectives of Change in Psycholinguistics.* Clevedon, UK: Multilingual Matters.

Hilborn, R.C. (2010). *Chaos and Nonlinear Dynamics: An Introduction for Scientists and Engineers.* DOI:10.1093/acprof:oso/9780198507239.001.0001 [accessed 19.07.2015].

Homburg, T.J. (1984). Holistic evaluation of ESL compositions: can it be validated objectively? *TESOL Quarterly*, *18*(1), pp. 87–107.

Housen, A. & Kuiken, F. (2009). Complexity, accuracy, and fluency in second language acquisition. *Applieed Linguistics*, *30*(4), pp. 461–473.

Housen, A., Kuiken, F. & Vedder, I. (2012). Complexity, accuracy and fluency. Definitions, measurements and researhc. In A. Housen, F. Kuiken & I. Vedder (Eds.), *Dimensions of L2 Performance and Proficiency* (pp. 1–20). Amsterdam/Philadelphia: John Benjamins Publishing Company.

Housen, A., Kuiken, F. & Vedder, I. (Eds.). (2012). *Dimensions of L2 Performance and proficiency. Complexity, Accuracy and Fluency in SLA.* Amsterdam/Philadelphia: John Benjamins Publishing Company.

Hunt, K. (1970). Syntactic maturity in school children and adults. *Monographs of the Society for Research in Child Development*, *35*(1), pp. 1–67.

Ishikawa, S. (1995). Objective measurement of low-proficiency EFL narrative writing. *Journal of Second Language Writing*, *4*, pp. 51–70.

Johansson, V. (2009). *Developmental Aspects of Text Production in Writing and Speech.* Lund: Department of Linguistics and Phonetics. Centre for Languages and Literature. Lund University.

Kaczmarek, C.M. (1980). Scoring and rating essay tasks. In J.W. Oller & K. Perkins (Eds.), *Research in Language Testing* (pp. 151–159). Rowley, MA: Newbury House.

Kaplan, D. & Glass, L. (1995). *Understanding Nonlinear Dynamics.* New York: Springer Publishing Company.

Kaufer, D.S., Hayes, J.R. & Flower, L. (1986). Composing written sentences. *Research in the Teaching of English*, *20*, pp. 121–140.

Kay, J. & Hanley, J. (1994). Peripheral disorders of spelling: The role of the graphemic buffer. In G. Brown & N. Ellis, *Handbook of Spelling: Theory, Process and Intervention*. Chichester: John Wiley.

Kormos, J. & Dénes, M. (2004). Exploring measures and perceptions in the speech of second language learners. *System*, *32*, pp. 145–164.

Kowal, I. (2008). Att mäta språklig medvetenhet. En datorstödd analys av självkorrigeringar. In P. Bukowski, G. Porwisz & I. Kowal (Eds.), *Perspektiv på svenska språket och litteraturen* (pp. 185–194). Kraków: Wydawnictwo Uniwersytetu Jagiellońskiego.

Kowal, I. (2009). Bedömning av metaspråklig medvetenhet. En longitudinell studie. In P. Juvonen (Ed.), *ASLA 22. Språk och lärande. Rapport från ASLA höstsymposium, Stockholm 7–8 November 2008. Language and learning. Papers from the ASLA symposium in Stockholm 7–8 November 2008* (pp. 157–171). Stockholm: ASLA.

Kowal, I. (2011). Online revisions in FL writing. General rules and individual differences. In J. Arabski & A. Wojtaszek (Eds.). *Individual Learner Differences in SLA* (pp. 309–320). Bristol: Multilingual Matters.

Kowal, I. (2012). Dynamika i struktura grupy w klasie językowej (U. Paprocka--Piotrowska, Ed.). *Neofilolog*, *39*(2), pp. 131–146.

Kowal, I. (2014). Fluency in second language writing: A developmental perspective. *Studia Linguistica Universitatis Iagellonicae Cracoviensis*, *131*(3), pp. 229–246.

Krashen, S. (1981). *Second Language Acquisition and Learning*. Oxford: Pergamon Press.

Kuhn, D. (1995). Microgenetic study of change: What has it told us? *Psychological Science*, *6*(3), pp. 133–139.

Kuiken, F. & Vedder, I. (2007). Cognitive task complexity and linguistic performance in French L2 writing. In M.P. Garcia-Mayo (Ed.), *Investigating Tasks in Formal Language Learning* (pp. 117–135). Clevedon: Multilingual Matters.

Kuiken, F. & Vedder, I. (2008). Cognitive task complexity and written output in Italian and French as a foreign language. *Journal of Second Language Writing*, *17*(1), pp. 48–60.

Kuiken, F., Mos, M. & Vedder, I. (2005). Cognitive task complexity and second language writing performance. In S. Foster-Cohen, M.P. Garcia-Mayo & J. Cenoz (Eds.), *Eurosla* Yearbook (Vol. 5, pp. 195–222). Amsterdam: John Benjamins Publishing Company.

Lado, R. (1961). *Language Testing: The Construction and Use of Foreign Language Tests: A Teachers' Book*. London: Longman.

Larsen-Freeman, D. (1978). An ESL index of development. *TESOL Quarterly*, *12*(4), pp. 439–448.

Larsen-Freeman, D. (1997). Chaos/complexity science and second language acquisition. *Applied Linguistics*, *8*(2), pp. 141–165.

Larsen-Freeman, D. (2002). Language acquisition and language use from a chaos/complexity theory perspective. In C. Kramsch (Ed.), *Language Acquisition and Language Socialization*. London: Continuum.

Larsen-Freeman, D. (2006). The emergence of complexity, fluency, and accuracy in the oral and written production of five Chinese learners of English. *Applied Linguistics*, *27*(4), pp. 560–619.

Larsen-Freeman, D. (2009). Adjusting expectations: The study of complexity, accuracy, and fluency in second language acquisition. *Applied Linguistics, 30*(4), pp. 579–589.

Larsen-Freeman, D. & Cameron, L. (2008). *Complex Systems and Applied Linguistics*. Oxford: Oxford University Press.

Larsen-Freeman, D. & Strom, V. (1978). The construction of a second language acquisition index of development. *Language Learning*, *27*(1), pp. 123–134.

Lee, K. & Karmiloff-Smith, A. (2002). Macro- and microdevelopmental research: Assumptions, research strategies, constraints, and utilities. In N. Granott & J. Parziale (Eds.), *Microdevelopment : Transition Processes in Development and Learning* (pp. 243–265). New York: Cambridge University Press.

Lennon, P. (1990). Investigating fluency in EFL: A quantitative approach. *Language Learning*, *40*(3), pp. 387–417.

Lennon, P. (1991). Error: Some problems of definition, identification, and distinction. *Applied Linguistics*, *12*(2), pp. 180–196.

Levy, C.M. & Ransdell, S. (1995). Is writing as difficult as it seems? *Memory & Cognition*, *23*, pp. 767–779.

Li, T.-Y. & Yorke, J. (1975). Period Three Implies Chaos. *The American Mathematical Monthly*, *82*(10), pp. 985–992.

Lo, J. & Hyland, F. (2007). Enhansing students' engagement and motivation in writing: The case of primary students in Hong Kong. *Journal of Second Language Writing, 16*, pp. 219–237.

Lorenz, E. (1963). Deterministic nonperiodic flow. *Journal of the Atmospheric Sciences*, *20*, 130–141.

Luelsdorff, P.A. (1990). Processing strategies in bilingual spellers. In J. Fisiak (Ed.), *Further Insights into Contrastive Analysis* (pp. 187–205). Amsterdam/ Philadelphia: John Benjamins.

Lundstrom, K. & Baker, W. (2009). To give is better than to receive: The benefits of peer review to the reviewer's own writing. *Journal of Second Language Writing, 18*, pp. 30–43.

Malvern, D., Richards, B., Chipere, N. & Durán, P. (2004). *Lexical Diversity and Language Development*. Houndmills: Palgrave Macmillan.

Manneville, P. (2004). *Instabilities, Chaos and Turbulence*. London: Imperial College Press.

Maxwell, J.C. (1865). A dynamical theory of the electromagnetic field. *Philosophical Transactions of the Royal Society of London*, *155*, 459–512.

McGraw-Hill Encyclopedia of Science & Technology. (1997). New York: McGraw-Hill.

Michel, M.C., Kuiken, F. & Vedder, I. (2007). The influence of complexity in monologic versus dialogic tasks in Dutch L2. *International Review of Applied Linguistics in Language Teaching*, *45*(3), pp. 241–259.

Miestamo, M. (2008). Grammatical complexity in a cross-linguistic perspective. In M. Miestamo, K. Sinnemäki & F. Karlsson (Eds.), *Language Complexity. Typology, Contact, Change* (pp. 23–41). Amsterdam/Philadelphia: John Benjamins Publishing Company.

Möhle, D. (1984). The comparison of the second language speech production of different native speakers. In H. Dechert, D. Möhle & M. Raupach (Eds.), *Second Language Productions* (pp. 26–49). Tübingen: Günter Narr.

Nas, G. (1975). *Determining the Communicative Value of Written Discourse Produced by L2 Learners.* Utrecht, The Netherland: Institute of Applied Linguistic.

Nauclér, K. (1980). *Perspectives on Misspellings: a Phonetic, Phonological and Psycholinguistic Study.* Malmö: LiberLäromedel/Gleerup.

Nichols, J. (2009). Linguistic complexity: A comprehensive definition and survey. In G. Sampson, D. Gil & P. Trudgill (Eds.), *Language Complexity as an Evolving Variable* (pp. 110–125). Oxford: Oxford University Press.

Norris, J.M. & Ortega, L. (2009). Towards an organic approach to investigating CAF in instructed SLA: The case of complexity. *Applied Linguistics, 30*(4), pp. 555–578.

Okada, T. (2005). A corpus-based study of spelling errors of Japanese EFL Writers with reference to errors occurring in word-initial and word-final positions. In V. Cook & B. Bassetti (Eds.), *Second Language Writing Systems.* Clavedon: Multilingual Matters.

Pallotti, G. (2009). CAF: Defining, refining and differentiating. *Applied Linguistics, 30*(4), pp. 590–601.

Pallotti, G. (2015). A simple view of linguistic complexity. *Second Language Research, 31*(1), pp. 117–134.

Palviainen, Å., Kalaja, P. & Mäntylä, K. (2012). Development of L2-writing: Fluency and proficiency. In L. Meriläinen, L. Kolehmainen & T. Nieminen (Eds.), *AFinLA-e Soveltavan kielitieteen tutkimuksia n:o 4* (pp. 47–59). AFinLA.

Paulus, T.M. (1999). The effect of peer and teacher feedback on student writing. *Journal of Second Language Writing, 8*(3), pp. 265–289.

Pienemann, M. & Håkansson, G. (1999). A unified approach towards the development of Swedish as L2: A processability account. *Studies in Second Language Acquisition, 21*(3), pp. 383–420.

Pienemann, M. (1998). *Language Processing and Second Language Development: Processability Theory.* Amsterdam: Benjamins.

Polat, B. & Kim, Y. (2013). Dynamics of complexity and accuracy: A longitudinal case study of advanced untutored development. *Applied Linguistics (Advance Access published July 13)*, pp. 1–25.

Polio, C.G. (1997). Measures of linguistic accuracy in second language writing research. *Language Learning, 47*(1), pp. 101–143.

Prigogine, I. & Stengers, I. (1985). *Order out of Chaos.* London: Flamingo.

Riggenbach, H. (1991). Toward an understanding of fluency: A microanalysis of nonnative speaker conversation. *Discource Processes, 14*, pp. 423–441.

Ruelle, D. (1978). Dynamical systems with turbulent behaviour. *Mathematical Problems in Theoretical Physics: Lecture Notes in Physics, 80*, 341–360.

Ruelle, D. & Takens, F. (1971). On the nature of tTurbulence. *Journal of Mathematical Physics, 20*, 167–192.

Schöner, G. (2009). Development as change of system dynamics: Stability, instability, and emergence. In M.S. John, P. Spencer, *Toward a Unified Theory of Development Connectionism and Dynamic System Theory Re-Consider.* DOI: 10.1093/acprof:oso/9780195300598.001.0001 [accessed 19.07.2015].

Scott, M. & Tucker, G. (1974). Error analysis and English-language strategies of Arab students. *Language Learning, 24*(1), pp. 69–97.

Segalowitz, N. (2010). *Cognitive Bases of Second Language Fluency.* New York: Routledge.

Selinker, L. (1972). Interlanguage. *IRAL; International Review of Applied Linguistics in Language Teaching, 10*(3), pp. 209–231.

Severinsson-Eklundh, K. & Kollberg, P. (1996). A computer tool and framework for analysing on-line revisions. In M. Levy & S. Randsell (Eds.), *The Science of Writing* (pp. 163–188). New Jersey.

Siegler, R. (2002). Microgenetic studies of self-explanation. In N. Granott & J. Parziale (Eds.), *Microdevelopment. Transition Processes in Development and Learning* (pp. 31–58). New York: Cambridge University Press.

Siegler, R. & Crowley, K. (1991). The microgenetic method. A direct means for studying cognitive development. *American Psychologist, 6*, pp. 606–620.

Skehan, P. (1996). Second language acquisition and task based instruction. In J. Willis & D. Willis (Eds.), *Challenge and Change in Language Teaching* (pp. 17–30). Oxford: Heinemann.

Skehan, P. (1998). *A Cognitive Approach to Language Learning.* Oxford: Oxford University Press.

Skehan, P. (2003). Task-based instruction. *Language Teaching, 36*, pp. 1–14.

Skehan, P. (2009). Modelling second language performance: Integrating complexity, accuracy, fluency, and lexis. *Applied Linguistics, 30*(4), pp. 510–532.

Skehan, P. & Foster, P. (2012). Complexity, accuracy, fluency and lexis in task-based performance. In A. Housen, F. Kuiken & I. Vedder (Eds.), *Dimensions of L2 Performance and Proficiency. Complexity, Accuracy and Fluency in SLA* (pp. 199–220). Amsterdam/Philadelphia: John Benjamins Publishing Company.

Spelman Miller, K., Lindgren, E. & Sullivan, K.P. (2008). The psycholinguistic dimension in second language writing: Opportunities for research and pedagogy using computer keystroke logging. *TESOL Quarterly, 42*, pp. 433–453.

Spoelman, M. & Verspoor, M. (2010). dynamic patterns in development of accuracy and complexity: A longitudinal case study in the acquisition of Finnish. *Applied Linguistics, 31*(4), pp. 532–553.

Strömqvist, S. (1996). *Discource Flow and Linguistic Information Structuring: Explorations in Speech and Writing.* Göteborg: University of Göteborg. Department of Linguistics.

Strömqvist, S. (1999). Production rate profiles. In S. Strömqvist & E. Ahlsén (Eds.), *The Process of Writing: A Progress Report* (pp. 53–70). Göteborg: Gothenburg Papers in Theoretical Linguistics.

Strömqvist, S. & Ahlsén, E. (1999). *The Process of Writing – A Progress Report.* Göteborg: Gothenburg Papers in Theoretical Linguistics.

Strömqvist, S. & Malmsten, L. (1998). *ScriptLog pro 1.04 – user's manual. Technical report.* University of Göteborg. Departement of Linguistics.

Strömqvist, S., Holmqvist, K., Johansson, V., Karlsson, H. & Wengelin, Å. (2006). What Keystroke Logging can Reveal about Writing. In K. Sullivan & E Lindgren *Computer key-stroke logging and writing: methods and applications*, pp. 45–72, Amsterdam, Elsevier.

Tarone, E. (1988). *Variation in Interlanguage.* London: Edward Arnold.

Tarone, E. (1989). On chameleons and monitors. In M. Eisenstein (Ed.), *The Dynamic Interlanguage* (pp. 3–15). New York: Springer Science+ Business media, LLC.

Thelen, E. & Bates, E. (2003). Connectionism and dynamic systems: Are they really different? *Developmental Science*, *6*(4), pp. 378–391.

Thelen, E. & Smith, L. (1994). *A Dynamic Systems Approach to the Development of Cognition and Action.* Cambridge, MA: The MIT Press.

Thelen, E. & Ulrich, B. (1991). Hidden skills: A dynamic systems analysis of treadmill stepping during the first year. *Monographs of the Society for Research in Child Development*, *56*(1), pp. 1–103.

Towell, R. (1987). Variability and progress in the language development of advanced learners of a foreign language. In *Second Language Acquisition in Context* (pp. 113–127). New York: Prentice Hall.

Towell, R., Howkins, R. & Bazergui, N. (1996). The development of fluency in advanced leartners of French. *Applied Linguistics*, *17*, pp. 84–119.

Trudgill, P. (2001). Contact and simplification. *Linguistic Typology*, Vol 5(2/3), pp. 371–374.

Uppstad, P. & Solheim, O.J. (2007). Aspects on fluency in writing. *Journal of Psycholinguistic Research*, *36*, pp. 79–87.

van Dijk, M., Verspoor, M. & Lowie, W. (2011). Variability in DST. In M. Verspoor, K. de Boot & W. Lowie (Eds.), *A Dynamic Approach to Second Language Development* (pp. 55–84). Amsterdam/Philadelphia: John Benjamins Publishing Company.

van Geert, P. (1991). A Dynamic Systems Model of Cognitive and Language Growth. *Psychological Review*, *98*(1), 3–53.

van Geert, P. (1994). *Dynamic Systems of Development. Change between Complexity and Chaos.* Hertfordshire: Harvester Wheatsheaf.

van Geert, P. (2007). Dynamic systems in second language learning: Some general methodological reflections. *Bilingualism: Language and Cognition*, *10*(1), pp. 47–49.

van Geert, P. (2008). The dynamic systems approach in the study of L1 and L2 acquisition: An introduction. *The Modern Language Journal, 92*(2), 179–199.

van Geert, P. (2009). Nonlinear complex dynamical systems in developmental psychology. In S. Guastello, M. Koopmans & D. Pincus (Eds.), *Chaos and Complexity in Psychology* (pp. 242–281). Cambridge: Cambridge University Press.

van Geert, P. & van Dijk, M. (2002). Focus on variability: New tools to study intra-individual variability in developmental data. *Infant Behaviour and Development, 25*, pp. 340–374.

van Gelderen, A. & Oostadam, R. (2005). Effetcs of fluency training on the application of linguistic operations in writing. *L1 – Educational Studies in Language and Literature, 5*, pp. 215–240.

Vann, R. (1979). Oral and written syntactic relationships in second language learning. In C.A. Yorio, P. Kyle & J. Schachter (Eds.), *On TESOL '79: The Learner in Focus* (pp. 322–329). Washington, D.C.: TESOL.

Vermeer, A. (2000). Coming to grips with lexical richness in spontaneous speech data. *Language Testing, 17*(1), pp. 65–83.

Verspoor, M., de Bot, K. & Lowie, W. (Eds.). (2011). *A Dynamic Approach to Second Language Development. Methods and Techniques.* Amsterdam/Philadelphia: John Benjamins Publishing Company.

Verspoor, M., Lowie, W. & van Dijk, M. (2008). Variability in second language development from a dynamic systems perspective. *The Modern Language Journal, 92*(2), pp. 214–231.

Verspoor, M., Lowie, W., van Geert, P., van Dijk, M. & Schmid, M.S. (2011). How to sections. In M. Verspoor, K. de Bot & W. Lowie (Eds.), *A Dynamic Approach to Second Language Development* (pp. 130–199). Amsterdam/Philadelphia: John Benjamins Publishing Company.

Weisstein, E.W. (2002). *CRC Concise Encyclopedia of Mathematics, Second Edition.* Chapman and Hall/CRC.

Wengelin, Å. (1999a). Pauses and editings in the written language production of adults with and without severe reading and writing difficulties. In S. Strömqvist & E. Ahlsén (Eds.), *The Process of Writing: A Progress Report* (pp. 71–86). Göteborg.

Wengelin, Å. (1999b). Spelling and grammar in dyslexic and deaf adults. In S. Strömqvist & E. Ahlsén (Eds.), *The Process of Writing – a Progress Report* (pp. 87–102). Gothenburg: Gothenburg Papers in Theoretical Linguistics.

Wengelin, Å. (2002). *Text Production in Adults with Reading and Writing Difficulties.* PhD thesis. Department of Linguistics. Göteborg University.

Wengelin, Å. (2007). The Word-Level Focus in Text Production by Adults with Reading and Writing Difficulties. In M. Torrance, L. van Waes & D. Galbraith (Eds.), *Writing nad Cognition. Research and Application* (pp. 67–82). Amsterdam: Elsevier.

Werner, H. (1956). Microgenesis and aphasia. *The Journal of Abnormal and Social Psychology*, *52*(3), pp. 347–353.

Wessa, P. (2015). *Free Statistics Software, Office for Research Development and Education*. Retrieved from http://www.wessa.net/ [accessed 21.07.2015].

Williams, J. & Evans, J. (1998). What kind of focus and on which forms? In C. Doughty & J. Williams (Eds.), *Focus on Form in Classroom Second Language Acquisition* (pp. 139–151). Cambridge: Cambridge University Press.

Wolfe-Quintero, K., Inagaki, S. & Kim, H.-Y. (1998). *Second Language Development in Writing: Measures of Fluency, Accuracy, and Complexity.* Honolulu: HI: University of Hawaii.

List of tables

List of figures

TECHNICAL EDITORS
Agnieszka Stęplewska, Renata Włodek

PROOFREADING
Jason Lowther

TECHNICAL PROOFREADING
Kinga Stępień

TYPESETTING
Regina Wojtyłko

Jagiellonian University Press
Editorial Offices: ul. Michałowskiego 9/2, 31-126 Kraków
Phone: +48 12-663-01-97, Fax +48 12-631-01-98